JESUS THE JEWISH

JESUS
THE JEWISH
THEOLOGIAN

BRAD H. YOUNG

Forewords by
Marvin R. Wilson and Rabbi David Wolpe

HENDRICKSON
PUBLISHERS

Copyright © 1995 by Hendrickson Publishers, Inc.
P. O. Box 3473
Peabody, Massachusetts 01961–3473
All rights reserved
Printed in the United States of America

ISBN 1–56563–060–2

First printing — June 1995

Photos on pages 46, 83, 84, 102, 118, 126 (top), 141, 142, 162
appear courtesy of the Israel Antiquities Authority and are
used with permission.

Library of Congress Cataloging-in-Publication Data

Young, Brad H.
    Jesus the Jewish theologian / Brad H. Young.
    Includes bibliographical references and index.
    ISBN 1-56563-060-2 (pbk.)
    1. Jesus Christ—Jewishness. 2. Jesus Christ—Biography.
    3. Jesus Christ—Teachings. 4. Jesus Christ—Messiahship.
    I. Title
    BT590.J8Y68 1995
    232—dc20   95-6016
                                                     CIP

With much appreciation for their friendship

and with my highest esteem,

this book is dedicated to

Dennis and Georgia Lee Clifton

Table of Contents

Part 3: THE JEWISH THEOLOGY IN JESUS' PARABLES

Part 4: THE JEWISH MESSIAH AND THE POLITICS OF ROME

Part 5: THE FUTURE MESSIAH

EPILOGUE

AFTERWORD

List of Illustrations

I express my deep appreciation to the Israel Antiquities Authorities for providing the photographs of these precious artifacts, archaeological remains, and manuscripts for publication here. All of these photographs are used with their courtesy and permission. I am grateful for their kind assistance in locating and reproducing these illustrative photographs from the life setting of the land of Israel. These Jewish antiquities enhance our appreciation of the material culture of the people.

Foreword

Rabbi David Wolpe

WHEN CHRISTIANS WRITE ABOUT JESUS, THEY WRITE with the weight of theology. When Jews write about Jesus, they write with the weight of history. For Judaism the life of Jesus is difficult to isolate from the rift it represented from Jewish history. All the rancor that followed— the pain and persecution, the tentative efforts at understanding sabotaged by hatred, the rejection, belittlement, and horror—is the prism through which Jesus has traditionally been refracted for the Jew. To see Jesus as he was is a difficult task because of the legacy left toward the Jewish people by Christianity.

This characterization may seem excessively harsh to a Christian reader. Surely there were times of cooperation and harmony? Indeed such times occurred, although they were fewer than we would hope. But the basic outline was essentially fixed for centuries. Jesus represents a break to Judaism; he is a Jew who became the fountainhead of another faith, a religious child that broke from its parent. Given the subsequent history, what parent could look upon such a child without ambivalence, at best?

Today we live in a new age. Understanding between Jews and Christians, although still not ideal, has reached a point unimaginable to our ancestors. Nonetheless no Jew who takes up his or her pen to write of Jesus can entirely escape the burden of that history. The exploration of Jesus' life and teachings can no more be objective for a Jew than it can for a Christian—although for quite different reasons.

Yet tolerance is a powerful liberator of ideas. In our time, as understanding grows, and respect spreads, Jews can begin anew to explore the life and teachings of Jesus.

Jesus was born to an age of teachers. It was a time of strong views and fractious debate. Time smooths out the wrinkles of the past, so that we begin to talk about "the views of the first century," although opening a newspaper today we see how various are human views in any given time. Later tradition imposes an orthodoxy that enshrines debate, and freezes it. Alliances, which are always shifting in real life, become fixed. Ideas that would have been understood then, seem heretical now.

Thus we are constrained by the rigidity of later perspectives. This makes it difficult to see Jesus in his original context. There is another reason why it is so hard to understand Jesus, and that is the simple complexity of any human story. A biographer once asked his audience to imagine, next time they read a biography, how accurate would be even their best friend's account of their own love life. Is there anyone who could, with pen and paper, really explain the twists and turns of your own private story? The human heart is so various and secretive that, even for the least complex among us, true explanation of our lives is elusive.

How much more complex is it to account for a character born 2,000 years ago into a different world, whose legacy is interpreted by so many strong-minded and independent followers? The mysteries of the human heart are overlaid with the detritus of history. A reclamation project seems hopeless.

Yet we do have a logical starting point. The place to begin searching for Jesus is in the world in which he grew. His roots were first-century Judaism. What was the world like for a first-century Jew?

Jesus was born at a critical time for the Jewish people. It was a time of transition from a tradition that was bound to a specific land, and a specific temple, into a portable tradition, one that Jews could carry with them throughout their wanderings. The diaspora was "invented" at the destruction of the first temple in 586 B.C.E. But the final break with the land was not until 700 years later, when the Bar-Kochba revolt was crushed by the Romans. After the destruction of the second temple, and the leveling of the land, Judaism proceeded to forge itself into a new model—rabbinic Judaism—which has survived and flourished until our day.

The greatest spirits of rabbinic Judaism, such as Hillel and Akiba, lived within 100 years of this time. The world into which Jesus was born, for all its problems, was bursting with religious creativity. First-century Judaism was filled with debate and diversity. Even within the confines of rabbinic Judaism, argumentation was the order of the day. To debate the meaning of life or the minutiae of the law was the reigning passion of rabbinic scholars. In a poignant talmudic passage, Rabbi Johanan mourns the loss of his colleague Resh Lakish because Rabbi Johanan can find no other rabbi who could so ably and vigorously disagree with him!

The rabbinic tradition is much studied today, but for a long time it was moribund in the Christian world. Christianity was concerned about Judaism up until the time of Jesus, but after that Judaism was irrelevant, a curio in the display case of world religions. Today, however, Christian scholars are beginning to understand that much of what Judaism preserved is what Jesus would have known. It may be that a fifth- or sixth-century rabbinic midrash—legend—perpetuates a tradition that Jesus would have taken for granted. In a world of oral transmission, the date something is finally written down can be haphazard—a product of pure chance. A rabbinic legend that survives in a tenth-century manuscript may have been known, assumed, or even alluded to by Jesus—and instantly recognized by his audience.

The world of first-century Judaism inherited much, but bequeathed even more to the generations that followed. Vivid apocalyptic imagery, elaborations of ancient law, stories and legends, gentle teachings of God's love, and ripe images of God's revenge—all of this and more swirled around the pious lives of first-century Judaism. And all of it took place in the confines of a Roman Empire with little more than a mild curiosity toward these God-intoxicated peasants.

Jesus lived in a textual world. Most important to Christianity is a life; most important to Judaism is a book. That is why the most popular work of Christian spirituality is Thomas à Kempis' *Imitation of Christ.* There is in Christianity an ideal life. But for Jesus himself, there was no such model. His own life was dictated by the notion of ideal texts. No Jewish spiritual work advises its reader to be like Moses; it counsels, rather, to try to follow the *writings* of Moses and his later interpreters.

Judaism was not only textual by choice—it was textual by virtue of the narrowness of the ancient world. We have a variety of informational sources—television, radio, an endless array of books. For the rabbis of the first century, intellectual energy was absorbed by the Bible. It was not simply that the Bible was memorized—it was their touchstone in every life experience. Life was sketched against a background of quotations embedded in the soul. Everything was referred back to the text, from daily work, to family, to extraordinary experiences. Rabbinic documents are so densely allusive not because the rabbis were straining to display erudition, but because the rabbis were educated Jews and as such lived those texts. The stories and laws of the Bible were common coinage. They were the yardstick against which life was ceaselessly measured.

Like any good teacher, Jesus began where the people were. His audience was rooted in texts. Why, in the Sermon on the Mount, does he begin "you have heard . . . but I say?" Because he is dealing with a people for whom the word is alive and ever present. Even to depart from the text, one must begin with it.

If we wish to really fathom what Jesus is talking about, we have to try to enter the minds of his listeners. Every speaker, no matter how universal, addresses a particular community; if we wish to understand Pericles, we must put ourselves in the minds of ancient Athenians; if we wish to grasp the oratory of Cicero, we must become members of the Roman Senate, and if we wish to hear Jesus, we must become ancient Jews.

That is why Jews and Judaism have so much to contribute to the understanding of Jesus. We have preserved the religious assumptions of his first listeners. We kept in our memory the texts that were real to our ancestors.

But the obstacles to sharing this knowledge are twofold, one on each side of the religious divide: Jews themselves are profoundly ambivalent, at best, concerning the character and destiny of Jesus, whom many see as having betrayed Judaism. Christians are reluctant to listen to Jews speak about Jesus, because he is, in Christian thinking, to be understood only in the light of Christian teachings and dogma.

Both Jews and Christians are caught in what we may call "the Borges syndrome." The great Argentinean writer Jorge Luis Borges pointed out that each new writer creates his precursors. That is, no one "knew" that Kierkegaard was an existentialist until later writers such as Kafka, Camus, and Unamuno came along to establish him as the fountainhead of a line of tradition. Now it is impossible to read Kierkegaard without his followers in mind. Similarly, Jesus cannot be read without see-

ing him as a precursor. How can we read Jesus without thinking of Paul, and Augustine, and Aquinas? Alternatively, how
can we read Jesus without thinking of the Crusades, the Inqui-
sition, and the blood libel?

The only way out of this impasse is the collaboration of scholars. Both Jewish and Christian scholars must transcend the
boundaries of their own communities; the former to examine
Jesus' life, and the latter to immerse themselves in the texts that
illuminate the world of Jesus and his audience.

That scholarly balancing act is the accomplishment of this
book. Dr. Young understands and appreciates the world of rabbinic midrash. His learning enables him to locate Jesus' teaching
in the context of the world in which he lived. Dr. Young has
mastered the texts which are the treasure-house of early Jewish
spirituality. In his scholarship and in his life, he has kept touch
with the very sources that nourished early Christians.

Thus this book illuminates anew how *Jewish* Jesus was. That
should come as no surprise to Jews or to Christians, although it
often does. Jesus grew from the soil of his people. In reading
this book I was struck again and again by how Jesus' teachings
were paralleled in my own tradition.

Of course I was also enlightened as to precisely where those
traditions diverged. Jesus did recast some of what he was given
by his own teachers. Dr. Young's book is not intended to dimin-
ish Jesus' teaching, but to show its roots.

One of the most exciting prospects of our age is the possibility that we might transcend our own parochialism to acknowledge spiritual richness wherever we find it. Fidelity to one's
own tradition does not mean we must be deaf to the music of
other faiths. Spiritual traditions East and West are talking not
merely past each other, but *to* each other. Nowhere is this more
important than in the dialogue between Judaism and Christianity, which has been so fraught with misunderstanding, animosity, and pain. In its origin, this is a family quarrel, and family
quarrels are notoriously intractable. They require that we wait
until passions have subsided somewhat and we can heed the
scriptural admonition of Isaiah, "Come, let us reason together" (Isa 1:18).

It has taken an unconscionably long time for Christians and
Jews to realize how much more unites than divides us. We
spring from the same remarkable recognition—that this world
was fashioned by a God who is remote yet near at hand, a God

who demands goodness, a God who grants love. These are the
teachings, spoken in so many different voices, that the reader
will find in Dr. Young's book. Through these voices we will not
only rediscover a world that once was; we will be inspired to
help create the world that might be.

Rabbi David Wolpe
Professor of Judaic Studies
Director of the Ostrow Library
University of Judaism
Los Angeles, California

Foreword

Marvin R. Wilson

To pick up a volume titled *JESUS THE JEWISH Theologian* may appear unusual to some Christians. Considering the general dejudaization of the modern church, such a reaction is understandable. Among many Christians, Jesus as a historic figure remains largely removed from Judaism and first-century Jewish culture.

This point was ever so starkly brought to my attention several years ago through a piece of Sunday School literature which came across my desk. It was written for grade school children and produced by a leading denominational publishing house. The part which caught my eye was a full-page drawing of Jesus. He was depicted as a boy and shown going up steps leading into a building. Underneath the drawing was this caption: "Jesus was a good Christian boy who went to church every Sunday." I scarcely could believe my eyes! Here were three glaring errors in one sentence: Jesus was a Christian, not a Jew; he attended church, not synagogue; and he went on Sunday, not the Sabbath. On seeing this I thought to myself, if this is what is being taught in certain church schools among the young, no wonder a problem persists today among many Christian adults. These Christians fail to grasp the Jewishness of Jesus and the Jewish background to the New Testament writings. Dr. Brad Young's book therefore is indeed timely for it helps today's church address an obvious need. This welcome text brings the reader face-to-face with a Jewish Jesus, his Jewish teachings, and his Jewish world.

Numerous centuries of anti-Jewishness and anti-Semitism within the church have created a great need for solid teaching material on the Jewish background to the Gospel accounts. The theological teachings of Jesus are Jewish to the core, rooted in the Torah of Israel. Brad Young has rightly observed that "by rejecting Judaism the church has missed Jesus." In this volume, Dr. Young places Jesus in his Jewish context. He permits the words of Jesus to glisten within their own Semitic setting. For the author, "Jesus is an insider promoting renewal and reform from within the system." Since many Christians are uninformed about the system, Dr. Young has done his readers a great service in introducing them to Jewish theological thought. Throughout the book he interacts extensively with the Hebrew Scriptures, the Dead Sea Scrolls, Josephus, early rabbinic literature, and other extrabiblical Jewish sources. What emerges, however, is not "Jesus the Jewish theologian" in any Western, systematic sense. Rather, in Jesus, Dr. Young presents an Eastern, or Semitic, theologian, one who employs a living, vibrant theology distinguished by such features as action, metaphor, mystery, quest for holiness in life, and the experience of the presence and power of God (not mere thinking about God) in the life of the individual. Brad Young is exceptionally well qualified to write this book on Jesus the Jewish theologian. The fact that he spent nearly a decade living in Jerusalem and had as his mentor in Gospel research a world-class Jewish scholar, David Flusser, makes for impressive credentials. Furthermore, in the world of biblical scholarship it is relatively rare to find a New Testament specialist so well trained in Hebrew language and early rabbinic literature, as well as the Greek Scriptures. In addition, Dr. Young's work with a coterie of Jewish and Christian scholars associated with the Jerusalem School of Synoptic Research has further sharpened his understanding of the words of Jesus within their first-century Jewish matrix.

Anyone who picks up this book and begins to study it will immediately recognize that it is not simply "more of the same"; it cannot be characterized as another "garden variety" book on the life and teachings of Jesus. The table of contents and generous supply of notes certainly reveal this fact. Through extensive use of Jewish sources Dr. Young has creatively shed new light on Jesus, master Jewish teacher and theologian. Brad Young gets behind the synoptic accounts and allows the Hebraic setting of the words of Jesus to shine through.

To look at the Gospel events and to hear the words of Jesus in their Jewish context should be the desire of every student of the New Testament. *Jesus the Jewish Theologian* helps make this possible. It opens many windows of fresh insight into the

Gospel accounts. Christians and Jews can profit much from reading this excellent book, a very readable and scholarly work. It will be my delight to commend this volume to a wide readership, for a Jesus robbed of or removed from his Jewish setting results in much misunderstanding about him.

Dr. Young's book will prove to be a useful tool in the hands of those who are eager to discover in detail how Jesus is a theologian, a rabbi who based his rich theology on Judaism. May this book have the long life it richly deserves.

Marvin R. Wilson
Ockenga Professor of Biblical and Theological Studies
Gordon College
Wenham, Massachusetts

Preface
Jesus and His Religious Heritage

From my youth onwards I have found in Jesus my great brother. That Christianity has regarded and does regard him as God and Savior has always appeared to me a fact of the highest importance which, for his sake and my own, I must endeavor to understand. . . . My own fraternally open relationship to him has grown ever stronger and clearer, and today I see him more strongly and clearly than ever before. I am more than ever certain that a great place belongs to him in Israel's history of faith and that this place cannot be described by any of the usual categories.

—Martin Buber

IN AN INTERNATIONALLY RECOGNIZED UNIVERSITY, A world-renowned New Testament scholar remarked to his students, "The first thing you must do to be a good Christian is to kill the Jew inside of you." One of the students raised her hand to respond to his statement with a question. The learned professor listened as she asked him, "Do you mean Jesus?"

His statement and her question must be taken seriously. They represent two quite divergent views of the beginnings of Christianity. Who is Jesus of Nazareth? Here I will argue that Jesus is a theologian. In fact Jesus based his theology upon Judaism. Jesus never rejected his cultural and religious heritage. As a devout Jew, he was loyal to his people. The Christian belief system, however, is built in part upon the teachings of Jesus, but it ignores their solid foundation in Jewish theology.

The world-renowned New Testament scholar viewed Judaism as the antithesis of everything he believed about Jesus and the beginnings of Christian faith. His theology betrays his antagonism toward Jewish belief and practice. But his student possessed greater wisdom. She demonstrated a keen awareness of the fact that Jesus himself was Jewish. In her eyes, Jesus was at one with his people. The religion of the Jews in the first century is the root which produced the fruit of Christian faith. Faith in Jesus, however, has sometimes made it difficult for Christians to understand and appreciate the faith of Jesus. The religion of Jesus and his people was Judaism. Christian faith in Jesus sometimes has alienated Jesus from ancient Judaism and has exiled him from his people. Today I sense a new openness and a strong longing to learn from the teacher of Galilee. People sincerely desire to know what Jesus wanted to say. Here we will endeavor to listen to Jesus' message as an audience in the first century would have heard and understood his words.

The audience is decisive. Theologians have read the Gospels as Christian literature written by the church and for the church. When Jesus is viewed among the Gentiles, the significance of Jewish culture and custom is minimized or forgotten altogether. But when Jesus is viewed as a Jew within the context of first-century Judaism, an entirely different portrait emerges. Indeed many divergent portrayals of Jesus have been given throughout history. In the essays concerning Jesus' life and teachings that follow, an increased sensitivity to the rich heritage of the Jewish people will be pursued. The Torah rooted faith in the one all-powerful God and a strong sense of national identity; and the homeland of a devout people created a setting in which Jesus taught and worked among his people. The historical sources and new archaeological evidence describing a distinct way of life must be carefully studied to understand the Gospels.

Today the Christian faithful have been challenged with the message of God's love for the Jewish people. The New Testament scholar who told his class "The first thing you must do to be a good Christian is to kill the Jew inside of you," betrays a view deeply rooted in some traditional church teachings. His starting point is very important. The professor begins with a rejection of Judaism. His student responds with a remarkable question. Her challenging reaction to his remark warns us against doing away with Jesus by rejecting his expression of religious faith and practice. Most certainly Jesus did not begin by rejecting Judaism. He is a Jewish theologian.

Jesus is inextricably linked to his people and their faith. To understand Jesus, we must learn to love his people and his religion. He came not to destroy but to fulfill. Hillel could have made the same statement, especially in the context of a proper interpretation of the Ten Commandments. Jesus placed the meaning of Torah on a firmer footing. As Jesus spoke to a Jewish audience, he treated serious issues relating to the proper interpretation of Torah.

Because a scholar's perception of Torah and Judaism in the first century vastly impacts his or her approach to early Christianity, the following essays on Jesus begin with a study of the text. The textual examination of Jesus' teachings in the Gospels is the starting point. Linguistic study, historical reflection, cultural heritage, and archaeological discovery must inform our views of Jesus. On the one hand, the study of ancient Judaism will certainly give rich insight into the beginnings of Christianity. On the other hand, Judaism possesses a message and purpose apart from Christianity and its origins; moreover, these are expressed by the faith of the Jewish people that is rooted in Torah.

Traditional Christian views of Torah, however, sometimes make it difficult to understand Jesus' teachings. One finds at least four different views of Torah. The first one is the Jewish view. Torah is divine wisdom, which teaches the knowledge of God and reverence for his will. Torah reveals God's nature. He is Creator and Master of the universe. God as revealed in Torah is sovereign over all. The second is the Christian view, which often describes the old law as a perverted legalism. At best, the Christian view of Torah can be ambivalent or negative. The third is the Christian view of the Jewish view. Perhaps this third view is the most abominable. As Christians we have not studied Judaism for its own sake. The Jewish view of Torah is described wrongly as a salvation-by-works religion, a simple earn-your-way legalistic religious system of oppression. The Jewish concept of God's compassion and his sovereignty is replaced with traditional, untutored prejudices. The fourth view, however, is essential, but it is routinely neglected. It is Jesus' view. How did Jesus view Torah? Like other rabbis and teachers, Jesus developed his own approach within the parameters of ancient Jewish faith and practice. Consequently, Jesus cannot be alienated from Judaism or exiled from his people. But one thing is clear. Those wanting to understand Torah must never reject the Jewish people and Judaism.

The present book is written for all readers interested in fresh insights into the Jewish beginnings of Christianity. My hope is that some results of scholarly reflection on the life and teachings of Jesus from leading scholars in Israel will be made more accessible to a wider circle of readers. The theme of Jesus the Jewish theologian unifies these chapters concerning the Jewish background to the life and teachings of Jesus. The beginnings of Christianity will never be properly understood by "killing the Jew inside of you," as the professor advised. Instead, the student's question should speak to us in the post-holocaust era. We must not "kill" Jesus by destroying his links to his people and his faith. For Jesus, Judaism was a vibrant belief in the true God. The traditional attitude of ecclesiastical teachings toward the Jewish sources of early Christianity too often has distorted the message of Jesus. He sought to reform and revitalize, not to destroy and replace.

Regrettably, the voice of Jesus has become muddled by the din of scholarly debate and the facade of church religion. The Jewish roots of Jesus' teachings lead to a fresh hearing of the ancient text. Overcoming the cultural and historical barriers that hinder the modern seeker is risky, but every effort to give us a clearer vision of Jesus is worth the struggle. I hope these studies will give greater clarity to the message of Jesus as we explore the Jewish roots of the Gospel texts. Our greatest challenge is to hear his authentic voice. Early Judaism provides the firm foundation for a proper understanding of Jesus and his Jewish theology.

Acknowledgements

MANY PEOPLE HAVE AIDED ME IN MY QUEST FOR learning and understanding. Here I would like to say thank you to special friends and colleagues who have contributed to my understanding of Jesus and assisted me in the writing of *Jesus the Jewish Theologian*. While every book is the result of many people working together, the present text is especially indebted to a number of outstanding specialists in Jewish and Christian studies who have influenced my research, encouraged my efforts, and often offered critical insight.

First and foremost, I must acknowledge the tremendous influence of Professor David Flusser of the Hebrew University. With respect to the origins of Christianity and early Judaism, Professor Flusser's work is crucial for any serious study of Jesus and the Gospels. I deeply cherish his warm friendship, keen wit, and sharp mind. For me, it has been a life-changing experience to sit at his feet and exchange words of Torah. No one who works with him will remain the same. His energy and vision have impacted my life forever. He has assisted me in understanding the life and teachings of Jesus. The authenticity of his scholarship, the intensity of his spirit, and the insight he possesses into the historical Jesus have been rich sources of inspiration and guidance. I have benefited from his counsel. I highly value his understanding of classical Greek, the Dead Sea Scrolls, rabbinic literature, and the Gospels.

I must also express my profound thanks to Dr. Robert Lisle Lindsey, who pioneered a Hebrew translation of the Gospel of Mark and made a fresh analysis of the interrelationships of the Synoptic Gospels. His analysis of the Greek text and knowledge of the Hebrew language have enhanced my study of the Gospels. During my stay in Jerusalem, Lindsey guided me and encouraged my research. Throughout his retirement years in Oklahoma,

I have benefited from our fruitful discussions. His friendship and scholarship have been my constant companions in writing this work.

Over the years, I have discussed a number of issues relating to parable study with Professor Shmuel Safrai of the Hebrew University. His insights have proved to be invaluable. Dr. Stephen R. Notley has read much of the text, making helpful recommendations. I admire his knowledge of the text and acquaintance with the geographical setting. Here in Tulsa, I have enjoyed active exchange with Rabbi Marc Boone Fitzerman of B'nai Emunah Congregation, and I have often benefited from his scholarly intuition and creativity. I esteem his friendship and appreciate his dedication for expanding understanding between Christians and Jews. From the Jewish-Christian dialogue group of Tulsa, Sheila Mudd has been kind enough to read the manuscript and offer valuable help.

My friend and colleague Joseph Frankovic has been a source of encouragement and help. He has read the entire manuscript and made important suggestions for improving the work. I value his scholarly insight, and I am grateful for his tireless effort. His editorial suggestions have made many arguments of the text clearer. I was privileged to have him in my classroom, and it has been rewarding to see him further his studies in the fine doctoral program at Jewish Theological Seminary. Few Christians possess his profound understanding of the relationship between the church and the synagogue. Frankovic's strong scholarship has made the book more accessible and refined many difficult issues.

Dr. Roy B. Blizzard has challenged many in the church to reevaluate their understanding of Jesus and early Judaism. I appreciate the way Dr. Blizzard and his wife, Gloria, have promoted scholarship, encouraged me, and helped students studying the beginnings of Christianity. They have stood behind many Christians who wanted to study Hebrew and develop meaningful relationships with the Jewish community. I value highly my discussions with him concerning Gospel scholarship and his thoughtful recommendations. A number of these studies appeared in a preliminary form in his journal, *Yavo Digest,* which reaches a wide audience in the Christian community. His daughter, Georgia Lee Clifton, has edited these studies and has made an outstanding contribution to the work. Dennis Clifton, her husband, has been an active participant in the scholarly endeavors. Their friendship has meant a great deal to my wife, Janice, and to me. I greatly appreciate the Blizzard family and their energetic efforts to further education and strengthen scholarship. I gratefully dedicate this book to Dennis and Georgia Lee Clifton.

I must mention my close working relationship with my faculty colleagues here in the School of Theology at Oral Roberts University. Dr. Roy E. Hayden has read much of the work and has given me strong encouragement. Dr. Howard Ervin has helped me refine some linguistic issues. Dr. Robert Mansfield read parts of the work and has helped in my effort. Our dean, Dr. Paul G. Chappell, possesses tremendous energy and dedication. His vision for excellence in scholarship and his appreciation for the Jewish roots of Christianity have contributed much to the writing of the book.

I am grateful to the Israel Department of Antiquities for its help in obtaining photographs of archaeological artifacts. The Israeli government and academic community have supported exploration and discovery. The antiquities authorities have been extremely helpful and supportive of academic exchange and advancement. I appreciate the use of their pictorial archives which illustrate the discussion of my book. My work at the Hebrew University has directed much of my involvement with this book while challenging some of our traditional misconceptions of first-century Judaism and Jesus' relationship to his people.

My dear friends Dr. Marvin Wilson and Rabbi David Wolpe each graciously agreed to write a foreword to the book. It was my desire that the book contain two forewords, one written by a Jewish leader and one written by a Christian. They are both scholars, but they are also leaders in their respective communities. I admire them for their scholarship and for their sacrificial service to the community. They have built bridges of understanding between Christians and Jews through example, giving of self, and academic exchange. My hope is that readers of the present book will seek out the fine scholarship of Marvin Wilson and David Wolpe. Dr. Wilson's book, *Our Father Abraham,* has been a favorite textbook among my students. Rabbi David Wolpe's thoughtful book, *Healer of Shattered Hearts,* has challenged Christians and Jews with a powerful portrayal of the divine nature. Christians need to hear Rabbi Wolpe's message, which paves the way for a new vision of Judaism and a fresh approach to the rich heritage which binds Christians and Jews together. As a Christian, I hope that the present book about Jesus will strengthen understanding between the faith communities of the church and the synagogue.

Much of my leisure time is devoted to writing and research. I highly value the dedication of my wife, Janice, and her involvement in projects like *Jesus the Jewish Theologian*. Our son, Matthew David, keeps us both very busy, and he is a joy to watch as he grows. My parents, Senator John and Claudeen Young, have strongly encouraged my academic work. I appreciate their understanding and strong support for these efforts.

It is my hope that the present work reaches both scholars and lay people and provides a firmer foundation for understanding Jesus in his first-century cultural setting. The strengths of the book are the fruit of many people working together. My life has been enriched with opportunities to interact with scholars as well as my students, all of whom have taught me so much. Time and space will not allow me to say thank you to many others who have provided necessary help in the production of the book. The give and take of scholarly exchange sharpens the point and refines the issue. The evidence, however, does not always permit a clear consensus of opinion. Any shortcomings of the book should be attributed to me.

List of Abbreviations

Most of the abbreviations used in the book should be familiar to the general reader. The *Encyclopaedia Judaica* has been consulted as a standard guide for many abbreviations. Below is a partial list of abbreviations to serve as a convenient reference.

AB	Anchor Bible
Ant.	*Jewish Antiquities* (see writings of Josephus)
b.	Babylonian as in Babylonian Talmud
b.	ben (son in Hebrew) or bar (son in Aramaic)
B. Bat.	*Baba Bathra*
B.C.E.	Before the Common Era, as B.C.
Ber.	*Berakhot*
C.E.	Common Era, as A.D.
chap.	chapter
ET	English translation
Ger.	German
Git.	*Gittin*
hal.	halakhah
Heb.	Hebrew
j.	Jerusalem as in Jerusalem or Palestinian Talmud
Jos.	Josephus
KJV	King James Version
LCL	Loeb Classical Library
LXX	Septuagint
m.	Mishnah
MS	manuscript
NASB	New American Standard Bible

NIGTC	New International Greek Testament Commentary
NIV	New International Version
NT	New Testament
NTG	New Testament in Greek (edited by the American and British Committees of the International Greek New Testament Project with the aim of providing a complete critical apparatus)
OT	Old Testament
PAM	Palestine Archaeological Museum
R.	Rabbi
Radak	Rabbi David Kimchi
Rashi	Rabbi Shelomo ben Yitzchak
RSV	Revised Standard Version
San.	*Sanhedrin*
Shab.	*Shabbat*
Ta'an.	*Ta'anit*
t.	Tosefta
TDNT	*Theological Dictionary of the New Testament*
Yeb.	*Yebamot*

Transliterations

Most of the Hebrew, Greek and Aramaic transliterations will follow the guidelines set forth on these two charts. Some inconsistency will appear in quotations and in some names. Generally the recognized English forms of Hebrew names has been followed. So instead of the transliterated form of the Hebrew name "Yehudah," the reader will find "Judah," the more common English form of the name.

GREEK

A α ą	a		Υ υ	u
B β	b		Φ φ	f
Γ γ	g		X χ	ch
Δ δ	d		Ψ ψ	ps
E ε	e		Ω ω ῳ	ō
Z ζ	z		αι	ai
H η ῃ	ē		ει	ei
Θ θ	th		οι	oi
I ι	i		υι	ui
K κ	k		ου	ou
Λ λ	l		ευ	eu
M μ	m		ηυ	ēu
N ν	n		ντ	nt
Ξ ξ	x		μπ	mp
O o	o		γκ	ngk
Π π	p		νγ	ng
P ρ ῥ	r rh		ʽ	h
Σ σ ς	s		ʼ	—
T τ	t			

HEBREW

Hebrew	Transliteration	Hebrew	Transliteration
א	not transliterated	ר	r
בּ	b	שׁ	sh
ב	v	שׂ	s
גּ	g	תּ	t
ג		ת	
דּ	d	ג׳	dzh, J
ד		ז׳	zh, J
ה	h	צ׳	tz
ו	v—when not a vowel	◌ָ	a
ז	z	◌ַ	a
ח	ch	◌ֲ	a
ט	t	◌ֵ	
י	y—when vowel and at end of words—i	◌ֶ	e
כּ	k	◌ֱ	e
ך‎,כ	kh	◌ְ	e (only *sheva na* is transliterated)
ל	l		
ם‎,מ	m	◌ִ	i
ן‎,נ	n	◌ִי	i
ס	s	◌ֹ	o
ע	not transliterated	וֹ	o
פּ	p	◌ֻ	u
ף‎,פ	f	וּ	u
ץ‎,צ	tz	◌ֵי	ei; biblical e
ק	k		

Introduction
Jesus the Jewish Theologian

*The Christian message, which in its origins intended to be an
affirmation and culmination of Judaism, became very early
diverted into a repudiation and negation of Judaism; obsolescence
and abrogation of Jewish faith became conviction and doctrine; the
new covenant was conceived not as a new phase or disclosure but as
abolition and replacement of the ancient one; theological thinking
fashioned its terms in a spirit of antithesis to Judaism. Contrast and
contradiction rather than acknowledgement of roots relatedness and
indebtedness, became the perspective. Judaism a religion of
law, Christianity a religion of grace; Judaism teaches a God of
wrath, Christianity a God of love; Judaism a religion of slavish
obedience, Christianity the conviction of free men; Judaism is
particularism, Christianity is universalism; Judaism seeks
work-righteousness, Christianity preaches faith-righteousness. The
teaching of the old covenant a religion of fear, the gospel of the new
covenant a religion of love.*

—Abraham Joshua Heschel

AS CHRISTIANS WE TEND TO VIEW PAUL AS THE
church's first theologian. I have become convinced
that this approach is theology at its worst. Christianity begins with Jesus. As a faith tradition, moreover, Christian belief must encompass all of the rich cultural and religious
heritage of its founder.

Jesus is a theologian. His rich genius and keen wit infuse
his colorful parables and creative teachings preserved in the
Gospel stories. Even though modern culture and religious per-
suasions make it difficult for a contemporary reader to comprehend his message in the same way that a Jewish listener could
in the first century, the theological depth of Jesus cannot be

overlooked. Jesus was every bit as much of a theologian as
the Apostle Paul. In fact, Jesus' training and experience as a
learned teacher of Torah far surpassed that of Paul the Jewish
apostle to the Gentiles.

The fact that Jesus was a Jew is seldom questioned today, but
its far-reaching ramifications for the interpretation of his life
are routinely passed over. Although Jesus was Jewish, his theology is sometimes treated as if he were Christian. But Jesus
never attended a church. He never celebrated Christmas. He
never wore new clothes on Easter Sunday. His cultural orientation was rooted deeply in the faith experience of his people. His
teachings concerning God's love and the dignity of each human
being were based upon the foundations of Jewish religious
thought during the Second Temple period. The more we learn
about this fascinating period of history, the more we will know
about Jesus. Jesus worshipped in the synagogue. He celebrated
the Passover. He ate kosher food. He offered prayers in the
temple in Jerusalem. The Jewish religious heritage of Jesus
impacted his life in every dimension of his daily experience.

Jesus must be understood as a Jewish theologian. His theology
is Jewish to the core. The tragic history of the relationship
between Judaism and Christianity makes it extremely difficult
to hear his forceful voice. The attacks of the church against
the synagogue have stripped Jesus of his religious heritage. As
Christians we have been taught wrong prejudices about Jews
and Judaism. Hatred for the Jewish people has erected a barrier
separating Jesus from his theology. Ethnically he may be considered a Jew, but religiously he remains a Christian who failed
to reform the corrupt religious system of the Jews. Such an
approach fails. Jesus is Jewish both in his ethnic background
and in his religious thought and practice.

A fresh approach to Jesus is urgently needed. Today Christians and Jews want to understand one another. In a post-
holocaust era one must hope that genuine love and mutual
respect will uproot the ever-present danger of prejudice and
bigotry. Jesus should be viewed as an integral part of Judaism
during his day.

The Jewish theology of Jesus surprises and amazes contemporary readers. The teachings of Jesus are intimately connected to
his Jewish background, which runs deeper than flesh and blood.
The Judaism of Jesus is represented in his profound theology of
God and the inestimable value of each person created in the

divine image. Jesus is Jewish. He is also a theologian. These two facts should never be separated: Jesus is a Jewish theologian.

While Jesus' theology is made known through his teachings and parables, the person is also made known through life events. In the Gospels the experiences of Jesus' life are described as a messianic drama. The birth was no ordinary birth. While similar to the common lot of humankind, it was an extraordinary event which heralds a new beginning. The baptism of Jesus was so much more than the common experience of John the Baptist's followers in the desert regions of Judea who went to immerse themselves in the river Jordan. Even in death, the experience of Jesus was distinctive, and when examining the life of Jesus the theologian, one must also carefully study his death. Death is the common experience of humanity, but in the Gospel story Jesus died to experience the resurrection.

Why was Jesus killed? In the age of Roman supremacy, political intrigue, and the intense strife between popular religious movements and diverse local authorities maintaining a balance of power, the question might even be asked in another way. Was Jesus killed because he was a bad Jew? Or was he killed because he was a good Jew? From a raw historical perspective, who should be blamed for his death? The cause for Jesus' execution in the Roman court of Pontius Pilate was infinitely more connected to politics and the determined policy of the imperial government, which sought to root out all Jewish messianic hopes, than it was related to a revolutionary theology or religious upheaval. Jesus' theology did not prompt his death. Jesus was killed as a devout Jew loyal to the heritage of his faith. The political circumstances of a difficult era of history, where Jews were persecuted for being devout, and, above all, where the old messianic hope had to be suppressed, describe the background for Jesus' trial and execution.

But the Gospels proclaim that Jesus rose from the dead. The tomb could not imprison the Jewish Messiah. The proclamation of the risen Lord became the essence of the preaching of the early church as enshrined in the Gospels. Jesus the Messiah gave prophetic predictions concerning the future. His messianic task could be completed only in two comings, one as the suffering servant and one as the eschatological judge.

In the following chapters I begin with the Gospel account of Jesus' life and teachings. The approach pursues a reading of the messianic drama of Jesus' life events, his kingdom proclamation, his theological foundation in parable illustrations, the conflict leading to his death, and his intriguing predictions concerning the future. Jewish parallels from sources that are contemporary with Jesus or throw light upon the original force of his word are examined. Such sources must be studied for their own message in their original context. But without a consideration of the Jewish parallels, the Gospels will forever be filtered through Western culture, and Jesus will be completely missed or greatly misunderstood. Jesus the Jewish theologian has changed the world forever. The world, however, including church leaders and outstanding scholars, often has missed Jesus. The original Jewish environment of his life promises to reveal a new vision of Jesus and his message.

PART 1

THE MESSIANIC DRAMA OF JESUS' LIFE EVENTS

One can no longer contrast belief in the Gospels themselves with belief in the Church, for the Gospels themselves came out of the Church. If they had their origins in the preaching and teaching of the Apostles and were constructed of units preserved and formed into shape by the local Christian churches, this means that he who bases his faith on the Christ of the Gospels is really basing his faith on what the early Church taught about Christ.

—Raymond E. Brown

1

The Birth of the Messiah
and the Song of the Angels

THE STORY OF JESUS' BIRTH IN THE GOSPELS RESO-
nates with Jewish beliefs concerning God's plan of
salvation and the promised coming of the messianic
deliverer. The birth of the Messiah is by no means an ordinary
affair. The event is marked by prophecy and angelic visitations.
The song of the angels as told in Luke 2:14 expresses the inward
yearnings of the Jewish people concerning the Messiah. These
words of praise and adoration which define the messianic task
have a rich Jewish background.

The threefold structure of the angelic song in the King James
Version of the Bible is well known and often quoted during the
Christmas season: 1. "Glory to God in the highest" 2. "on earth
peace" 3. "goodwill toward men." Most modern translations,
however, have a variant twofold version of the angelic song:
1. "Glory to God in the highest" 2. "Peace on earth toward men
of goodwill." The first version emphasizes the universal meaning of the coming of the Messiah. Goodwill is for all people.
The second version indicates that his coming is reserved for
people who are worthy, that is, "men of goodwill." The difference between these two versions of the song is more significant than is often realized. David Flusser has argued strongly
for the first version, that is, the three-part pronouncement of
the angels.[1] Below we shall examine the Jewish background to
the birth of the Messiah in the Gospels and the meaning of the
song of the angels in order to understand the nature of the messianic task.

The texts of the Gospels are grounded in the rich diversity of
Jewish messianic thought which characterized the late Second
Temple period.[2] When studying the Gospels, one must seek
to become aware of Jesus' distinctive message about his task.

Grounding this task in the expectations and traditions of first-century Judaism also includes certain distinct and innovative features. The song of the angels, "Glory to God in the highest, peace on earth, goodwill toward men" or as other translations have rendered it, "Glory to God in the highest, peace on earth toward men of goodwill," has become a point of scholarly disagreement.[3] As we examine the meaning of the birth of the Messiah in the context of ancient Jewish thought, the better reading of the threefold blessing for the angelic song will become clear. First the background of the story of the birth of the Messiah must be viewed within its historical and cultural context.

Important biblical figures chosen by God to carry out special tasks in salvation history often have unusual circumstances surrounding their births. The profile of such personalities in the Bible usually includes an account of the individual's miraculous birth. Frequently a miracle baby is considered to be destined for greatness in God's higher purposes. Salvation and redemption are made possible because God sets apart an individual even from the womb to be anointed for the divine task.

For instance, the Old Testament contains a number of miracle births. Abraham and Sarah miraculously give birth to Isaac.[4] The Scripture teaches, "The LORD visited Sarah as he had said, and the LORD did to Sarah as he had promised. And Sarah conceived, and bore Abraham a son in his old age at the time of which God had spoken to him" (Gen 21:1–2). Isaac had a unique task to fulfill in the divine plan. In addition to Isaac's birth, the births of Samson, who saved the people from the Philistines, and Samuel, who served as an anointed prophet, were also described as miraculous events (Judg 13:3, 24; 1 Sam 1:2, 20). Many rabbis felt that even Moses was a miracle baby.[5] Isaac, Samson, Samuel, and certainly Moses all played special roles in the divine plan.

According to the rabbis, prophecy and divine intervention accompanied the birth of Moses. Like the child Jesus, whose unique mission prophecies foretold,[6] Moses was the subject of a prophecy spoken by his sister Miriam. Before Moses was born, Miriam predicted the destiny of her baby brother. Moses became a model for the messianic idea. The Talmud tells about Miriam, who prophesied, saying, "In the future my mother will give birth to a son who will save Israel." At the time when

Moses was born, the whole house was filled with light. Her father stood up and kissed her on the head. He said to her, "My daughter, your prophecy has been fulfilled."[7]

Miriam prophesied about the task before Moses. God would use her infant brother to save Israel. The struggles of the family to protect the child from the Egyptian Pharaoh, who desired to kill all the Hebrew children, served the higher purpose of redeeming the people of Israel from slavery.

The stories of Jesus' birth are preceded in Luke's Gospel by the account of John the Baptist's family and his miraculous birth. John the Baptist also had a role to play. Perhaps Luke employed a source about the life and ministry of John for the record of these events.[8] In any case, the episodes in the Gospel of Luke indicate the manner in which God used the longings of an ordinary family like Elizabeth and Zechariah, the mother and father of John the Baptist, to fulfill the divine strategy. They wanted a baby. When they prayed, God supernaturally intervened, and John the Baptist was born. His mission was to prepare the way for Jesus. Amazingly, the personal anguish of a barren family hoping for the birth of a child gave way to the higher purpose in God's divine plan to prepare for the coming of Jesus.

The shepherds who were watching their flocks by night were common Jewish laborers. One cannot be certain of their status in society but it seems that shepherds were not highly esteemed.[9] Some suggest they were tending some of the sacrificial animals for the temple, but this is not implied in any way by the text. Unlike the account of Matthew where great wise men from the East are told of the coming king, the humble shepherds experienced the manifestation of angels who sang a blessing that described the purpose of Jesus' birth.[10] In light of the descriptions of supernatural happenings associated with important figures in Jewish history, the angels' appearance and their hymn of praise are very much a part of the fabric of Hebrew thought for the messianic idea. The anticipation that the birth of the Messiah would be heralded by the angels of the divine presence was by no means foreign to popular thinking in the first century.

The difference between the two-part version of their song, "Glory to God in the highest and on earth peace toward men of goodwill," and the threefold blessing, "Glory to God in the highest and on earth peace, goodwill toward men," is of tremendous importance for the understanding of Jesus' messianic task. In Greek the difference between the two translations is actually only one letter. The word for "goodwill" in Greek, *eudokia,* in the nominative case supports the threefold translation. The merciful goodwill of God is designated for all people. When the one Greek letter, sigma (ς pronounced like the *s* sound in English), is added to the end of the word, *eudokia,* it is put in the genitive case and would be translated, "toward men of goodwill." The translation as a genitive, *eudokias,* accounts for the two-part version of the song. Reliable Greek manuscripts of Luke preserve both versions of the text, that is, with the sigma (in the genitive case) and without it (in the nominative case).[11] With the sigma, the text describes the nature of the people by the genitive case. Peace is promised only to people of goodwill, or as the Revised Standard Version translates, "among men with whom he [God] is pleased!" The word *eudokia* "goodwill" in Greek is a translation of the Hebrew term *ratzon* (e.g., in LXX 1 Chron 16:10; Ps 5:12).

The Dead Sea Scrolls use this term, *ratzon,* quite frequently. David Flusser has studied the word in the Dead Sea Scrolls and observed that it became a technical term for the sectarian theology of predestination in the community.[12] The elect are predestined to receive God's goodwill. Only they receive his benevolent favor. This specialized meaning of *ratzon* "goodwill," as Flusser has observed, departs from the sense of the word which occurs in the Hebrew Scriptures, where divine favor is more universal. At least traditional Jewish interpretations do not restrict the meaning of the word *ratzon* "goodwill" as does the Dead Sea community. Bruce Metzger comments in regard to the two-part text, "Prior to the discovery of the Dead Sea Scrolls it was sometimes argued that 'men of [God's] good pleasure' is an unusual, if not impossible, expression in Hebrew."[13] With the discovery of the Dead Sea Scrolls, however, the expression has been found in the Hebrew of the sect. Since both readings are possible in Hebrew and both texts have strong support in the textual tradition, the task of determining which one of these variants is the better reading is indeed difficult.

Here, the context in the Gospel of Luke and the background from Jewish liturgy provide strong support for the threefold text of Luke 2:14:

1. "Glory to God in the highest"

2. "On earth peace"

3. "Goodwill toward men."

The angel who appears to the humble shepherds says to them, "Fear not: for behold, I bring you good tidings of great joy which shall be to all people" (v. 10). The phrase "which shall be to all people" does not limit the message of peace to a select group.[14] In Flusser's study of the theology of the Dead Sea sect, he has pointed out that this sectarian community understood God's goodwill *(ratzon)* as restricted to the members of their elect group. God's peace and goodwill could not be offered to anyone else. Everyone outside their limited number was predestined for eternal punishment. The concept of free will was not accepted by this group. They believed that an individual is not able to make the decision whether or not to follow the path of God. In their view, a person already possessed a spirit, either good or evil, which predetermined the individual's relationship to God. Therefore, they used the expression "men of goodwill" as a technical term for members of their own religious order.[15] The wider Hebrew meaning of the term as found frequently in the Bible was ignored by the Dead Sea community. It is easy to understand how later Christian scribes may have been drawn to the genitive form of *eudokia* because it expressed their understanding of a limited salvation for those predestined for God's goodness. The threefold text for the birth of the Messiah, which proclaims God's goodwill to all people, however, most certainly is supported from the context in Luke 2:10. The glad tidings are for all people. Clearly the three-part version of the blessing in Luke 2:14 is the preferred translation. The King James Version renders a fine translation of the threefold text.

In the larger Jewish background of the text, Flusser has noticed also the strong similarities the threefold text of Luke shares with traditional liturgical blessings. For example, there is the description of the praise of the angels in Isaiah 6:3, when they cry out, "Holy, Holy, Holy is the LORD of hosts: the whole earth is filled with his glory." The Lord is called holy three times. The three-part structure of blessings as well as the rule of threes in storytelling is a well-known characteristic of folktales and a familiar literary device.[16] In the praise of the angels who surround the heavenly throne, the word "holy" is used three

times in Isaiah. The Aramaic Targum of this passage provides
insight into the ancient Jewish understanding of the text of
Isaiah. Moreover, it forms a remarkable parallel to Luke 2:14.[17]
Again a three-part structure emerges from the song of the angels. The Targum of Isaiah says,

1. "Holy in the highest heaven, the house of his Presence"

2. "Holy upon the earth, the work of his might"

3. "Holy for endless ages is the Lord of hosts:
   the whole earth is full of the brightness of his glory."

The song of the angels to the shepherds concerning the birth of
the Messiah reflects the three-part litany of the angels in
Isaiah's vision in Jewish tradition. The first blessing contains the
strongest words of praise for God who is portrayed as the all-
powerful king enthroned on high. "Glory to God in the highest"
from Luke is parallel to "Holy in the highest heaven, the house
of his Presence," from the Targum of Isaiah. The second blessing in Luke, "On earth peace" is echoed in the next blessing in
Isaiah, "Holy upon earth the work of his might." The most
important of the phrases in Luke, "goodwill toward men," finds
parallel in the third part of the angels' song in the Targum of
Isaiah, "the whole earth is full of the brightness of his glory."
   The message of the angels for the birth of the Messiah is
universal. The all-powerful God of heaven seeks to establish
peace on earth and express his merciful will for all people. His
divine favor is provided for all humanity. To understand fully
the good tidings of the angels, one must recall the Hebrew
meaning of peace. It is wholeness and completeness. Jesus is
said to be the Prince of Peace. The word "prince" could refer to
an official in government. During Jesus' day, governmental officials were in charge of war. Jesus, however, is not the minister
of war. He is the Prince of Peace who brings wholeness and
salvation for all the people. The goodwill of God is not restricted to those few who are predestined, but for all who receive God's divine favor. According to Jeremias, "goodwill"
(Heb. *ratzon*), appears 56 times in the Hebrew Old Testament.
In at least 37 instances, it refers to God's good pleasure.[18] It is
his higher purpose for those he created. The word "goodwill"
denotes God's blessing and his divine favor. In Deuteronomy
33:24 "satisfied with goodwill" is paralleled by "full with the
blessing of the LORD." Goodwill is a blessing of the Lord.

The word "goodwill" possessed deep meaning for the Jewish people in the first century. Not only is the term used in Old Testament passages like Deuteronomy 33:24, but in the Jewish literature around the time of Jesus it signifies God's desire to express his merciful benevolence to humanity. In the Psalms of Solomon, "goodwill" describes God's goodness: "To us and to our children, O Lord our Savior, be your goodwill *[eudokia]* forever; we shall not be moved forever."[19] Divine favor is expressed when God's good pleasure is accomplished. His will is done. Thus in the Lord's Prayer Jesus instructs his disciples to pray, "Thy will be done." This word for will is the same term, *ratzon,* in Hebrew. It denotes God's higher purpose and his good pleasure. It expresses what God truly desires. He wants people to experience his peace and salvation. The birth of the Messiah means that peace, divine wholeness, is made known to people. God's merciful will is revealed for all of humanity in the coming of Jesus. His coming was for "all people" as indicated in Luke 2:10. The "goodwill" in the song of the angels refers to God's divine favor which is being revealed in the birth of Jesus the Messiah. The mission of Jesus resonated with the song of the angels, "Glory to God in the highest, on earth peace, goodwill toward men!"

NOTES

1. David Flusser, "Sanktus und Gloria," in *Abraham unser Vater: Festschrift für Otto Michel zum 60. Geburtstag* (ed. O. Betz, M. Hengel, and P. Schmidt; Leiden: Brill, 1963) 129–52; reprinted now in D. Flusser, *Entdeckungen im Neuen Testament* 1.226–44. The approach of Flusser is favored by Jean Daniélou, *The Infancy Narratives* (New York: Herder and Herder, 1968) 63.

2. See the important study, R. E. Brown, *The Birth of the Messiah* (New York: Doubleday, 1977; revised, 1993) 425–27.

3. While David Flusser (see note 1) has argued convincingly for the three-part song of the angels, the more accepted position today is by far the two-part version of the song. This position has appeared in numerous studies. See for example, E. Vogt, " 'Peace among Men of God's Good Pleasure' Luke 2,14," in *The Scrolls and the New Testament* (ed. K. Stendahl; New York: Harper, 1957) 114–17; J. A. Fitzmyer, " 'Peace upon Earth among Men of His Good Will' (Luke 2:14)," *Theological Studies* 19 (1958) 225–27; and also Randy Buth, "The Sons of His Will," *Jerusalem Perspective* (November/December 1989) 6–7. Fitzmyer's treatment presents the evidence for this view clearly. See also his fine

commentary, J. A. Fitzmyer, *The Gospel according to Luke* (AB 28; New York: Doubleday, 1981) 1.410–12. None of these studies, however, deals with the compelling evidence cited by Flusser for accepting the three-part song of the angels in Luke 2:14. In the present short chapter, only portions of Flusser's arguments will be presented.

4. Gen 18:10; 21:1–3; on Ishmael see also Gen 16:11.

5. See the discussion of David Daube, *The New Testament and Rabbinic Judaism* (1956; reprint, Peabody: Hendrickson, 1994) 5–9. See the excellent and intriguing study by Allan Kensky, "Moses and Jesus: The Birth of a Savior," *Judaism* 42 (1993) 43–49.

6. See Luke 2:25–38.

7. B. *Megillah* 14a and see parallel traditions b. *Sotah* 13a; Mechilta de Rabbi Simeon bar Yochai on Exodus 15:20 (Epstein and Melamed, p. 100); Exodus Rabbah 1:22; Numbers Rabbah 13:19; Midrash Mishle 14.

8. It would not be surprising if a source similar to the Gospel stories about Jesus was written about the life of John the Baptist and circulated among his followers. The stories about John the Baptist's birth could have been a part of such a text. In the prologue to Luke's Gospel, Luke explains that he used sources available to him that could throw light upon Jesus' life. Though a Baptist source has not survived the centuries, such a literary work may have circulated widely during the period.

9. As Fitzmyer, *Luke,* 1.408, correctly notes, "News of the birth of the Messiah is first made known, not to religious or secular rulers of the land, but to lowly inhabitants of the area, busy with other matters." The good news is not given to the high and mighty power brokers of that day but to the common folk.

10. Joseph Frankovic has suggested that the universal message of the angelic hymn is supported by the fact that the angels appear to humble shepherds who were regarded as a dubious lot (private communication). Were shepherds widely esteemed as "men of goodwill"? The wise men would be more suitable for such a descriptive term, but not shepherds.

11. For a consideration of the textual evidence see Bruce Metzger, *A Textual Commentary on the Greek New Testament* (New York: United Bible Societies, 1975) 133; and Fitzmyer, *Luke,* 1.411. Both Metzger and Fitzmyer see stronger textual support for the two-part text. But the correctors of Sinaiticus and Vaticanus as well as L, Θ, and patristic evidence should not be dismissed lightly. It is easier to explain how scribes would change the nominative form into the genitive for their theological purposes than to imagine that the sigma of the genitive case was deleted to make the text more universal in outlook. For further evidence see *The New Testament in Greek. The Gospel according to St. Luke* (ed. American and British Committees of the International Greek New Testament Project; Oxford: Clarendon, 1984) 1.39–40.

12. See Flusser, "Sanktus und Gloria," 130 and 149.

13. Metzger, *Textual Commentary,* 133. It is clear that both texts are possible in Hebrew. However, the sectarian thought of the religious order stands behind the construction of the phrase in the Hebrew of the Dead Sea Scrolls. The more direct Hebrew reconstruction, *ratzon le-bene adam,* as would be in the threefold text of the song of the angels, is far better.

14. In the least, the phrase from Luke 2:10, "to all the people" (Greek *panti to lao* or in Hebrew *lakol haam*), refers to all the people of Israel, which is more universal than the restrictive "men of goodwill." The words of the angel of the Lord in Luke 2:10, "I bring you good news of a great joy which will come to all the people," portray an event in salvation history for the entire nation.

15. The term, "men of goodwill" *meanshe ratzon* (literally "from men of goodwill"), appears only once in an unpublished Dead Sea Scroll fragment 4Q418 (PAM 41.908; see S. Reed, M. Lundberg, E. Tov, and Stephan J. Pfann, *The Dead Sea Scrolls on Microfiche* [Leiden: Brill, 1993], and also R. Eisenman and J. Robinson, *A Facsimile Edition of the Dead Sea Scrolls* [Washington, D.C.: Biblical Archaeology Society, 1991], vol. 1, plate 506). The terms "sons of thy goodwill" *bene ratzon-chah* (1QH 4.32f., 11.9) and "the chosen of goodwill" *bachire ratzon* (1QH 8.6), published some time ago from the Thanksgiving Scroll, have led a number of scholars to think that the phrase "men of goodwill" is idiomatic Hebrew. These word constructions, however, reflect the high sectarian and exclusive theology of the Dead Sea Scrolls. On one occasion, David Flusser wrote to me, "In my opinion, such a phrase as 'men of goodwill' cannot be said in Hebrew" (private communication). That such a phrase appears in the Dead Sea Scrolls does not mean necessarily that it is fine idiomatic Hebrew. As Bruce Metzger observed, "Prior to the discovery of the Dead Sea Scrolls it was sometimes argued that 'men of God's good pleasure' is an unusual, if not impossible, expression in Hebrew" (Metzger, *Textual Commentary,* 133). The evidence from the Dead Sea Scrolls must be weighed and evaluated in light of all considerations. I tend to agree with Flusser that the phrase "men of goodwill" is exceedingly difficult if not altogether impossible in Hebrew. The scrolls reflect the theological outlook of the sect, and this particular Hebrew construction is somewhat strained. They see men of goodwill as the sons of light in their community who are predestined to receive salvation. In ancient Jewish teachings, however, it was more acceptable to speak about God's goodwill.

16. The three-part nature of storytelling as in the parable of the Good Samaritan, for instance, where one sees (1) Priest (2) Levite and (3) Samaritan does not prove the point—but it does strengthen the other evidence in favor of "goodwill toward men" in Luke 2:14 (cf. Exod 20:4). On the parables, see also H. McArthur and R. Johnston, *They Also Taught in Parables* (Grand Rapids: Zondervan, 1990) 132–34.

17. See especially Flusser, "Sanktus und Gloria," 151.

18. See J. Jeremias, "*Anthropoi eudokias* (Lc 2, 14)," *Zeitschrift für die neutestamentliche Wissenschaft* 28 (1929) 13–20. See especially p. 16.

19. Psalms of Solomon 8:39. See R. H. Charles, *The Apocrypha and Pseudepigrapha of the Old Testament* (Oxford: Clarendon, 1977) 2.642. Most authorities agree that the Psalms of Solomon were originally composed in Hebrew and translated into Greek. See R. Wright, "Psalms of Solomon," in *The Old Testament Pseudepigrapha* (ed. J. Charlesworth; New York: Doubleday, 1985) 2.640.

2
The Baptism of the Messiah

IN ONE OF THE MORE FAMOUS AND WIDELY READ
books on the life of Christ, David Friedrich Strauss
(1835) argued that Jesus was baptized because he had
repented of his sins and felt the need for purification.[1] After all,
the baptism of John was for repentance. Why else would Jesus
seek baptism from John? On the other hand, by way of contrast
to Strauss' argument, New Testament teachings portray Jesus as
the anointed one of God who did not commit a sin. In addition,
the Gospel accounts of Jesus' baptism concentrate on describing
the surrounding events and the voice from heaven rather than
treating the issue of why Jesus was baptized.[2] Now a study of
the Dead Sea Scrolls, as well as a careful study of the rabbinic
literature and the writings of the first-century Jewish historian
Josephus, give us a fresh look at the story of Jesus' baptism.[3]
For a proper perspective we must view the episode through the
eyes of first-century Jews.

JESUS AND THE SPIRIT

The true significance of the baptism emerges through the
special description of the event and the powerful message given
through the heavenly voice. In this regard Luke is of immense
value because of the Third Gospel's strong emphasis on the
sonship of Jesus. As we shall see, Moffatt's translation, being
based on the better Greek texts, actually makes a direct reference to the messianic thought behind Psalm 2:7, "You are my
son, today I have begotten you." This chapter will examine this
all-important episode from Jesus' life in light of its Jewish background. The Jewish sources more clearly picture first-century
Israel and the deeper meaning of the baptism as an event in the
life of Jesus. One fact is certain from Strauss' book: John the
Baptist is a central figure in the Gospel accounts, and the role

of his controversial ministry in the wilderness when he called the people to repent from their sins and enter the waters of baptism prepared the way for the career of the coming one.

JOHN THE BAPTIST AND THE DEAD SEA SCROLLS

The Gospels portray John the Baptist as a passionate Hebrew prophet who announces that someone greater is coming. John hates sin. He preaches holiness with a fire that stirs the heart of everyone hearing his message. He invites the people to the waters of the Jordan River for a baptism of repentance.

Recently the Dead Sea Scrolls have afforded rich insight into John's thinking. The ancient scrolls outline special rules for the new members of the Dead Sea community. Required to undergo intensive training, careful screening, and arduous testing, in many ways new members had to prove their holiness and election as the "sons of light" before they were admitted. For example, new initiates had to surrender all their worldly goods and donate their money to the community fund before they were accepted into the fold of the Dead Sea sect. Members of the Qumran community also practiced baptism.

According to their view of baptism, the individual must be holy before ritual immersion. If the heart had not been washed through personal piety and holiness, the water of baptism would not purify the flesh. The Dead Sea sect emphasized ritual purity and practiced water baptism by immersion.[4] Archaeologists have discovered many ritual immersion pools at Tel Qumran where most scholars locate the headquarters of the Dead Sea sect. These numerous baptismal pools were designed according to the specifications of Jewish religious law.

At Qumran the individual seeking baptism had to be pure from sin before going into the water: "They shall not enter the water . . . unless they turn from their wickedness: for all who transgress His word are unclean."[5] Turning to God by recognizing the truth of the sect's teachings and by observing the commandments according to the community's interpretation of the law was required of all members. Baptism would not be administered for someone who was not living the proper life according to the community's standard. The *Community Rule* determines the law for the one seeking purification in baptism,

He shall not be reckoned among the perfect; he shall neither be purified by atonement, nor cleansed by purifying waters, nor sanctified by seas and rivers, nor washed clean with any ablution. Unclean, unclean shall he be. For as long as he despises the precepts of God he shall receive no instruction in the Community of His counsel.[6]

Notice the reference to the purifying waters of seas and rivers. In the Jewish teachings of the Mishnah, living water—defined as rivers or seas—was the highest grade of cleansing for ritual immersion (m. *Mikvaot* 1:6). The person was required to be immersed in living water which could be collected from rain or rivers. In a similar way, John the Baptist baptized in the river, which is considered living water. It is, however, also significant that the Dead Sea sect required religious purity before baptism. The individual seeking baptism was required to turn from wickedness before entering the waters of ritual immersion. Repentance preceded baptism in the Dead Sea community.

John the Baptist employed the same standard. The one who desired baptism was required first to turn from sin and then approach the waters with a pure heart. Repentance prepared the way for baptism. In that regard the pure life of Jesus was not a hindrance but rather a prerequisite for John's baptism. Josephus explains that in John's teachings repentance purified the soul while baptism cleansed the body. Josephus remarks concerning John the Baptist:

For Herod had put him [John the Baptist] to death, though he was a good man and had exhorted the Jews to lead righteous lives, to practice justice towards their fellows and piety towards God, and so doing to join in baptism. In his view this was a necessary preliminary if baptism was to be acceptable to God. They must not employ it to gain pardon for whatever sins they committed, but as a consecration of the body implying that the soul was already thoroughly cleansed by right behavior.[7]

John called on the people to practice piety and pursue a lifestyle of right conduct. The center of John the Baptist's activities was located close to the geographical area of Tel Qumran and near the caves where the Dead Sea Scrolls were discovered. Moreover, John's theological understanding of baptism seems to be similar to the approach taken to the ritual immersion practiced by the Dead Sea sect. Was John a member of the Dead Sea community? Scholars debate this question. While many similarities exist between John and the Dead Sea sect, the sharp differences are equally impressive. For example, Luke's Gospel even describes tax collectors and soldiers who went into the wilderness to hear John and repented of their sins.

The major center of the Dead Sea community was located near John's activities. Tax collectors or soldiers who sought membership in the Dead Sea community would be required to sell everything, drop out of society, and join the ascetic life of the holy congregation. After a probationary period of testing, and if they proved worthy, they would be accepted. According to Luke, John the Baptist gave a different answer to people who desired forgiveness. When the tax collectors asked John, "What shall we do?" they were seeking a true relationship with God through repentance. They wanted to renew a proper relationship with their Father in heaven. John said to them, "Collect no more than is appointed you" (Luke 3:13). The soldiers asked him the same question, "What shall we do?" He challenged them with the exhortation, "Rob no one by violence or by false accusation, and be content with your wages" (Luke 3:14). In stark contrast to the religious community at Qumran, John did not even ask tax collectors and soldiers to leave their questionable occupations and drop out of society. He did not stipulate that they sell all their possessions and join his group of disciples who waited for the last days in the wilderness. Instead his prophetic message implored the people to live a holy life in the mainstream of society. The religious mindset at Qumran could not tolerate John's approach. They believed that salvation was reserved for the select few who joined their strict ascetic life of discipline and revealed themselves as the true sons of light. Everyone else should be hated.[8]

Despite such differences, John's view of baptism coincides with the teachings of the Dead Sea community. Perhaps he was familiar with their doctrine. He may even have been a member of the sect at one time. His rejection of their sectarian hatred and exclusive approach to faith in God, however, makes it impossible to associate him directly with their movement. John the Baptist possessed a passion for righteousness. He proclaimed God's favor for *all* of Israel. He was not a member of the Dead Sea sect during his ministry of preaching to the people and baptizing the ones who repented of wrong. He would never accept the exclusive doctrine of the Qumran sect. As a prophet, he wanted everyone to repent; further, he believed in the choice of the individual rather than in a predetermined fate for all the sons of light and the sons of darkness. John the Baptist preached divine goodness for all who would reform their lives before the coming judgment. He encouraged those who accepted his message to be active in the mainstream of society by living a life of holiness and bringing redemption in everyday life.

JOHN THE BAPTIST AND JESUS

Jesus went to John the Baptist to be baptized. Luke's version describes Jesus as being baptized with all the people. The most distinctive feature of Luke's description of the baptism, however, is the divine voice. Only the Gospels of Matthew and John hint at the reason for Jesus' baptism.[9] Matthew's version offers more information about the interaction between Jesus and John the Baptist. In Matthew, John asked Jesus to baptize him. Jesus, however, persisted in the request for baptism. He explains that he must fulfill all righteousness. In his identity with the totality of human need, he submitted to baptism in order to affirm the process of redemption which was in action as a result of John's prophetic career. Luke's portrayal drives home the message. Jesus is with all the people, thus demonstrating his total identification with all humanity.

Moffatt's translation of Luke's version of the baptism is based upon a well-reasoned reading of important Greek manuscripts which describe Jesus and his special mission. One must study carefully Luke's description of Jesus' baptism in light of ancient Jewish thought.

> Now when all the people had been baptized, and when Jesus had been baptized and was praying, heaven opened and the holy Spirit descended in bodily form like a dove upon him; then came a voice from heaven, "Thou art my son, the Beloved, to-day have I become your father" (Luke 3:21–22 according to Moffatt's translation).

THE VOICE AND THE MESSAGE

The voice in Moffatt's translation refers to Psalm 2:7—"You are my son, today I have begotten you"—and also to Isaiah 42:1, where "my chosen" (*bachiri* in Hebrew) is synonymous to "my beloved." In reality, a much improved translation of the voice in the key verse of Moffatt's translation is:

"You are my son, the chosen, today I have brought you forth."

This translation enables the listener to hear the allusions to the Hebrew Scriptures. It makes a distinction between the voice of the transfiguration and the Western reading of the text of Jesus' baptism which hints at Psalm 2:7 and Isaiah 42:1.[10] Quite probably some church fathers were concerned that the reference to Psalm 2:7 in Luke's version might be misleading. They feared that it would be understood as teaching that Jesus was adopted as the Son of God on the occasion of his baptism. The adoptionist theology which claimed that Jesus was merely a good man who was adopted as God's son because of his personal piety was rejected by the leaders of the early church. Properly understood, however, the reference to Psalm 2:7 had little to do with a systematic theology of adoption.

In Hebrew thought, Psalm 2 refers to the Lord's anointed. It is a messianic text. It tells about the presentation of God's anointed. It proclaims, "You are my son, today I have begotten you." Originally it probably made reference to the king of Israel who was God's representative on earth to bring freedom to the people. They were protected and preserved by God whose son served as king. In the time of Jesus, however, the son was identified with the future deliverer who would fulfill the divine plan of redemption. He would be presented to the people as God's representative for change. He would minister healing and wholeness to human need.

A better translation of Psalm 2:7 at the baptism would render the Hebrew verb usually translated, "I have begotten thee" as, "I have brought thee forth."[11] God is like a midwife who delivers the child and presents him for all the world to see. Jesus did not become the child of God at the baptism. He was presented, however, at that time to the people. All who hear the story are called to wonder in awe at the heavenly voice and its message. The voice hints back to two great texts from the Hebrew Bible. The first is Psalm 2:7, a passage believed to describe the anointed one of God who would bring salvation for the people. In verse 2, the psalmist explains, "The kings of the earth set themselves . . . against the LORD and his anointed (mashicho)." The second text is Isaiah 42:1, which also speaks about the chosen one who is the anointed servant of the Lord: "Behold, my servant, whom I uphold, my chosen, in whom my soul delights; I have put my Spirit upon him, he will bring forth justice to the nations." The second text from Isaiah 42:1 is crucial for the baptism. It refers to Spirit empowerment for service. At the baptism Jesus is presented to the people and empowered by the Spirit to fulfill his difficult mission.

THE SPIRIT AND THE MESSIAH

The Jewish background enriches our comprehension of this momentous episode in the life of Jesus. It should be remembered that a voice from heaven was well known during the period. Sometimes an echo voice, referred to in rabbinic texts as a daughter voice, *bat kol,* was likened to the sound of a chirping bird or the cooing of a dove.[12] Some teachers thought it was an echo of the voice of God himself. With the decline of the work of the latter prophets, the people were dependent upon guidance from the daughter voice. When the prophet of the final redemption appeared, the Holy Spirit would return and prophecy would be renewed for the people. Then the redemptive process would be put forward with powerful force.

In Jewish literature a heavenly voice sometimes proclaims the divine will. In the Talmud a well-known story is related about the famous Rabbi Jose.

> Rabbi Jose says, I was once traveling on the road, and I entered into one of the ruins of Jerusalem in order to pray. Elijah of blessed memory appeared and waited for me at the door till I finished my prayer. After I finished my prayer, he said to me: Peace be with you, my master and teacher! And he said to me: My son, why did you go into this ruin? I replied: To pray. He said to me: You ought to have prayed on the road. I replied: I feared lest passers-by might interrupt me. He said to me: You ought to have said an abbreviated prayer. Thus I then learned from him three things: One must not go into a ruin; one may say the prayer on the road; and if one does say his prayer on the road, he recites an abbreviated prayer. He further said to me: My son, what sound did you hear in this ruin? I replied: I heard a divine voice, cooing like a dove, and saying: Woe to children on account of whose sins I destroyed My house, burnt My temple and exiled them among the nations of the world![13]

As in the Gospel story of Jesus' baptism, Rabbi Jose hears a divine voice during prayer. In the baptism of Jesus, the Holy Spirit

descends upon Jesus like a dove. A voice from heaven proclaims Jesus' mission. Rabbi Jose also hears the sound of a voice
during prayer which communicates an important message. The
voice is likened to the cooing of a dove. The message deals with
the national catastrophe of the destruction of the temple which
left the holy city of Jerusalem in ruins. The story illustrates that
the voice from heaven and descriptive elements like the cooing
of a dove also appear in Jewish literature from late antiquity.

Contrary to popular belief, in Jewish thought the dove is not
always associated with the Holy Spirit. In the story of Rabbi
Jose, the cooing of a dove describes the sound of the echo voice.
Not infrequently the dove refers to the people of Israel.[14] The
prophet Hosea likened the Jewish people to a dove. They were
taken into Egypt but God was planning their redemption. The
exiled dove was going to come home (Hos 11:11). In another
rabbinic story, however, Rabbi Simeon b. Zoma does describe
the action of the Spirit of God during the creation of the world
by comparing the movement of the Spirit to that of a dove. In
the creation account of Genesis, the Spirit is said to hover
(merachefet) over the waters.

Rabbi Simeon b. Zoma meditated upon the passage and ex-
pounded on his understanding,

> "I was contemplating the Creation [and have come to the conclusion]
> that between the upper and the nether waters there is but two or
> three finger breaths," he [Zoma] answered. "For it is not written
> here, 'And the Spirit of God' blew, but 'hovered,' like a dove flying
> and flapping with its wings, its wings barely touching [the nest over
> which it hovers]."[15]

Zoma was dealing with the story of creation and pondering its
deeper meaning. The Spirit hovered over the waters like a dove
flying over its nest. Surely it would be wrong to conclude from
this story that the Holy Spirit is always symbolized by a dove in
Jewish thought. The movement of the Spirit, however, can be
compared to the way a dove flies gracefully over its nest in a
hovering motion.

Perhaps this is the point at the baptism of Jesus. The phenomenon of the Spirit's descent is of greater import than supposed symbolism. God's Spirit is moving and empowering Jesus.
It is so tangible and real in the dimension of human experience
that a dove descends upon him. The Spirit empowerment for
service is of prime significance at the baptism of Jesus. Al-

though sometimes the dove is thought to symbolize the Holy Spirit or the people of Israel, it actually opens a vista into the supernatural realm. The appearance of the dove creates an increased awareness of awe because of the momentous action of the Spirit's descent. God has empowered Jesus for service.

The rabbis sometimes associated the bestowal of the Spirit with the coming of the Messiah. The anointed one of God would receive the divine power to accomplish his mission. Interestingly, even when discussing the work of the Spirit at the creation of the world, the ancient rabbis believed that the process of redemption is hinted at by an implied reference to the Messiah. They offer this interpretation of Genesis: " 'The Spirit of God hovered,' this alludes to the spirit of Messiah, as you read, 'And the Spirit of the Lord shall rest upon him' (Isa 11:2)."[16] In their creative method of biblical interpretation, the rabbis read Genesis 1:2, "the Spirit of God was hovering over the face of the waters," and they associated it with the words of the prophet in Isaiah 11:2, "And the Spirit of the LORD shall rest upon him." In the mind of the rabbis, the "him" in Isaiah 11:2 is none other than the anointed one of God, the promised Messiah. Of course, it is important to remember that the messianic idea was complex and diversified. Passages of Scripture like Genesis 1:2 and Isaiah 11:2 received different interpretations and were not always associated with the coming of the Messiah. Nevertheless, messianic interpretations of these texts are regularly reflected in ancient Jewish biblical commentary on the Hebrew text.

Rooted in the Jewish belief that God is good, the messianic idea develops from a sense of past history and future destiny. Just as God saved his people in the past, he will deliver them again. In the past he used an anointed prophet like Moses. In the future he will use a chosen servant empowered by the Holy Spirit. The glory of the divine presence *(Shekhinah)* is revealed in the work of the future prophet who will be anointed to accomplish the task. According to early Jewish teachings, however, many sages of Israel believed that the prophetic time, when the Holy Spirit spoke through the prophets and worked miracles of deliverance, had ended. When the latter prophets of the Bible died, the Holy Spirit was taken away. The daughter voice, or heavenly echo, was thought to replace prophetic inspiration. The Holy Spirit, it was taught, had been removed until the proper time for the renewal of prophecy. When the time is

right and the people are prepared, the prophetic ministry of the
Holy Spirit will be renewed. Most probably the process would
be initiated by a charismatic personality such as the Messiah. At
that time, the Spirit will work God's higher purposes during the
messianic age.

> Our Rabbis taught: Since the death of the last prophets, Haggai,
> Zechariah and Malachi, the Holy Spirit [of prophetic inspiration]
> departed from Israel; yet they were still able to avail themselves of
> the heavenly voice *(Bat-kol).* Once when the Rabbis were met in the
> upper chamber of Gurya's house at Jericho, a heavenly voice *(Bat-
> kol)* was heard, saying: "There is one amongst you who is worthy that
> the *Shekhinah* [Holy Spirit] should rest on him as it did on Moses, but
> his generation does not merit it." The Sages present set their eyes on
> Hillel the Elder. And when he died, they lamented and said: "Alas,
> the pious man, the humble man, the disciple of Ezra [is no more]."[17]

This intriguing story from the Talmud possesses many striking
similarities with the baptism of Jesus. One immediately notices
the description of the Holy Spirit, the heavenly voice, and a
special and pious individual. In the Talmud the person is Hillel.
In the Gospel the special individual is Jesus.

In the talmudic story a heavenly voice was heard in a gather-
ing of the sages. There is a person who is worthy to be endowed
with the Spirit like Moses. The far-reaching ramifications of this
declaration are astonishing. The story seems to reveal a keen
sensitivity for God's redemptive plan. As God's instrument,
Moses was used to redeem the people from slavery. He was
used to bring salvation to God's people. Whoever is endowed
with the Spirit of God will fulfill the task of the anointed prophet
like Moses (Deut 18:18). One such person was sitting in the
midst of the sages on that occasion. He was worthy of the task.
Although the divine presence *(Shekhinah)* as revealed in the
Holy Spirit was taken from Israel when the prophets Zechariah,
Haggai, and Malachi had died, a new prophet like Moses would
renew the Spirit and bring about the redemption of the people.
All the eyes of those present were fixed upon Hillel. He was
worthy to receive the prophetic endowment, but his generation
was not. The sages expected that God would initiate the redemptive process when the people were prepared and the right
leader was ready. Piety is the emphasis of the story.

Now from some of the previously unpublished Dead Sea
Scrolls, a clearer picture of the messianic idea is emerging.

S. Wise and J. Tabor have called attention to the Hebrew text
of scroll 4Q287, which they translate, "The Holy Spirit rested on
His Messiah." In another scroll fragment the anointing of the
Messiah for healing the sick and proclaiming divine favor to the
poor is described.[18] While much more research is needed for a
better understanding of these texts, the reference to Spirit empowerment for ministry, however, is an important insight for the
Gospel account of the baptism of Jesus. John the Baptist bap-
tizes Jesus. The heavens open, recalling the experience of the
Hebrew prophet Ezekiel (Ezek 1:1). The dramatic descent of
the dove accompanies the miraculous event. God has spoken.
Jesus is made known and his work begins.

David Flusser observes that the background of the event lies
in ancient Judaism. Many of the descriptive elements and extraordinary phenomena that accompany Jesus' experience point
toward his messianic task; moreover, they have their parallels in
Jewish literature. Flusser observes, "Echoing voices were not an
uncommon phenomenon among the Jews of those days, and
frequently these voices were heard to utter verses from Scripture. Endowment with the Holy Spirit, accompanied by an ec-
static experience, was apparently no unique experience among
those who were baptized in John's presence in the Jordan."[19] It
is important to remember that the Gospels were written for a
Jewish audience and that they describe common experiences of
the people. The message of the divine voice at the baptism,
however, focuses attention on the special mission of Jesus. He is
God's Son, the empowered servant of the Lord.

Strauss suggested that Jesus needed baptism because of his sin
just like everybody else. But the Gospel accounts emphasize the
phenomena surrounding this experience because he is no ordinary person. A. Gilmore has noted,

> Jesus' baptism illustrates, as does His working at the carpenter's
> bench, His tiredness, hunger, temptation and sorrow, how completely
> He entered into the life of man; and He being what He was, the first
> step involved the last. In that sense plainly, the baptism, like the
> incarnation itself, already involved the cross—logically, and theo-
> logically, though not necessarily as something always consciously
> foreseen.[20]

Certainly Jesus could pray all the prayers for the day of atonement or offer sacrifice on Passover. He entered into the religious experience like every devout Jewish person during the

Second Temple period. The Gospel of Luke seems to portray this element more clearly. As all the people are being baptized, Jesus enters the water for baptism. He totally identified with every aspect of human experience.

On the other hand, no one should mistake identification with *identity*. Jesus is reaching out to all people and identifying with humankind. But he is the Son of God in a mysterious and wonderful way. Jesus is unlike any person, and yet he is like every human being. His sonship as portrayed from Psalm 2:7 is proclaimed through a heavenly voice. The son is like the father, and the father is like the son. One must understand divine grace and mercy by observing Jesus' life and teachings. At the baptism he is empowered by the Spirit to fulfill the messianic task. He came as a minister who would help hurting people in need of healing. We must see Jesus among his people. He involved himself with human experience and identifies with each person's need even to the point of submitting himself to John for baptism.

The baptism of Jesus grants rich insight into the Jewish background of the life setting of first-century Israel. The Dead Sea Scrolls, Josephus, rabbinic literature, and the Gospels vividly portray the experiences of the Jewish people. The messianic idea in ancient Israel envisioned the coming of the prophet who would be endowed with the Holy Spirit in order to fulfill the divine purpose. Jesus' baptism dramatically portrays his presentation to the people and the beginning of his ultimate mission. At the waters of baptism, Jesus is empowered by the Spirit. He is destined to accomplish the messianic task as the kingdom of heaven is advanced in his life and teachings.

NOTES

1. David Friedrich Strauss, *The Life of Jesus Critically Examined* (reprint, Philadelphia: Fortress, 1972) 237–39. Though Strauss' work was first published in German in 1835, some of the difficult questions he raised concerning the life and teachings of Jesus have yet to be answered satisfactorily by subsequent scholars.

2. See Matt 3:13–17; Mark 1:9–11; Luke 3:21–22; and John 1:29–34. Here I have made use of the fine translation of James Moffatt, *A New Translation of the Bible* (London: Hodder & Stoughton, 1948).

3. See David Flusser, "The Baptism of John and the Dead Sea Sect," in *Essays on the Dead Sea Scrolls* (ed. C. Rabin and Y. Yadin; Jerusa-

lem: Hekhal Ha-Sefer, 1961) 209–39 (Hebrew) and W. Brownlee, "John the Baptist in Light of the Dead Sea Scrolls," in Stendahl, *The Scrolls and the New Testament.*

4. Today the identity of the Dead Sea community continues to be debated among scholars. Personally, I am convinced that they were Essenes. For a fresh discussion see Todd Beall, *Josephus' Description of the Essenes Illustrated by the Dead Sea Scrolls* (Cambridge: Cambridge University Press, 1988) and James VanderKam, "The People of the Dead Sea Scrolls: Essenes or Sadducees?" *Bible Review* (April, 1991) and now VanderKam's *The Dead Sea Scrolls Today* (Grand Rapids: Eerdmans, 1994) 71–92.

5. See the *Manual of Discipline* (1QS) 5.13–15 (J. Licht's Hebrew version, 132–33) and the English translation of G. Vermes, *The Dead Sea Scrolls in English* (Baltimore: Penguin, 1988) 1QS 5, p. 68. Vermes has titled the *Manual of Discipline* the *Community Rule* in his English rendering of the Hebrew text. Compare also the same idea which is conveyed by the teaching, "He shall be cleansed from all his sins by the spirit of holiness uniting him to His truth, and his iniquity shall be expiated by the spirit of uprightness and humility. And when his flesh is sprinkled with purifying water and sanctified by cleansing water, it shall be made clean by the humble submission of his soul to all the precepts of God." See Vermes, *Dead Sea Scrolls in English*, 1QS 3.4–6, p. 64.

6. See Vermes, *Dead Sea Scrolls in English*, 1QS 3.4–6, p. 64. See also David Flusser, *Jesus* (New York: Herder and Herder, 1969) 25–43.

7. Josephus, *Ant.* 18.116ff. (18, 5,2), Loeb edition, 80ff.

8. See the *Community Rule* (1QS) 1.11, ". . . that they may love all the sons of light . . . and hate all the sons of darkness . . ." (Vermes, *Dead Sea Scrolls in English*, 62). I am grateful to David Flusser who has helped me understand the relationship between John the Baptist and the Essenes. See also Flusser, *Jesus*, 25.

9. Luke adds the details concerning Jesus' prayer and the description of the dove in a bodily form. In Matthew John tries to prevent Jesus. He asks Jesus to baptize him. Jesus explains that he must fulfill all righteousness. He affirmed the process of redemption which was being realized in John's movement. As he taught them concerning the coming one, John the Baptist called on the people to return to God. On the messianic idea, see Joseph Klausner, *The Messianic Idea in Israel* (New York: Macmillan, 1955) and James Charlesworth, ed., *The Messiah* (Minneapolis: Fortress, 1992).

10. In other versions the heavenly voice at the baptism is the same as at the transfiguration, Matt 17:5; Mark 9:7; Luke 9:35. On the manuscript evidence see *The New Testament in Greek: The Gospel according to St. Luke,* 1.68f. Bruce Metzger, *Textual Commentary,* 136, also

discusses the manuscript evidence. Neither Moffatt nor I would be able to agree with Metzger's conclusions, however.

11. Noted Hebrew language and New Testament scholar Robert L. Lindsey has argued for this translation (private communication). This textual reading was accepted by A. Huck and maintained by Heinrich Greeven, *Synopse der drei ersten Evangelien* (Tübingen: J. C. B. Mohr, 1981) and also by M. E. Boismard and A. Lamouille, *Synopsis Graeca Quattuor Evangeliorum* (Paris: Peeters, 1986).

12. See Saul Lieberman, *Hellenism in Jewish Palestine* (New York: Jewish Theological Seminary, 1962) 194–99 and Richard Steven Notley, "The Concept of the Holy Spirit in Jewish Literature of the Second Temple Period and 'Pre-Pauline' Christianity" (Ph.D. diss., Hebrew University, 1991) 160–81. The Tosafot of b. *Sanhedrin* 11a regard the "Daughter Voice" as an echo of the voice of God.

13. See b. *Ber.* 3a.

14. See the rabbinic parable where the Jewish people fleeing Egypt are compared to a dove fleeing from a hawk, *Mechilta* on Exod 14:9–14, Lauterbach, 1.211.

15. Genesis Rabbah 2:4 (English translation of Soncino Press, 17–18). See also the variant readings in Albeck's Hebrew edition, 1.16–17.

16. Ibid.

17. See b. *San.* 11a (English translation of Soncino Press, 46) and see also j. *Sotah* 24b, chap. 9, hal. 14; b. *Sotah* 48b, 33a; b. *Yoma* 9b. In the context it is important to remember that others in later generations are also thought to be worthy for the *Shekhinah* to rest upon them.

18. See S. Wise and J. Tabor, "The Messiah Text," *Biblical Archaeology Review* (November/December, 1992) 62. Roy Blizzard has impacted my understanding of these texts. In the study of the Dead Sea Scrolls, Blizzard has emphasized the larger context in ancient Judaism and the Hebrew Scriptures (private communication). In reality, some qualification is needed for the translation by Wise and Tabor. The manuscript is quite fragmentary, and it is difficult to know who is meant by the translation "His Messiah." Conceivably, the manuscript could refer to a priest, prophet, or royal ruler as well as to a messianic deliverer who is anointed with the Holy Spirit. The Holy Spirit empowers the individual for service. See Reed, Lundberg, Tov, and Pfann, *The Dead Sea Scrolls on Microfiche,* PAM 43.314.

19. See Flusser, *Jesus,* 29.

20. See A. Gilmore, *Christian Baptism* (London: Lutterworth, 1959) 94–95.

3

The Temptation of Jesus

T HE TEMPTATION OF JESUS FOLLOWS THE SPIRIT'S
descent at his baptism.' After the high spiritual experience at the waters of the Jordan River, Jesus
comes into direct conflict with the power of evil. Satan dramatically appears on the scene and presents Jesus with an opportunity to achieve the higher purpose of redemption without the
pain of the cross. In fact, Jesus is confronted with the issue of
the divine nature. Satan is not asking Jesus to prove himself.
Rather than trying to prove that Jesus is the Son, as affirmed at
the baptism, the test concerns God and his purpose. The temptation of Jesus focuses on the divine character and the messianic
task. Who is God? How will his redemptive purpose be accomplished? In Greek Satan's questions imply a real condition; they
could even be translated, "Since you are the Son of God . . ."[1]
Jesus did not have to prove his sonship to Satan.

On the contrary, the issue of the three temptations centers on
the nature of God and the identity of the one worthy of complete trust and total faith commitment. In the Hebrew Bible
God alone is worthy of worship and love (Deut 6:4–5). The
episode of the temptation of Jesus in the Gospels is arguably
one of the most misunderstood of all stories in the documents
which relate his life and teachings (Matt 4:1–11; Mark 1:12–13;
Luke 4:1–13). Nonetheless, the wilderness experience of Jesus
proved crucial for revealing his original mission and defining
the messianic task. In the passage one encounters the personal
struggle of Jesus as he confronts the power of evil. Here the
center of attention will rest on the oft-neglected final temptation, according to Luke's Gospel, whose setting is on a lethal
height in the temple complex (Luke 4:9–11).[2]

After his Spirit empowerment at the waters of baptism and
the call for his work to begin, Jesus is tested by Satan. With
Jesus' call into service, according to Luke, the Spirit leads Jesus

into the wilderness to be tempted.[3] Like Moses and Elijah who fasted for forty days, Jesus abstains from both food and water, relying upon divine sustenance during this period[4] of preparation. The prophet in the wilderness seeks clarity of vision for his task. When Jesus is physically weakened, Satan comes to tempt him with food. In many ways Jesus is depicted as the representative of the people Israel, who were tested by God for forty years in the wilderness to see what was in their heart (Deut 8:3–6). Designated Son of God at the baptismal scene (Luke 3:22, 38), Jesus goes into the wilderness in much the same way as the nation entered trial in its desert wanderings.[5] There Jesus enters into conflict with evil.

> And you shall remember all the way which the LORD your God has led you these forty years in the wilderness, that he might humble you, testing you to know what was in your heart, whether you would keep his commandments, or not. And he humbled you and let you hunger and fed you with manna, which you did not know, nor did your fathers know; that he might make you know that man does not live by bread alone, but man lives by everything that proceeds out of the mouth of the LORD (Deut 8:2–3).

The background for the story is found in the Hebrew heritage of the Jewish people. These verses would come to the minds of Jesus' disciples as they listened to the story of the temptation.

One of the greatest mistakes interpreters make is failing to recognize that the test is real. Like the people in their desert wanderings, Jesus is tested. Jesus could well have failed in the same way.[6] Sometimes it is wrongly claimed that Jesus could have turned the stone into bread, or that he could have received the rule of this world from Satan, the god of this world, and he would have been saved by the angels if he had taken the proverbial step of faith and cast himself down in a suicidal jump from the height of the temple. Nothing could be farther from the truth. The temptation is portrayed as an authentic test having the potential to undermine completely the redemptive work of the Messiah. Satan, the master deceiver, earnestly wants these temptations to foil the ultimate divine plan.

All the temptations inherently deny the oneness of God. The original Jewish audience would have heard the *Shema Yisrael* in the background, an echo of the great affirmation of the people's historic faith, "Hear O Israel, the LORD our God, the LORD is one" (Deut 6:4). The passage is related not only to Israel's temptation because of its context in Deuteronomy 6:4 but also to the temptation of the Son of God who represents his people and quotes from Deuteronomy 6–8 in his struggle with evil.[7] Satan is asking Jesus to worship him and recognize his power. Such an act would deny the God of Israel and would defy the teachings of Torah. The Lord is one and God alone is worthy of worship and total trust. The basis of the test was to acknowledge who God is. The Lord is God, and God alone should be worshipped; this is the deeper significance of these three temptations.

The temptation was real. Each time Jesus is tempted to deny the lordship of his Father. Satan tells Jesus that by defying God he will achieve a good purpose. The first temptation denied God's provision. God had sustained Jesus during his fast; to accept Satan's challenge would have been a confession that God's provision was insufficient. Jesus responds with Scripture: "Man shall not live by bread alone." Similar circumstances prevailed when the people of Israel wandered through the desert relying upon God to provide them with manna.

The second temptation, according to Luke 4:5f., involved the sovereignty of God.

> And the devil took him up, and showed him all the kingdoms of the world in a moment of time, and said to him, "To you I will give all this authority and their glory; for it has been delivered to me, and I give it to whom I will. If you, then, will worship me, it shall be yours."

In the same way as God showed Moses the land of Israel in a moment of time (Deut 34:1f.), the devil showed Jesus the kingdoms of the world. The devil promised to place them under Jesus' authority and give him the glory of such power—on the condition that Jesus worship him. According to Daniel 7:13ff., only God has the authority over his creation. He alone is the King of the universe, and the authority of Satan is limited (cf. Job 1:9–12). According to the Jewish conception of God's sovereignty, such a claim by Satan was based upon a false presupposition. Satan cannot give what belongs to God. Hence the real nature of this test was to deny the lordship of God and to enter into idolatrous worship of the devil. Again Jesus responds with Scripture (Luke 4:8): "It is written, 'You shall worship the Lord your God, and him only shall you serve' " (Deut 6:13). This quotation from Torah comes from the larger context of Israel's *Shema,* "Hear O Israel, the LORD our God, the LORD is one" (Deut 6:4).

The final temptation in the temple is the culmination of this decisive episode in the career of Jesus. Jeremias suggested that Jesus used this story to warn his disciples against accepting political success in the short term instead of achieving the higher purposes of God for his kingdom in the long-range plan. The setting in life might even be the Passover seder of the Last Supper.[8] While the Synoptic Gospels do tell the story of the temptation, they remain silent as to when such a teaching passed on to the disciples. In theory, the Last Supper would be the perfect occasion. The rich imagery of the story's background in the wilderness would be appropriate in the order of the Passover discussion. The crisis of Jesus' death loomed in the darkness of the night. The threat of false messianic expectations must be overcome. The disciples could well be tempted to follow political ambitions rather than focus on the work of God's kingdom. The Zealots, on the one hand, believed that God's reign could be established through military resistance and active political involvement. Jesus, on the other hand, preached a message of healing through God's redemptive power. The divine reign comes from God alone. Similar temptations to find a shortcut to achieving the divine purpose could reemerge in the future.

Standing upon the wing (*epi to pterygion* in Greek or *kanaf* in Hebrew) of the temple, the deceiver now quotes Scripture, attempting to entice Jesus into accepting the easy way to success. "Wing of the temple" more literally translates the more familiar term, "pinnacle of the temple." Christian legend locates the site of Jesus' final temptation upon the so-called pinnacle of the temple on the southeastern corner of the Herodian retaining wall. This tradition is most probably incorrect. In the minds of the Gospel writers, the wing of the temple must have been more centrally located. Perhaps Jesus was situated upon the height of the sanctuary, which would have provided greater visibility. While no archaeological evidence has suggested the point, some identifiable part of the architecture may have depicted the wings of the divine presence surrounding the temple and protecting it. In all events, the visibility of the spot would be greater if the temptation were staged in the inner sanctuary, which towered above the city some 150 feet.[9] If only Jesus would cast himself down from the lethal height, the people would flock to his movement. God would save him. After all, the promise of the psalm says that the angels will shield him from all harm. Certainly God would protect him. Psalm 91 speaks of divine protection under God's "wings" of refuge (v. 4) in the sanctuary. The "wing of the temple" evokes the image of God's constant protection. Satan quotes a portion of the psalm, endeavoring to entice him to jump. The temple is the symbol of sanctuary, shelter, and security. No one could die under the wing of the temple, which represented God's protection of His people. But the devil omitted the reference in Psalm 91:11 which stated, "in all thy ways," which could be understood to mean in the normal or natural ways in which a human being walks and not if one suicidally casts oneself down from a tremendous height. Jesus' words from the Torah affirm the divine character and human responsibility. Against the force of Satan's temptation, Jesus counters, "You shall not tempt the LORD your God" (Deut 6:16).

But the true nature of the final temptation can be understood only in light of the messianic beliefs of the period. The temple was closely related to the activities of the messianic deliverer who would use the forum of its sacred courts to proclaim his message of deliverance. A Jewish midrash—though of later date—describes the actions of the Messiah in the temple.

> Our teachers taught, at the time when the King Messiah will appear, he will come and stand upon the roof of the temple. He will proclaim to Israel and will say to the humble, "The time of your redemption has arrived! If you do not believe—behold my light which shines upon you . . ." (Pesikta Rabbati 36).[10]

If this tradition, or a similar one, existed in the time of Jesus, it would clarify the place and the nature of Satan's test. It suggests that the temptation really centered on the nature of the messianic task. Standing upon the roof (wing?) of the temple, the Messiah would declare, "The time of your redemption has arrived!" Satan was asking Jesus to reveal himself as the Messiah by appearing in supernatural power in the temple where all would recognize the nature and purpose of his mission.

In another reference from an early historical source, the tradition concerning the Messiah's appearance in the temple is mentioned in a powerful allusion. Josephus describes the destruction of the temple in 70 C.E. as the tenth Roman legion crushed the nationalistic hopes of the Zealots to overthrow foreign rule and to establish an autonomous religious kingdom.

Because the Zealots believed that somehow divine intervention would save their cause, they could overcome their fear of the superior military strength of imperial Rome. They hoped for a messianic deliverance. The notorious Zealot ringleader, Simon bar Giora, fought bravely against the Roman foe, but when he realized that there was no hope of winning the battle for Jerusalem and the temple, he sought to escape. Josephus reports that Simon and his faithful friends employed some stone cutters and tried to escape through the secret underground tunnels of the temple. Josephus explains that when he realized that any attempt was hopeless,

> Simon, imagining that he could cheat the Romans by creating a scare, dressed himself in white tunics and buckling over them a purple mantle arose out of the ground at the spot where on the temple formerly stood (Josephus, *War* 7.27–30).

The people who saw him froze in fear, probably imagining that he was the promised messianic deliverer. Perhaps the Messiah had appeared on the scene after all.

The reference from Josephus indicates that indeed messianic hopes surrounded the temple complex. Josephus' words, "at the spot," seem to refer to the temple compound and quite possibly to a position like the wing.

The final temptation with all its ramifications for the history of salvation moved to an intense climax. Would Jesus be deceived by Satan and choose the quick way to redemption? No. The kingdom Jesus taught about is founded upon the oneness of God and the need to establish his reign of peace. Succumbing to Satan's enticement would defy God.

For Christians Jesus is called the Prince of Peace. He brings the highest redemption through the seeming defeat of the cross. Kings are not known for their humility. Jesus' power is not like political royalty. Only Jesus could turn death's defeat upon a cruel Roman cross into a victory for God and for his people. Jesus did not succumb to the temptation to deny the lordship of his Father in an attempt to found a new political regime. Nonetheless, he was determined to establish his kingdom by accomplishing the higher purposes of God. Jesus calls upon all people to obey God. He did not become a political messiah but redefined the nature of the messianic task. The strong answer, "it is written," resounds in the human experience in the face of any temptation to sin. Satan cloaked the wrong in the garment of the right by appealing to a higher purpose. Jesus' firm vision of the character of God, however, mocks Satan's attempt to cause Jesus to stumble and fall. The entire episode teaches about God and his redemptive purpose. "Thou shalt have no other gods before me."

NOTES

1. See Fitzmyer, *Luke*, 1.515.

2. On the issues relating to the synoptic problem, see my *Jesus and His Jewish Parables* (Mahwah, N.J.: Paulist, 1989) 129–63. Matthew changes the order of the three temptations. The climax of the threefold temptation is best preserved in Luke (compare also the three types of temptations in 1 John 2:16).

3. See Luke 4:1. Only Luke records that the Spirit directed Jesus, which betrays his own emphasis (see also Luke 1:41, 61; Acts 2:4; 4:8, 31; 9:17; 13:9).

4. See Exod 34:28; 1 Kgs 19:8. A normal Jewish fast was abstinence from both food and water; see A. Evan Shoshan, *Dictionary*, 1127 (Hebrew) and cf. m. *Yoma,* chap. 8. Thus it was considered miraculous for someone to go without food and water for forty days. Only God could sustain Jesus for such a fast, and to turn a stone into bread would deny God's provision and his lordship.

5. See B. Gehardsson, *The Testing of God's Son* (Lund, Sweden: Gleerup, 1966).

6. For a different view, see the fine work of John Nolland, *Luke* (Word Biblical Commentary; Dallas: Word, 1989) 1.179. Nolland argues, "That Jesus as Son of God has power to make stones bread is doubted neither by the Devil nor by Jesus himself." While this traditional approach is understandable and supported by many, the essence of the temptation was probably infinitely more serious. Far more was at stake than using the privilege of Sonship for selfish purposes.

7. One must carefully read Deut 6–8 for a full appreciation of the connection.

8. See J. Jeremias, *The Parables of Jesus* (London: SCM, 1972) 123. Jeremias perceptively suggests that the story could have been told to the disciples during the Last Supper. The Passover is filled with references to the wilderness experience of ancient Israel. Jeremias observes, "The temptation-stories are words of Jesus in which, in the form of a *mashal*, he told his disciples about his victory over the temptation to present himself as a political Messiah—perhaps in order to warn them against a similar temptation." Hence, it is in the passion of Jesus which follows the Last Supper that victory is won. Jeremias concludes that

Jesus "asserts against his opponents—now, at this very hour, Satan is conquered, Christ is greater than Satan!"

9. The temple stood ninety feet high for the sanctuary itself and sixty feet for the surrounding priestly chambers and structures. After the Empire State Building and the numerous skyscrapers which form the skyline of modern cities, Westerners have tended to lose appreciation for the marvels of ancient architecture. Like the pyramids of Egypt, the Jewish temple must have been an awesome structure to behold. Because of the topography of Jerusalem, the grandeur of Herod's architectural design would be an overwhelming vision of beauty towering above the city with an impressive height and the gleam of pure gold.

10. P. Billerbeck, *Kommentar zum Neuen Testament aus Talmud und Midrasch* (Munich: C. H. Beck, 1978) 1.151. For me, the most important study ever written about the temptation of Jesus appeared in David Flusser, "Der Versuchung Jesu und ihr jüdischer Hintergrund," *Judaica* 45 (1989) 110–28.

4

Miracles, Proclamation, and Healing Faith

THE GOSPELS RECORD MANY MIRACLES IN THE LIFE of Jesus. He often used the occasion of a miracle to proclaim the active force of God's reign. "But if it is by the finger of God I cast out demons," Jesus declares, "then the kingdom of God has come upon you."[1] Jesus' ministry of healing helped hurting people and demonstrated the power of God's grace. The teaching of Jesus, however, is as important as the miracle in each of these episodes. The story of the miracle is often accompanied by a proclamation of truth. Sometimes the message affirms the faith of the person seeking help. One must recognize the miracle, the message, and the healing faith involved in these events in Jesus' ministry.

Unfortunately, as Christians we have seldom discovered the Jewish background for the miracle ministry of Jesus. First it must be emphasized that the Jewish sources describing miracles should be studied carefully and understood in their specific context. The Jewish worldview embraced the concept of miracles. God's dominion is unlimited. In his book *The Rabbinic Mind* the esteemed Jewish scholar Max Kadushin observed, "Indeed, it is hardly an exaggeration to state the presence of *Nissim* [miracles] was, in a sense, the expected order of things."[2]

A careful study of the miracles of Jesus in light of the Jewish background can greatly enhance one's perception of miracles, the meaning of Jesus' proclamation of the kingdom, and the essence of true faith. The healing faith that appears in the Gospel stories stirs modern readers just as it excited and puzzled believers in antiquity. The Jewish people have a strong heritage of the sovereignty of God who is good and who works miracles to save and to help his people.

According to the Gospels, Jesus performed many miracles. He
worked miracles of nature. He stilled the storm and walked
on water. He performed exorcisms and set people oppressed
by demon power free. He healed people from their physical
disorders.

THE JEWISH BACKGROUND OF GOSPEL MIRACLES

Early Jewish sources tell of similar miracles. Of course the
Hebrew Bible is filled with accounts of God's supernatural acts.
Some of these miracles are redemptive, such as the parting of
the Red Sea in the mighty deliverance of the people of Israel
from Egyptian bondage (Exod 14:21–31). Others are more personal, like the extension of King Hezekiah's life when he prayed
for healing (Isa 38:1–8). But the Talmudic literature also tells
stories of miraculous cures and of answers to prayers for rain to
end a devastating drought. The people of Israel were keenly
aware of God's presence and his sovereign power. The Jewish
scholar Geza Vermes has even graphically described what he
called "Charismatic Judaism" as a pious religious movement in
which people believed in miracles and experienced supernatural
answers to prayer.[3]

While the miracles in the Gospels have been questioned by
rationalists and modern skeptics, the evangelists and their early
readers clearly viewed Jesus as a miracle-worker. Many of the
early rabbis associated with the so-called charismatic stream of
ancient Judaism were also known for their miracles. Solomon
Schechter pointed out the importance of understanding miracles
in religious faith. In fact, most of the miracles recorded in the
Hebrew Bible also have parallels somewhere in the talmudic
literature. In the worldview of the rabbis, God could not be
exiled from human existence. Solomon Schechter's insights are
worth repeating:

> Despite the various attempts made by semi-rationalists to minimise
> their significance, the frequent occurrence of miracles will always
> remain, both for believers and sceptics, one of the most important
> tests of the religion in question; to the former as a sign of its superhu-
> man nature, to the latter as a proof of its doubtful origin. The student
> is accordingly anxious to see whether the miraculous formed an es-
> sential element of Rabbinic Judaism. Nor are we quite disappointed
> when we turn over the pages of the Talmud with this purpose in view.

There is hardly any miracle recorded in the Bible for which a parallel might not be found in the Rabbinic literature.[4]

The miracle-working rabbis were celebrated for their humility and piety. Like those about Jesus, stories about them include references to women and children. In the story below, God answers the prayer of Abba Chilkiah's saintly wife before that of the pious and humble rabbi. They are both praying for rain, but the rain clouds form where she is beseeching God for his mercy. The Jewish people believed in miracles. Many were farmers, and the agricultural life of the people made them especially sensitive to God's activities in nature. Even if the farmer did all his work perfectly, he still had to depend upon divine favor for a bountiful harvest. The weather and other conditions of nature, which were all controlled by God, could help the farmer or destroy his crops. Thus, it is not surprising to find many stories about the need for rain in talmudic literature.

Abba Chilkiah was a grandson of Choni the Circle Drawer [Onias], and whenever the world was in need of rain, the Rabbis sent a message to him. He prayed and rain fell. On one occasion, there was an urgent need for rain and the Rabbis sent to him a couple of scholars to ask him to pray for rain. . . . He said to his wife, I know the scholars have come on account of rain, let us go up to the roof and pray, perhaps the Holy One, Blessed be He, will have mercy and rain will fall, without having credit given to us. They went up to the roof. He stood in one corner and she in another. At first the clouds appeared over the corner where his wife stood. When he came down he said to the scholars, Why have you scholars come here? They replied: The Rabbis have sent us to you, Sir, to ask you to pray for rain. Thereupon he exclaimed, "Blessed be God, who has made you no longer dependent on Abba Chilkiah." . . . Sir, why did the clouds appear first in the corner where your wife stood and then in your corner? He answered, Because a wife stays at home and gives bread to the poor which they can at once enjoy whilst I give them money which they cannot enjoy immediately. Or perhaps it may have to do with certain robbers in our neighborhood. I prayed that they might die, but she prayed that they might repent [and they did]![5]

This miracle story, which describes the answer to prayers for rain, is surrounded by the legendary piety of Abba Chilkiah and his wife. She is praised because of her concern for the poor. In his humility Abba Chilkiah tries to avoid the notoriety and praise from the community that resulted from the miraculous answers to his prayers.

Many wonder-workers in Jewish literature are blood relatives
of Choni the Circle Drawer, who is an outstanding example of
this religious piety.[6] Most miracles in Jewish literature are miracles of nature. In times of severe drought, the pious Jewish
wonder-worker prayed, and God answered.

> Once they said to Choni the Circle Drawer, "Pray that rain may fall."
> He answered, "Go out and bring in the Passover ovens that they be
> not softened [by the rain]." He prayed, but the rain did not fall. What
> did he do? He drew a circle and stood within it and said before God,
> "O Lord of the universe, your children have turned their faces to me,
> for that I am like a son of the house before you. I swear by your great
> name that I will not stir from here until you have mercy upon your
> children." Rain began to fall drop by drop. He said, "I have not
> prayed for such rain, but for rain that will fill the cisterns, pits, and
> caverns." It began to rain with violence. He said, "I have not prayed
> for such rain, but for rain of goodwill, blessing, and graciousness."
> Then it rained in moderation.[7]

When the people needed rain, the pious rabbi would be asked
to pray to end the drought. By drawing a circle in the dirt,
standing in the middle of it, and telling God he would not move
until rain fell, Choni exhibited tremendous nerve. But Choni
was a very pious and saintly individual. He calls himself a
"son of the house," which in some ways is similar to the self-
awareness of Jesus. God answered these prayers, and it was
considered a great miracle when the rain came.[8]

Among charismatic rabbis, prayers were offered for healing
as well as for rain. The pious rabbi Chanina ben Dosa was
able to tell whether his prayer for healing was going to be
answered by the feeling or intensity he experienced during the
prayer.

> Concerning R. Chanina ben Dosa, it is told that when he prayed for
> the sick, he would say: "This one will live and this one will die." They
> asked him, "How do you know?" He answered, "If my prayer is
> fluent in my mouth, I know that the (person who is ill) is favored; if
> not I know that the illness is fatal."[9]

Chanina ben Dosa prayed for many sick people. Sometimes a
miracle of healing occurred, and at other times his prayer was
not answered. He was able to discern whether his request had
been accepted by God when his prayer was fluent in his mouth.
On one occasion his renowned and highly esteemed Torah master, Johanan ben Zakhai, asked him to pray for his sick son.

Why did a learned teacher and community leader like Johanan ben Zakhai seek out a humble rabbi such as Chanina ben Dosa to pray for the healing of his own son?

> Again it happened when R. Chanina ben Dosa went to Rabban Johanan ben Zakhai to study Torah, the son of Rabban Johanan ben Zakhai became sick. He asked him, "Chanina, my son, pray for him that he may live." He put his head between his knees, and prayed, and he lived. Rabban Johanan ben Zakhai said, "Even if ben Zakhai had squeezed his head between his knees all day long no attention would have been paid to him from heaven!" His wife said to him: "Is then Chanina greater than you?" He replied to her, "No! But he is like a servant before the king and I am like a prince before the king."[10]

Johanan ben Zakhai did not experience such miraculous answers to prayer. His wife asked him why. His reply underlines the tension between the more scholastic rabbis and the popular wonder-workers like the pious Chanina ben Dosa. He is like a household servant before the king, but Johanan ben Zakhai is like a minister in the cabinet. The description of Chanina ben Dosa as a servant of the king is very much like some of the terms used to describe Jesus.

On yet another occasion, the son of Rabbi Gamaliel was sick. Rabbi Gamaliel sent two of his disciples on a mission to ask Chanina ben Dosa to pray for his son to be healed. On this occasion Chanina ben Dosa prayed and recognized that his prayer had been answered because of the intensity of feeling. He declared that the son had been healed. Rabbi Gamaliel's disciples were shocked at Chanina ben Dosa's sensitivity. They noted the time when Chanina declared that the healing happened and later discovered that the boy had been healed at the very same hour.

> Our rabbis have taught: Once it happened that Rabban Gamaliel's son was sick, he sent two disciples to Rabbi Chanina ben Dosa that he might pray for him. When he saw them, he went to the upper room and prayed. When he came down, he said to them: "Go for the fever has departed from him." They asked him, "Are you a prophet?" He replied to them, "I am no prophet, nor am I a prophet's son, but this is how I am favored. If my prayer is fluent in my mouth, I know that he (the person who is ill) is favored. If not, I know that (the illness) is fatal." They sat down, and noted the hour. When they came to Rabban Gamaliel, he said to them: "By the worship! You have neither taken from it nor added to it, but this is how it happened. It was at that hour that the fever left him and he asked us for water to drink."[11]

Much like the healing of the centurion's servant who "was healed in the selfsame hour" (Matt 8:13), the son of Gamaliel was healed at a distance, and Rabbi Chanina ben Dosa was able to tell when the miracle happened.[12]

An important and interesting point of similarity between many of these stories and the Gospels is found in the tension one discovers between the charismatic wonder-worker and the religious establishment. The more scholastic rabbis often criticized the pious wonder-worker. Thus when Choni prayed for rain by drawing a circle in the dirt and telling God that he would not stir from the circle until God answered, he was criticized by Simeon ben Shetah, the leader of the Pharisees. Despite this, in theology Choni would be considered a Pharisee. In theology Jesus was also close to the Pharisees. Note the words of Simeon's criticism:

> Simeon ben Shetah sent to him saying, "If you had not been Choni I would have pronounced a ban against you! But what shall I do to you?—You importunest God, and he performs your will; like a son who importunes his father and he performs his will; and of you the Scripture says, 'Let thy father and thy mother be glad, and let her that bore thee rejoice' " (Prov 23:25).[13]

One finds similar criticism of Jesus. He heals on the Sabbath. He does not break the Sabbath law; however, he does go as far as possible to alleviate suffering on the Sabbath. Most religious authorities would have agreed with Jesus that just as preservation of life takes precedence over the laws regarding the Sabbath rest, so also healing, as an extension of saving life, takes precedence. But Simeon criticizes Choni for his extremes. After all, Choni petulantly drew a circle in the dirt, stood within it, and said he would not leave the circle until God answered his prayer. This was a daring act. Simeon ben Shetah says, "What shall I do to you?" but can do nothing because Choni did not violate the law. Jesus worked miracles. What shall be done to him? Nothing should be done because he did not violate the law. The tension between the miracle-worker and the scholastic rabbi is clear.

JESUS THE HEALER

Jesus' healing ministry is based on the great value of each individual person. One of the best examples of the power of

Jesus and of healing faith is seen in the story of the healing of the paralytic (Matt 9:1–8; Mark 2:1–12; Luke 5:17–26). Before Jesus worked a miracle he made a powerful pronouncement. Jesus simply states, "Take heart my son, your sins are forgiven" (Matt 9:2). He proclaims forgiveness for this paralyzed person. The tension emerges. Though criticism comes forth, Jesus deals with the friction. Jesus is able to answer these critics by establishing the validity of his teachings through action. In the end all the people glorify God for the miracle. They recognize God's goodness.

The healing of the paralytic is a clear case of Jesus' miracle-working ministry. The paralytic is carried to Jesus by the paralytic's faithful friends. He is unable to walk and is dependent upon others. His condition could easily have caused feelings of rejection and guilt. Often the cause of sickness was wrongly attributed to sin. Did this suffering person's sin cause his illness? Jesus' pronouncement of forgiveness gives to the hurting individual acceptance, which is a healing in and of itself. The grace of God comes forth in full force when Jesus works a miracle of healing. He does not condemn. Jesus speaks a word as the power of forgiveness and acceptance begins a process. The key verse in this passage, and indeed for the entire miracle-working ministry of Jesus, is found in his words, "Take heart my son, your sins are forgiven" (Matt 9:2). By forgiving the paralyzed person's sins in this dramatic proclamation, Jesus gives him the love, acceptance, and forgiveness that he desperately needs.

In Jewish texts true faith, like that of the paralytic and his friends, must be based upon the sovereignty of God. The rabbis give an example from the experience of the people of Israel in the wilderness. When the people were infested with snakes, God commanded Moses to make a fiery serpent to bring a cure. According to the rabbis, the fiery serpent itself had little to do with the healing. The healing came to those bitten by the snakes, because of their belief in God. Their faith was not in the serpent, but in God.

"And the LORD said to Moses: Make a fiery serpent" (Num 21:8). Now does a serpent kill or a serpent keep alive? It merely means this: When Moses did this, the Israelites would look at him [Moses] and believe in Him [God] who commanded Moses to do so; then God would send healing.[14]

Faith begins with God. God is good. He is sovereign. Faith in God must never be confused with faith in faith. In the ministry of Jesus, healing begins with God and his goodness. Jesus gave love and acceptance as a vehicle for the healing of the paralytic. Jesus pronounced forgiveness by enacting God's grace. Like a prophet, Jesus acted out a living parable. He simply spoke the word, and the man walked. Healing faith in the Gospels focuses not upon the problem but upon God, by recognizing God's goodness and mercy. In the Gospels, Jesus teaches people to "Have faith in God" (Mark 11:22 and see Matt 6:25–34).

The rabbinic parallels to the Gospel story of the healing demonstrate the rich cultural heritage for the events in the life of Jesus. They are very similar to the Talmud's stories of miraculous healings. In many ways Jesus would be at home among the ranks of Choni the Circle Drawer. In other ways, he is in a class all by himself. His profound self-awareness goes beyond the humble piety of these rabbis, though to be sure, Jesus stressed humility in word and deed. By way of contrast, the miracles of Jesus were never performed as a result of prayer.[15] He merely speaks the word and the miracle happens. In that respect the healing ministry of Jesus is unparalleled.[16] In the case of the paralytic, he pronounced the word of grace through forgiveness, and the healing happened.

Perhaps the people could not grasp the full meaning of the words of Jesus until he healed the paralytic. Then they perceived God's goodness and gave glory to God. The heritage of the Jewish people acknowledges God's grace. The pious would pray, "Blessed is he who has not sinned, but if one has sinned— he will be forgiven."[17] In his love God forgives and heals people in need.

David Flusser has demonstrated that this blessing reflects an early Jewish benediction that is said when God works a miracle. When God blesses, the people are to respond, "Blessed be God who has done so great wonders for the children of men."[18] When Jesus healed the paralytic, the people gave praise to God. While they recognized the unusual authority given to Jesus, they gave praise to the God who healed the paralytic of his infirmity.

All good comes from God. In Jewish tradition, when someone benefits in any way from God's creation, that one is required to give thanks to God. The earth belongs to the Lord (Ps 24:1), and each time a person is blessed by God's goodness from this world he or she is bound to give praise to God. All belongs to him. One receives God's grace with thanksgiving and praise. Faith must be God-centered, focused upon his goodness and grace.

Faith in God and his grace is total trust in the Creator of heaven and earth. Faith acknowledges who God is and commits everything into his power. The miraculous healings of the Gospels revealed God's kingdom. The kingdom comes in full force when Jesus works a miracle of healing because it is the finger of God that brings deliverance and openly displays divine sovereignty. God's plan is designed to bring wholeness and healing to every area of an individual's life.

Jesus forgives the paralytic and heals him through the spoken word of his authority. Jesus' pronouncement of forgiveness as a result of faith in God's sovereignty displays Jesus' supreme authority. The people respond by giving praise to God. The kingdom, namely, the kingly sovereignty of God's supernatural power, has been realized by the miracle of healing.

NOTES

1. Luke 11:20 and Matt 12:28.

2. See Max Kadushin, *The Rabbinic Mind* (New York: Bloch, 1972) 156–57: "Thus, to mention several, it is told that R. Phinehas ben Ya'ir caused the waters of a river to divide on three occasions; that at the prayer of Nakdimon ben Gorion the day was lengthened and the sun shone in heaven; that, in answer to the prayer of Honi, the Circle Drawer, rain fell, and likewise, at different times, in answer to the prayers of others. Some of the Tannaim were said to have been 'accustomed to *Nissim* [miracles],' and this phrase is applied not only to famous teachers like Nahum of Gimzo and Simeon ben Yohai, but also to the wife of R. Hanina ben Dosa."

3. Geza Vermes, *Jesus the Jew* (London: Collins, 1974) 58–82. See especially David Flusser, *Judaism and the Origins of Christianity* (Jerusalem: Magnes, 1988) 535–42.

4. Solomon Schechter, *Aspects of Rabbinic Theology* (New York: Schocken, 1961) 5–6.

5. B. *Taʿan.* 23a and parallels. The piety of Beruria, the wife of Rabbi Meir, is also celebrated in a similar story in b. *Berakhot* 10a. See also the study of the form of the rabbinic miracle story as it relates to the Gospels in Laurence J. McGinley, *Form-Criticism of the Synoptic Healing Narratives* (Woodstock, Md.: Woodstock College, 1944) 96–118.

6. The story of Choni is discussed more fully in the chapter "Faith as *Chutzpah!*"

7. M. *Ta'an.* 3:8. See also the foreword by David Flusser to R. L. Lindsey, *A Hebrew Translation of the Gospel of Mark* (Jerusalem: Baptist House, 1973) 5.

8. Josephus mentioned Choni and the way he was exploited during the civil war. His powerful prayers were sought for military victory of one brother fighting against another. "Now there was a certain Onias [Choni the Circle Drawer], who, being a righteous man and dear to God, had once in a rainless period prayed to God to end the drought, and God had heard his prayer and sent rain; this man hid himself when he saw that the civil war continued to rage, but he was taken to the camp . . . and asked to place a curse on Aristobulus and his fellow rebels, just as he had, by his prayers, put an end to the rainless period. But when in spite of his refusals and excuses he was forced to speak by the mob, he stood up in their midst and said, 'O God, king of the universe, since these men standing beside me are Thy people, and those who are besieged are Thy priests, I beseech Thee not to hearken to them against these men nor to bring to pass what these men ask Thee to do to those others.' And when he had prayed in this manner the villains . . . who stood round him stoned him to death." Josephus, *Ant.* 14.22–24.

9. M. *Ber.* 5:5.

10. B. *Ber.* 34b.

11. Ibid.

12. See John 4:46–54. The parallel in Luke 7:1–10 does not mention the hour.

13. M. *Ta'an.* 3:8.

14. See Mechilta de Rabbi Ishmael on Exod 17:11 (Horovitz 179; Lauterbach, 143).

15. The only exception to this might be the story in John 11 concerning the raising of Lazarus. However, the prayer that he said for the others is not exactly parallel.

16. Meyer wisely warns against minimizing the importance of miracles in the study of the life of Jesus. See Ben F. Meyer, *Aims of Jesus* (London: SCM, 1979) 158:

> A minimizing attitude toward the miracles would be especially mistaken if it presupposed their reducibility to the popular prodigies of the surrounding world, Jewish or Greek. The miracles of Jesus were not magic. They were evoked by his word in a context of religious faith. They signified the reign of God in a way that illuminated its relation to world and history and bodily life precisely as fulfilment; as harvest, wedding, and banquet, as *Weltvollendung*, not the mere end but the consummation and re-creation of the world.

17. See t. *Sukkah* 4:2 and parallels. The saying was associated with the pious ones of old, which may be a description of religious faithful ones in the circle of Choni. I am grateful to David Flusser who called my attention to this rabbinic teaching.

18. See Pseudo-Philo 26:6; see M. R. James, *The Biblical Antiquities of Philo* (Hoboken, N.J.: KTAV, 1971) 154. On this blessing see David Flusser, *Judaism and the Origins of Christianity*, 535–42. Concerning the early Jewish miracle-workers, see Flusser's chapter, ibid., 543–51. It is similar to other blessings like "Blessed (is He) who has given (a portion) of His glory to flesh and blood" or "Blessed (is He) who has given (a portion) of His wisdom to flesh and blood" (b. *Ber.* 58a). See my chapter written with David Flusser, "Messianic Blessings in Jewish and Christian Texts," ibid., 280–300.

Lintel for the House of Study (synagogue) of Eleazer Hakapar.
Photo courtesy of the Israel Antiquities Authority.

"Seat of Moses" from Chorazin Synagogue.
Photo courtesy of the Israel Antiquities Authority.

PART 2

THE JEWISH ROOTS OF JESUS' KINGDOM THEOLOGY

For to us there are two kinds of hard saying: there are some which are hard to understand and there are some which are only too easy to understand. When sayings of Jesus which are hard in the former sense are explained in dynamically equivalent terms, then they are likely to become hard in the latter sense. Mark Twain spoke for many when he said that the things in the Bible that bothered him were not those that he did not understand but those which he did understand. This is particularly true of the sayings of Jesus.

—F. F. Bruce

5

"The Kingdom Suffers Violence . . ." or "The Kingdom Breaks Forth . . ."

JESUS VIEWED THE KINGDOM OF HEAVEN AS AN ACTIVE force in the world that was energized by God's power. He experienced the ever-growing intensity of divine favor in his teaching and healing work among people with great needs. The keen awareness of the divine presence at work in everyday life is strongly felt in such sayings of Jesus as, "But if it is by the finger of God that I cast out demons, then the kingdom of God has come upon you," and also especially, "From the days of John the Baptist until now the kingdom of heaven has suffered violence, and men of violence take it by force."[1] In the Gospel tradition, Jesus is portrayed as experiencing the force of God's reign as he teaches the people. How can these verses be properly interpreted in the historical setting of Jesus' life's work?

The ministry of Jesus was anything but ordinary. He expelled demons and ministered to ailing people as he challenged his disciples with a teaching message that centered conceptually on God's reign. What happened was extraordinary. The men and women in his band of followers experienced God's reign dynamically in a personal encounter. People helped other people as they followed Jesus and dedicated themselves to God. Nowhere is the theme of God's reign as a powerful healing force being unleashed in a hurting world more apparent than in the sayings of Jesus concerning John the Baptist. The prophets functioned until John, but now God's kingdom "suffers violence." As we will see, instead of "suffers violence," the action words "the kingdom of heaven *breaks forth*" are much closer to the original meaning of the text.[2] God's kingdom is advancing forcefully from within the dynamic movement itself, as people embrace the teachings of Jesus and put them into practice.

While in prison John sent two of his disciples to ask Jesus a question. Was he indeed the coming one, or should they expect someone else? Jesus had to explain his mission and the role that John's ministry had played to prepare for it. In the work of John, the climax of the ministry of all the prophets has been attained. Now John has made a breach in the wall which opens an entrance for and prepares the way for the ministry of Jesus. Two towering figures are profiled in this description of the redemptive work, John the Baptist and Jesus himself. But what does "suffer violence" really mean? How is it related to the kingdom of heaven and to the mission of Jesus? Without a sound approach to the translation of the Gospels, we lose something of great value from the words of Jesus because they are robbed of the rich imagery of the original language.

The art of Bible translation always impacts theology and culture. The King James translation of Matthew 11:12, "From the days of John the Baptist until now the kingdom of heaven suffereth violence, and the violent take it by force," has influenced many Christian theologians and has even found expression in Western culture. This saying of Jesus has been improperly translated, wrongly understood, and often removed from its original context concerning John the Baptist. Most of the time the verse has been given one of two interpretations. First, it was thought to describe how the kingdom was being attacked by men of violence. Second, and perhaps even more unfortunately, some scholars have suggested that Jesus advocated violence as a part of his kingdom message. They contend that he was one of the Zealots or was like them in the way in which he advocated force to attain political goals. But how can the disciples of Jesus be characterized as "men of violence" like the Zealots on the one hand and as "peacemakers" on the other? This saying of Jesus must be translated properly and studied within its original Jewish setting during the first century, when John the Baptist's ministry coalesced with the work of Jesus. Here it will be seen that John acts as the breaker who makes a breach in the wall. Through the opening John makes, the kingdom of heaven breaks forth from within. Jesus and his mission are the focal point of the phrase, "the kingdom of heaven breaks forth." The prophets lead up to John the Baptist, who then prepares the way for Jesus. But now the movement of Jesus' followers dynamically advances as a force for healing and wholeness in a suffering world.

How can the kingdom of heaven suffer violence? The verse does not make sense according to its translation in the KJV. Nevertheless, because of the popularity and the authority accorded to recognized versions of the New Testament, often revisions are viewed with skepticism. Even when the various accepted versions disagree, new translations of the Greek text are not always welcomed. The New International Version, for instance, translates the saying of Jesus as, "From the days of John the Baptist until now the kingdom of heaven has been forcefully advancing, and forceful men lay hold of it." Probably the NIV has more nearly captured the meaning of Matthew 11:12 than any of the other English translations. Here a new translation of the Greek text similar to that of the NIV will be suggested. The question of the Hebrew original of this saying of Jesus becomes of inestimable value when the Old Testament background is seen in Micah 2:13, "The breaker who opens the breach rises up before them. . . ." The tremendous significance of careful Bible translation should never be taken for granted. Each word warrants careful study. The idea that the kingdom of heaven is forcefully advancing as portrayed in the NIV is much nearer to the original meaning of the text. Since the kingdom-of-heaven message dominates the teachings of Jesus, Matthew 11:12 is essential for a proper approach to the Gospel. Each Greek word and its background in Hebrew, as well as the Jewish thought during the first century, must be examined to understand fully the teaching of Jesus concerning the kingdom in this text.

THE RIGHT TRANSLATION: "THE KINGDOM BREAKS FORTH . . ."

The Greek verb which is translated "suffers violence" in the KJV is *biazō*. "Suffers violence" is not a good translation. As has been noted, the New International Version rendered this Greek verb as "forcefully advancing." This translation of *biazō* is more appropriate than the passive idea from "suffers violence" because the active meaning correctly conveys both the force associated with the verb and also mentions the progressive movement of the divine reign. At times, the Hebrew verb *paratz*, which means "to break forth," was translated by the Greek verb *biazō* in the Septuagint.[3] The idea conveyed by the

Greek verb *biazō* certainly includes the action of "breaking forth."[4] Moreover, the Hebrew background of this saying of Jesus actually denotes an action of breaking out with strong force. The best rendering of the term in this context is "breaks forth."[5] The action originates from within and moves outward. It is a reflexive type of action which is found in the middle voice of the Greek language. The kingdom's source of power is an internal rather than an external source. Likewise, the single word *biastai*, a noun derived from the same Greek verb, is translated as "the violent" in the KJV and "forceful men" in the NIV. However, since *biastai* comes from the same verb *biazō* and is closely related to Micah 2:13, it should be rendered as "the breakers," that is, the ones making the breach wider as they break out from within the wall. They are the ones who are breaking out with the kingdom. Unquestionably, the entire saying of Jesus is connected to the words of the prophet Micah:

> He who opens the breach (the breaker, *haporetz*) will go up before them; they will break through *(partzu),* and pass the gate, going out by it. Their king *(malkam)* will pass on before them, the LORD at their head (Micah 2:13).

Of great significance here are the two major figures, "He who opens the breach" and "their king." "He who opens the breach" is one word in Hebrew, "the breaker," *haportez*. Both of them are connected to Jesus' saying, "The kingdom of heaven breaks forth. . . ." The first part of the verse from Micah 2:13, "He who opens the breach (the breaker, *haporetz*) will go up before them," is related to the words of Jesus, "From the days of John the Baptist until now, the kingdom of heaven breaks forth. . . ." The one who causes the kingdom to break forth is John the Baptist. Concerning him, Flusser writes, "With John the end-time begins—the decisive eruption into the history of the world."[6] John is the breaker *(haporetz)*. He opens the breach.

The mental image created by the verse in Micah 2:13 portrays a sheepfold full of sheep. When shepherds tend their sheep in the land of Israel, they often erect makeshift fences for a sheepfold. They will gather stones and build a temporary holding pen. The shepherds might design a full circular enclosure, or they might adapt an already existing natural barrier like a cave in the side of a rocky hillside. They will build the stone wall barricade in a semicircular fashion that will seal off the cave or other natural enclosure. In John 10:9, the Gospel records Jesus' words, "I am the door [of the sheepfold]." Literally, he lies in the entrance way of the holding pen. The good shepherd may actually form a human gate as he sleeps at the opening to the sheepfold. Shepherds work diligently to protect and care for their flocks, even risking their lives for the well-being of their sheep. The art of shepherding a herd in the land of Israel frequently required the use of an enclosed sheepfold to protect the livestock at night.

After the sheep have been confined all night in the limited space of the makeshift sheepfold, the animals are anxious to break out. In the morning the shepherd will knock down a section from the piled-up stones. He will break open the barricade wall which penned up the sheep all night in a protective enclosure. Anxious to be released from the holding pen, the sheep will rush out as quickly as possible, knocking down more stones from the makeshift fence in order to break outside.

While, in the historical context of Micah, the prophet may have had Jewish exiles held in foreign captivity in mind, the word picture of a shepherd making a breach in a makeshift sheepfold fence possessed rich metaphorical possibilities for describing the process of redemption. In the Hebrew mind, God would use two individuals, like the breaker and the king according to Micah 2:13, in order to make a way for the release of the captives. In the same way that sheep are anxious for release after a night of confinement within the sheepfold, the people will respond to the divine initiative, "they will break through (*partzu*), and pass the gate, going out by it. Their king (*malkam*) will pass on before them, the LORD at their head" (Mic 2:13). Not only are two key figures mentioned in Micah, but also the prophet Malachi refers to the prophet Elijah who would prepare the way for the coming of the Lord. When speaking about John the Baptist, Jesus quotes Malachi: "This is he of whom it is written, 'Behold, I send my messenger before thy face, who shall prepare thy way before thee' " (Matt 11:9–10).

Very meaningful for understanding the relationship between "the kingdom breaks forth" (*poretzet*, in Hebrew, *biazetai*, in Greek) and the "ones breaking out" (*portzim*, in Hebrew, *biastai*, in Greek) is the fact that Micah 2:13 refers both to the breaker (*haporetz*) and the ones who break forth (*partzu*) with him. The action in the verse is decisive. The breaker makes a breach and the ones inside the sheepfold break forth from within. The idea of persecution, namely, that the sheep inside the fold are under attack after the breach has been made, is not possible.

A major focus of Micah 2:13 is the king. He leads the ones breaking out of the fold with the Lord himself at the head of them. The two key players in the dramatic action described in the verse are the breaker and the king. David Flusser has demonstrated that these two figures play a prominent part in Jewish expectations pertaining to the coming of redemption. Flusser observes, "Elijah was to come first to open the breach, and he would be followed by those who broke through with their king, the Messiah."[7]

So far we have seen that the first part of the verse is better translated, "From the days of John the Baptist until now the kingdom of heaven breaks forth. . . ." But the second half of the saying of Jesus also raises some serious questions. The NIV translates it as "and forceful men [the breakers] lay hold of it." The KJV says, "and the violent take it by force." The Greek verb translated by "lay hold of" (NIV) or "take by force" (KJV) is *harpazō*. How should these two words, *biastai* "forceful men" (NIV) and *harpazō* "lay hold of" (NIV), best be translated?

In consideration of this question, R. L. Lindsey has looked to the second part of the same saying of Jesus in its parallel version from Luke 16:16, "and every one breaks out with it." The NIV of Luke 16:16 reads, "and everyone is forcing his way into it."[8] Lindsey is certainly correct in translating Luke 16:16, "and every one breaks out with it." But what about the Matthean version? In Lindsey's view, the verb *harpazō*, "lay hold of" or "take by force," was used descriptively by the editor of Matthew's Gospel. The verb was added to the source of Matthew's text as it was edited. According to Lindsey, in Hebrew the best rendering of the saying is, *meyame yochanan hamatbil vead atah malchut shamayim poretzet vekol poretz bah,* "From the days of John the Baptist until now, the kingdom of heaven breaks forth and everyone breaks forth with it." This reconstruction of the saying draws together Matthew 11:12a, "From the days of John the Baptist until now, the kingdom of heaven breaks forth," and Luke 16:16b, "and everyone breaks forth with it."[9] His reconstruction is certainly one possible approach. There is another.

With respect to Lindsey's well-reasoned position, the second part of Matthew's text also makes good sense. A first-century

Jewish reader of the Gospel story would hear the Hebrew idiom from the source text of Matthew 11:12b. The term *harpazō* may convey the idea of "to pursue" in the sense of, "But seek [pursue] first his kingdom and his righteousness" (Matt 6:33). The Greek verb *harpazō* is sometimes translated in Hebrew by terms like *gazal* "to steal," *lakach* "to take," and *lakad* "to capture" (biblical Hebrew) or even by *natal* "to take" or *tafas* "to grasp, or catch" (postbiblical Hebrew). Probably the Greek verb could actually be used for terms in Hebrew like *radaf* "to pursue" or even *bakesh* "to seek." I believe that *radaf* "to pursue earnestly" is the best translation. The text could be translated into Hebrew, *meyame yochanan hamatbil vead atah malchut shamayim poretzet vehaportzim rodfim [mevakshim] otah*, "From the days of John the Baptist until now, the kingdom of heaven breaks forth and those breaking forth are pursuing [seeking] it" (Matt 11:12). This translation brings out the meaning of the Greek text. The concept conveyed by this translation of the verse in Matthew would be similar to the words of Psalm 34:14, "seek peace and pursue it" *(bekesh shalom verodfehu).* In the Dead Sea Scrolls, the Hebrew word *radaf* "to pursue earnestly" is often used in a similar way. The members of the congregation in the Judean desert are exhorted to pursue earnestly wisdom and righteousness.[10] The essence of Matthew 11:12b dynamically portrays the ones breaking out of the sheepfold. They actively pursue the divine purposes in life with all their strength.

In any case, the controlling idea of the second part of the saying focuses on the higher values of God's reign. The ones breaking forth with the kingdom of heaven pursue the principles of God's reign with all their might. They possess an intensity for the work of the Lord. The rule of God is sought in every part of their lives. They become subjects of the king, accepting the yoke of the kingdom of heaven and seeking to see the redeeming power of healing love penetrate a world full of people in need of God.

JOHN'S DOUBTS ABOUT JESUS

John had doubts about Jesus. The question that John sent to Jesus through his disciples, "Are you the one who is to come, or should we look for another?" is perplexing in light of the

Gospel accounts concerning the baptism of Jesus. At the waters of baptism, John is portrayed in the Gospels as a witness to the voice from heaven. In Matthew he first refuses to baptize Jesus because he knows who Jesus is. But later while in prison, John the Baptist commissions two of his disciples to approach Jesus with the very serious question concerning the nature of Jesus' own mission. Why did John begin to entertain such strong doubts?

John's skepticism concerning the ministry of Jesus was rooted in Jewish messianic expectation. The issue really involved definition and understanding of the messianic task. John, as others during the period, anticipated the coming of a deliverer—but not one quite like Jesus. It was thought that the anointed one would be more like King David than a suffering servant. He would break the cruel yoke of foreign oppression that Rome and its puppet rulers had placed upon the Jewish people. John the Baptist probably anticipated a messianic figure who would bring freedom from the political oppression of Rome. The world had been so corrupted by its political and economic systems that a reform of the people was not enough. A supernatural intervention by God was needed.

While the Hebrew prophets envisioned a great return of the people to God and social reforms to solve the problems of the common people, the Jewish apocalyptists anticipated a complete transformation of the world order. A new Jerusalem is required, not merely a city reformed or renewed from within. John the Baptist seems to be much more eschatologically minded, which is to say that he expected the end times to come suddenly with the appearance of the one designated for the task. The one who is coming, John explained, possesses a greater task than the forerunner who announces his coming. John acts as his forerunner and announcer. He prepares the way for his coming. But John is not worthy to untie the coming one's sandals. The one who comes will baptize with the Holy Spirit.

The colorful images of judgment in the minds of the Hebrew prophets and apocalyptists are prominent in the words of John recorded in the Gospels. The wicked would be burned in the fires of punishment, and the righteous would be baptized with the divine favor of the Holy Spirit. The grace of God would be demonstrated to the people looking for his supernatural intervention. They must return to the Lord with a sincere heart. The lifestyle they pursue must change. They must follow a new righteous way of living. While earlier in the Gospel record John recognized Jesus as the person who would bring about a change in the world order, he began to doubt whether Jesus was the coming one. Perhaps he should anticipate someone else?

John wanted to learn more about Jesus' self-awareness. On three occasions in the Synoptic Gospels we find clear and direct descriptions of Jesus' approach to the question of his messiahship. "If you are the Messiah, tell us," Caiaphas directs Jesus (Luke 22:67). Jesus himself asks Peter, "But who do you say that I am?" (Luke 9:20). Here, for a third incident, John the Baptist poses the question to Jesus, "Are you the one who is coming, or do we expect someone else?" The issue raised on these three occasions still reverberates through history. What did people say about Jesus? What did Jesus say about himself? In all three instances from the Synoptic Gospels, a reply is given which is culturally conditioned. In each case the writers of the record recognized the strong significance Jesus gave to his mission. He is not the one a person would expect, if he or she were looking for a general to reestablish the political kingdom of King David. But if a person seeks a healer of needy people like the servant of the Lord from Isaiah, then he or she will not be disappointed. The times and the seasons are in the hands of the Father, and the final judgment will complete the task. The self-consciousness of Jesus was embedded in his view of the servant of the Lord in the writings of the Hebrew prophets. John the Baptist, in contrast, longed to see the vision of the eschatological judgment realized. John is really a tragic figure. He is a victim of his own theology.[11]

The doubts of John revolved around his view of the messianic task. The term "coming one" he probably understood more as an eschatological judge. The coming one would be like the Son of man described in the apocalyptic visions of Daniel or the book of Enoch. The coming one would stand before the Ancient of Days to receive all authority and power. Daniel gives a vivid description, "I saw in the night visions, and behold, with the clouds of heaven there came one like a Son of man, and he came to the Ancient of Days and was presented before him. And to him was given dominion and glory and kingdom" (Dan 7:13–14). The same title, "Son of man," is used for the coming one in the book of Enoch. Although the book of Enoch was not accepted by the church and the synagogue as a sacred writing to

be included in the Bible, it was widely read by the Jewish
people during the time of Jesus. It tells us a great deal about
how people viewed the coming one. For example, one passage
reads, "And the sum of judgement was given to the Son of man,
and he will cause the sinners to pass away and be destroyed
from off the earth. . . . For that Son of man has appeared, and
has seated himself on the throne of his glory. . . ."[12] Like Daniel,
the book of Enoch described the coming one as the Son of man
who would be God's judge in the end of time. Because John the
Baptist speaks about the coming one who will baptize in the
fires of judgment and whose winnowing fork is in his hand as
the axe is laid to the root, he probably anticipated a sudden
apocalyptic change in which the Son of man would establish an
entirely new world order. The sinners would be destroyed, and
the righteous would be baptized in the Holy Spirit. God's redemption would be consummated in a dramatic eruption into
history. The divine intervention into the natural course of human affairs would decisively bring judgment upon the present
corrupt world order. The righteous would be saved and the
wicked damned.

Whatever hopes John had for Jesus at the waters of the Jordan where he baptized so many, his expectations concerning the
coming one were not being fulfilled in the ministry of Jesus.
While imprisoned by Herod Antipas in the fortress of Machaerus on the eastern bank of the Jordan river just north of the
Dead Sea, John became skeptical about Jesus, his message, and
his mission.[13] Perhaps as his own fate hung in the balance of an
unjust political and judicial system, he longed to see the vision
of Daniel fulfilled. All of the Hebrew prophets and visionaries
had looked for the coming one. Who is he? When will he
appear? In John's mind, if Jesus were the promised coming one,
then he should move ahead with his mission. The time is short.
Jesus was not doing what John thought the coming one should
do. Like many others during the time of the Second Temple as
well as throughout history, John expected a different type of
messiah. Jesus' answer to John's disciples is not what John
wanted to hear. At the very least, Jesus' answer conveys a
threatening challenge to John the Baptist. It tells us, moreover,
about how Jesus viewed the messianic task. His view of the
coming one and that of John the Baptist's expectations are far
from synonymous.

THE WARNING OF JESUS

The stern warning of Jesus, "Blessed is he who does not stumble over me," carries a nuance in Hebrew having a much stronger force than English or Greek translations convey. The strong words form an awesome threat. They caution John the Baptist against serious wrongdoing. To answer the question of John, Jesus says, "Go tell John what you see and hear." Then he refers to well-known passages from the prophet Isaiah (29:18–19 and 35:5–6) which describe the ministry of the servant of the Lord more as a healer of suffering humanity than as the final judge who pronounces sentence upon the wicked and the just. Instead of taking the winnowing fork in his hands to bring judgment, Jesus is binding up the wounds of people in a hurting world. The poor hear the good news of the divine favor which is brought through the ministry of Jesus and his disciples.

The verb "to stumble" in the response of Jesus is a strong word for John. It means to sin or fail in a serious matter. John had missed the significance of Jesus' work. Jesus told John's disciples to go and tell him what they had observed as eye-witnesses to the ministry of Jesus and to caution him, "Blessed is he who does not stumble over me." In reality Jesus was both defining the messianic task and giving a stern warning. He was earnestly inviting John to accept his mission as it was being fulfilled in the midst of the people. As he begins to praise John, "There is none born among women greater than John the Baptist," he also notes that the least in the kingdom of heaven is greater than John. John the Baptist has been left behind. He is excluded from the kingdom movement. Jesus gives John an alarming warning. Although he represents the last of the prophets who yearned for the appearance of the anointed one, John has not understood the messianic task as defined by Jesus. His misunderstanding has its origins in the plurality of messianic expectations of first-century Judaism. John embraced an incorrect eschatological scenario which hindered him from joining Jesus' kingdom movement.

JEWISH MESSIANIC EXPECTATIONS

Views concerning the coming of the Messiah during the days of the Second Temple period were diverse and far from

monolithic.[14] The fact that in the Gospel record even John the
Baptist misunderstood the purpose of Jesus makes it clear that
he was not alone. Many expected a greater political dimension
to the work of the Messiah. In some circles a political messiah
like King David was expected, along with a second messiah who
would be more of a spiritual leader like the priest. Perhaps the
most difficult aspect of the mission of Jesus was the fact that he
would be crucified. Little evidence from the Second Temple
period suggests that the people were looking for a messianic
figure who would be killed. On the one hand, Jesus spoke about
the Son of man who would be rejected and turned over to the
Gentiles who would crucify him. On the other, he referred to
the future coming of the Son of man who would fulfill the role
of righteous judge and king of the nations. But in the interim
period Jesus was like an itinerant rabbi who taught the people
and healed their infirmities.

For many religious and secular people, the life work of Jesus
would have been difficult to understand fully in the context of
Israel's plurality of messianic expectations. Groups such as the
Sadducees and the priests would not even go so far as to expect
a messianic figure. Others, like the Pharisees, looked for divine
assistance in hard times. Popularly many people expected God
to liberate Israel from its Roman oppressors, just as God had
delivered his people from their slavery in Egypt. At that time
God used Moses to save the people from bondage to a foreign
power. Moses was the mediator between God and the people.
He functioned as a prophet who taught the people and worked
miracles. The people were liberated from Egypt as they believed in the Lord and in Moses his servant. In any case, the
people listening to Jesus discussed John the Baptist in terms of
his prophetic role.

They were accustomed to considering numerous traditions associated with divine strategies to bring salvation from foreign
oppression. As can be seen from the Dead Sea Scrolls, the
reading of the Hebrew prophets was often applied directly to
the life situation of the people. When they read Deuteronomy
18:18, "I will raise up a prophet from among their brethren, like
unto thee [Moses]," they did not think only of Joshua the historical successor to Moses but looked rather to the coming of
the prophet who would work a new miracle of redemption by a
second exodus in their days. In late antiquity many Jewish readers studied the Hebrew Scriptures but kept their eyes on current

developments in their common experience with their corrupt political oppressors. In their hearts of faith, they believed God had something better for his people. A second prophet like Moses would bring about the change. How everything would take place, however, was a subject for wide speculation and open discussion.

In spite of such great diversity in Judaism, Jesus sent John an alarming warning, "Blessed is he who does not stumble over me." When Jesus speaks to the crowds concerning the role of John the Baptist, he uses terms of high esteem by calling him a prophet who is like Elijah. He likens the ministry of John to the great in-breaking of the kingdom of heaven. Regardless of the diverse opinions concerning the coming of the Messiah, Jesus is hinting at common traditions that would have been widely known, even if some of the people would have viewed the popular beliefs about the coming of the Lord's anointed with skepticism or indifference. The rich multiplicity of messianic ideas that circulated during the Second Temple period provided a forum for exchange and lively discourse.

Although opinions fluctuated greatly among the learned as well as the less educated, the pervading Jewish belief in the goodness of the one God of Israel fostered the idea that he would not allow his people to suffer indefinitely. When the people read the texts of the Hebrew prophets, they believed that God was telling them about their generation and the unfolding of his ultimate purpose, namely, the salvation of his people Israel. Not surprisingly, Micah 2:13 and Malachi 3:1 were drawn together and studied as prophecies describing the events that would lead up to the coming of the anointed deliverer. Two towering figures could be seen in the words of both Micah and Malachi. Not only did Jesus call John the Baptist the prophet Elijah from Malachi, but he also hinted at contemporary beliefs concerning the coming of the Messiah. Both Elijah and the Messiah emerge from popular Jewish interpretations of Micah 2:13.

Two figures were anticipated. The first would be like Elijah. He would lead a tremendous spiritual renewal among the people which would prepare the way for the coming of the Messiah himself. The scenario of Elijah as forerunner and the Messiah as prophetic deliverer who comes after him possesses deep roots in the diversified teachings concerning the redemption of the people during the time of Jesus. The profiles of these two redemptive figures are described in dramatic detail. The

ancient scholars of the Hebrew Bible possessed a vivid awareness of the divine purpose in their interpretations of the Hebrew prophets. The eternal passion of the prophets is felt in the
popular Jewish exposition of their prophecies.

ELIJAH COMES FIRST

The passion of the prophets and their role in the higher purposes of God are mirrored in the words of Rabbi Johanan, "All
the prophets prophesied [all the good things] only for the days
of the Messiah; but as for the world to come, 'no eye has seen,
O God, besides thee, what you have prepared for those who
wait for him' (Isa 64:4)."[15] The main feature of the message of
the prophets was identified by the rabbis as the days of the
Messiah. The anxious waiting for the Messiah is felt in these
words. Concerning John the Baptist, Jesus said, "All the prophets prophesied until John." The ultimate reason for the work of
the prophets was to point beyond their days. From the time of
John the Baptist until now, the kingdom of heaven breaks forth,
and if one can understand it properly, John fulfills the role of
Elijah who was designated to prepare the way before the coming of the anointed Redeemer.

Malachi mentions Elijah by name when speaking about the
future day of the Lord. The prophet Elijah is also referred to in
the blessing of the Haftorah reading from the Hebrew prophets
in the worship of the ancient synagogue. The powerful role of
Elijah is reflected in the words of Malachi 4:4–5.

> Remember the law of my servant Moses, the statutes and ordinances
> that I commanded him at Horeb for all Israel. Behold, I will send you
> Elijah the prophet before the great and terrible day of the LORD comes.
> And he will turn the hearts of fathers to their children and the hearts
> of children to their fathers, lest I come and smite the land with a curse.

At the conclusion of the words of the prophet, Elijah himself is
portrayed in his special role in the divine plan. But Jesus quoted
the passage from Malachi, "Behold, I send my messenger to
prepare the way before me, and the Lord whom you seek will
suddenly come to his temple; the messenger of the covenant in
whom you delight, behold, he is coming, says the LORD of
hosts" (Mal 3:1–2). Two figures appear in the verse: (1) my
messenger and (2) the Lord.

As in Malachi 3:1, two important characters emerge from the reading of Micah 2:13: "The breaker (*haporetz*) who opens the breach rises up before them; they will break through (*partzu*), and pass the gate, going out by it. Their king (*malkam*) will pass on before them, the LORD at the head of them." In Micah, the two figures are portrayed by the designations (1) the breaker and (2) their king. These two characters, the breaker and their king, were popularly interpreted as referring to Elijah and the Messiah. A beautiful description of the future redemption is preserved in the homiletical midrash, Pesikta Rabbati, which is filled with early Jewish teachings about the holy days as well as with rich Bible exposition.

> When the Holy One, blessed be He, redeems Israel. Three days before the Messiah comes, Elijah will come and stand upon the mountains of Israel. . . . In that hour the Holy One, blessed be He, will show his glory and his kingdom to all the inhabitants of the world: He will redeem Israel, and He will appear at the head of them, as is said, he who opens the breach [the breaker, *haporetz*] will go up before them; they will break through and pass the gate, going out by it. Their king will pass on before them, the LORD at their head (Micah 2:13).[16]

The vivid portrait of the final redemption of the people of Israel portrays the coming of Elijah as a forerunner of the Messiah. Both Elijah and the Messiah are described here in a Jewish midrash which speaks about the glory of God's kingdom and which quotes Micah 2:13 as a proof text. The importance of the word "the breaker" (*haporetz*) in Micah 2:13 and the mention of the kingdom of heaven as "breaking forth" in the words of Jesus concerning John the Baptist and Elijah become clearer. In Hebrew the same word is used for both the "breaker" and the action of the kingdom, which is described as "breaking forth" ("suffers violence" in the KJV, and "advancing forcefully" in the NIV).[17] John the Baptist is like the breaker. But another Jewish parallel to the saying of Jesus is even more precise. It is quoted from an earlier source by the medieval Jewish exegete Rabbi David Kimchi (Radak) as he explains the meaning of Micah 2:13. Ancient Jewish commentators were keenly aware of the two outstanding figures in the verse, the breaker and the king. Radak comments upon the interpretation of Micah 2:13 by quoting an earlier Jewish source.

> In the words of our teachers of blessed memory and in the Midrash,
> it is taught that "the breaker" is Elijah and "their king" is the branch
> of the son of David.[18]

The king in Micah is identified as the branch of the son of
David, terminology so often associated with Israel's messianic
hope. He is the king Messiah. The action verb from the Gospel
saying, "the kingdom of heaven breaks forth," is connected to
the prophecy of Micah concerning "the breaker." In popular
Jewish discussions concerning the coming of the Messiah, biblical scholars thought that the change in society had to begin
through a period of preparation for the messianic age. The way
for the coming of redemption would be preceded by a prophet
who would have a ministry like Elijah. The king Messiah
would then come to complete the task. Jesus viewed the great
spiritual awakening resulting from John's prophetic ministry as
the preparation for his own work. David Flusser explains it so
well when he discusses his own insights into the relationship
between Radak's commentary on Micah 2:13 and John the
Baptist.

> David Kimchi [Radak] put the following interpretation upon this
> verse: "The one who opens up the breach" is Elijah and "their king"
> is the scion of David. According to this interpretation, which Jesus
> seems to have known, Elijah was to come first to open the breach,
> and he would be followed by those who broke through with their
> king, the Messiah. According to Jesus, the Elijah-John has already
> come, and those men who have the courage of decision now take the
> kingdom by force.[19]

The sheepfold has been broken wide open by the work of
John the Baptist. The drama which is unfolding with John's
prophetic preaching was already foreseen by the ancient Hebrew prophets. The kingdom of heaven has decisively broken
onto the scene with the healing ministry of Jesus. He teaches
the people to love God and to esteem each person with the
great human dignity which must be given to everyone created in
the divine image. The earlier vision of the prophets has been
fulfilled with John the Baptist, who serves as a major turning
point in the sacred history of divine redemption. But now the
kingdom of heaven breaks forth with vigor and power. The
spiritual renewal possesses a supernatural potency as the intensity of the divine favor brings wholeness to a world suffering

from the outside forces of oppression and the inner needs for healing. Jesus then must be identified with the image of the king from Micah 2:13.

David Flusser has called our attention to the early Hebrew commentary on Micah 2:13 and how it throws light upon the sayings of Jesus concerning the kingdom, the role of John the Baptist, and Jesus' own ministry. Flusser's scholarly intuition led him to associate the Jewish interpretation of Micah's words, "the breaker who opens the breach," to the teaching of Jesus, "the kingdom of heaven breaks forth." From this vantage point the saying affords profound insight into how Jesus viewed himself and his messianic task.

Interestingly, as early as the seventeenth century a Christian scholar, Edward Pococke (1604–91) arrived at the exact same conclusion, also based upon a reading of Radak's commentary on Micah. Pococke was an outstanding scholar and impressive linguist. For five years (1630–35) he served as English chaplain at Aleppo and certainly had access to a wealth of Jewish literature. It is not outside the realm of possibility that he would have discussed the Hebrew commentary of Radak concerning Micah with eminent Sephardic rabbis in Aleppo. Such a conversation would have been conducted in Arabic, a language in which Pococke was also fluent. Pococke explained the importance of Radak's commentary for a proper understanding of the relationship between John the Baptist and Jesus.

> To him that was promised to be as such, and was exhibited as such, and hath made good in himself what was promised, well may the title of הפרץ *(Haporets)* in this, or indeed in both senses agree. But if any think, that by הפרץ *(Haporets), the breaker*, and מלכם *(Malcam), their King*, should be meant two distinct persons, let him hear, what the Ancient *Jews* (as cited by the modern) say, for exposition of this place. *Haporets, the Breaker*, that is *Elias*, and *Malcam, their King*, that is *the Branch*, the Son of *David*; and then observe, what our Saviour himself hath taught us, that *John Baptist* was that *Elias* which was to come.[20]

After discussing the language of Micah 2:13 and the Jewish interpretation of it by Radak, Pococke comments upon the significance of the prophecy for the Gospel of Matthew. John the Baptist is Elijah, and Jesus is the branch, the son of David. The kingdom is portrayed because people are breaking forth with the tremendous spiritual renewal that resulted from John's ministry. Pococke continues:

> *that from the daies of John the Baptist, the Kingdom of Heaven suf-*
> *fered violence, and the violent took it by force. Mat.* 11:10, 12. Men
> breaking as it were, and passing through the gate, by his preaching
> repentance laid open, that they might go in and out: and it will be
> easy to apply to him this title of *the breaker*: and so we have in the
> words, a most illustrious prophecy of Christ, and his forerunner *John*
> *the Baptist.*[21]

As a philologist, Pococke recognized the great importance of
biblical languages for a proper understanding of the Gospels.
Although Flusser and Pococke use much different words to
explain the relationship between Jewish interpretations of Micah 2:13 and the sayings of Jesus concerning John the Baptist
and the kingdom, they both have argued the case. John is identified with the breaker. Jesus is claiming to fulfill the role of the
branch, the son of David. Hence both a twentieth-century Jewish scholar, David Flusser, and a seventeenth-century Christian
scholar, Edward Pococke, independently arrived at very similar
conclusions. The facts should be more important than the scholar's religious orientation. They both learned from the Jewish
literature.[22]

To sum up the results of our linguistic and historical study of
this difficult saying of Jesus, "From the days of John the Baptist
until now, the kingdom of heaven suffereth violence and the
violent take it by force," a better translation of the text viewed
within its original Jewish context makes the message of Jesus
concerning John the Baptist and the kingdom of heaven so
much clearer. According to Lindsey, linguistically a much better
translation would be, "From the days of John the Baptist until
now, the kingdom of heaven breaks forth and everyone breaks
forth with it" (Matt 11:12a and Luke 16:16b). In keeping more
closely with Matthew's version, the verse is best translated,
"From the days of John the Baptist until now, the kingdom of
heaven breaks forth and those breaking forth are pursuing
[seeking] it" (Matt 11:12).

Historically, it has been seen that some Jewish interpretations
of Micah 2:13 and Malachi 3:1ff. taught about two important
individuals who would fulfill the redemptive plan of God. Jewish Bible interpreters expected a prophet like Elijah who would
call the people to repentance. He would turn the hearts of the

children toward their heavenly Father as each would prepare for the day of the Lord. The second figure in the plan of redemption would be the branch, the son of David. Like David, he would bring peace and freedom to his people. When Jesus referred to John as the breaker, he was comparing him to Elijah who was to come. As a result of John's work as the breaker, the kingdom of heaven was now breaking forth within Jesus' own ministry of healing. The people experience the power of God. They hear the message of Jesus and are challenged to put it into practice. As the branch, the son of David, Jesus is the healer of needy humanity and a teacher of discipleship in the kingdom of heaven. Hence if John is Elijah, then Jesus is the branch, the son of David. The promised anointed one had come. Jesus reveals his sublime task and strong self-awareness. John the Baptist did not need to look for another. Clearly Jesus claimed to be the anointed one of God. He was saying that he is the Messiah.

JOHN THE BAPTIST AND MODERN CHRISTIANS

Today it is difficult for us to express unconditional love to religious people outside our own denominational setting and theological orientation. This is especially true when Christians consider orthodox Judaism as a vibrant faith. Orthodox Judaism is an authentic witness to the historical faith of Jesus. However, faith in Jesus can erect an impassable barrier against the ones who so meticulously endeavor to preserve historic Jewish faith and practice which is rooted in the divine promises, eternal covenants, and the enduring community of believers who live as Jesus lived. They practice the great-grandchild faith of ancient Judaism. Like Jesus who lived the religious life of his people, modern Jews cherish and observe their ancient faith.

For contemporary Christians the unconditional love which Jesus taught to his disciples must characterize their attitudes to modern expressions of Jewish faith. We need to understand why multitudes of Jews in the first century rejected Jesus. After all, even John the Baptist, who stands upon the pinnacle of the Hebrew prophets, entertained doubts about him. The issue of the messianic task was not cut and dried.

On the other hand, sometimes members of the modern Jewish community have not always appreciated the importance of Jesus for Christians who believe that he is the culmination of God's redemptive plan. His work is not completed. But as the suffering servant of the Lord, he came as a healer and teacher. According to Christian belief, the death of Jesus possesses the power of atonement for sins and transgressions. His promise to return and complete the messianic task forms a foundational doctrine of the church which is not so far removed from many traditional Jewish teachings concerning the coming of the Messiah. While some members in both communities express doubts at times about the supernatural coming of the Messiah, both Christians and Jews wait. Hence waiting on God—for the Messiah's first appearance for the Jewish people and his second for the Christian community—is a shared human experience in both faith traditions. The religious heritage of Judaism and Christianity gives common cause to members of the synagogue and the church. Both long together for godlike wholeness in a tormented world filled with injustice.

Multitudes of first-century Jews accepted Jesus as the promised Messiah. Many others rejected him. After two thousand years of disputation and a tragic history of suspicion, the time is ripe for a long overdue mutual acceptance in sincere love and genuine respect. Wrongly Christians have persecuted the Jewish people. Today as each faith community comes to an understanding of the historical context where members of the first-century Jewish people both accepted and rejected Jesus as Messiah and Lord, we make one small step toward interfaith understanding. Is it possible for modern Christians to show a measure of sympathy for John the Baptist and his sincere doubts even after he baptized Jesus? In light of the fact that Jesus taught about and described his messianic task to an audience with a plurality of messianic expectations, this is perfectly understandable. On the other side of the coin, members of the Jewish community seem more willing to recognize that Jesus' life and ministry satisfied the messianic expectations for many of their ancestors. But as Christians it is more difficult for us to honor the sincere beliefs of our Jewish brothers and sisters who, somewhat like John the Baptist, doubt whether Jesus fulfilled the messianic task. Can Christians accept and affirm members within the household of the Jewish community who do not confess faith in Jesus but who do live the faith of Jesus? The uncompromising message in Jesus' teaching about love must overcome theological prejudice. Both Judaism and Christianity preach the pursuit of peace. Christians and Jews are enriched when they listen to each other in genuine respect.

THE MESSIANIC HOPE

The Jewish messianic hope is above all rooted in the deep belief that the one true God is concerned about human suffering and that he will send someone to help. That someone will be like Moses, who brought liberation when Israel was a slave in Egypt. Israel needed a miracle to escape the torments of slavery. Moses was called to fulfill the mission. Messianic deliverers will be somewhat like Moses. They are anointed to alleviate the suffering of needy people. In a sense, Jesus raised up disciples to continue his ministry. They break forth with the message of God's reign. The messianic task of an anointed community is found as they fulfill the mission to relieve the sufferings of lost and broken humanity. The divine love for his creation must be expressed by finite human beings. God uses a Moses with all of his human weaknesses to bring hope to the camp of slaves.

The messianic hope of the followers of Jesus focuses both on his mission to help people and on his future coming. The task before the disciples of Jesus is great. His mission is revealed in the actions of his disciples who exemplify his teachings. They follow their teacher in observing his commandments. His promise to return and complete the messianic work of redemption was strong in the minds of his early followers. As the years have passed, the belief in his second coming sometimes has waned. For many, however, it remains a vibrant hope and a sure promise. But the work of the Messiah has been entrusted to the anointed community of faith. As members of a messianic community, his followers are anointed to fulfill the task of the Messiah until he returns. Christians are called to model love, forgiveness, and acceptance by following the example of Jesus.

From the time of John, the preparation was being made. Now the kingdom of heaven breaks forth, and all are breaking out with it. The rule of God challenges each new generation with the dynamic message of Jesus.

The kingdom should not be confined to the end times. Jesus, moreover, never advocated violence or political domination to achieve the goals of the divine rule. In the saying of Jesus examined here, his disciples are not being attacked; neither are they to be described as suffering violence or as violent people. He was not teaching violence or force as an acceptable method of operation. Jesus emphasized love, forgiveness, and acceptance. The kingdom is the power of God at work to help people. Jesus came to save. He came to teach a way of life. He taught his disciples to follow his example.

Jesus says, "For all the prophets and the law prophesied until John; and if you are willing to accept it, he is Elijah who is to come" (Matt 11:13). All the prophets look ahead to his coming. The kingdom of heaven is God's reign. It is seen in the activities of Jesus after John had prepared the way. The divine reign is realized when God's people receive his power to accomplish his purpose. This power is not reserved for the end times; rather, the kingdom breaks forth in the present as men and women experience God's redemptive power in their lives. They share what God has done for them as they help others. Jesus came to bring salvation and healing to hurting people in a world wracked by urgent human need.

NOTES

1. Luke 11:20; Matt 12:28; Matt 11:12; Luke 16:16. Study the passages in context. See the Beelzebub controversy, Matt 12:22–30; Mark 3:22–27; Luke 11:14–23, and the question of John the Baptist, Matt 11:2–15; Luke 7:18–28; 16:16.

2. For a summary of different views of commentators, see W. D. Davies and Dale Allison, *The Gospel according to St. Matthew* (International Critical Commentary; Edinburgh: T. & T. Clark, 1988), 2.254–56 and also G. R. Beasley-Murray, *Jesus and the Kingdom of God* (Grand Rapids: Eerdmans, 1986) 91–96. Davies and Allison understand the saying as referring to the kingdom of God's being attacked during the struggle between good and evil in the end times. They view the first phrase as a passive, meaning that the kingdom is under attack, although the Greek word can also be understood as a middle, which would describe an action from within the kingdom itself. While they prefer an interpretation which refers to the persecution of the preachers of the kingdom during the eschatological trial, they concede that " 'the kingdom of God breaks in with power, with force' may be a possible translation." Beasley-Murray agrees with an

eschatological emphasis for the verse, but he argues for a middle meaning in translation for the first part of the verse. In this point he is surely closer to the original meaning of the text. He suggests "The kingdom of heaven is powerfully breaking out (into the world), and violent men are strongly attacking it" as the proper translation. While his argument for the middle meaning, "the kingdom of heaven is powerfully breaking out," is strong, the second part of the translation may not convey the proper approach. At least the parallel in Luke 16:16b, "and every one enters it violently" (RSV), seems to describe *not* those who are attacking the kingdom but rather those individuals who are striving with forceful effort to enter into it. At least this is the way the translators of the RSV have understood (rightly) the Greek, εἰς αὐτὴν βιάζεται *(eis autēn biazetai).* Hence the NIV translates Luke 16:16b, "and everyone is forcing his way into it." Compare John Nolland, who accepts this approach, *Luke* 3.821. These questions will be discussed further. Here we suggest, with R. L. Lindsey (private communication), that a translation such as "The kingdom of heaven is breaking forth and every one breaks forth with it" is much closer to the original idea of the passage (see esp. Flusser, *Jesus,* 38–40 [Ger.], 40 [ET]).

3. Compare the important discussion concerning the wording of Matt 11:12 in Daube, *New Testament and Rabbinic Judaism,* 285ff. Though Daube recognizes *paratz* as a possible translation of *biazō* as reflected also in the LXX, he shows great caution when he concludes, "Any suggestion as to the original structure is bound to be conjectural" (p., 300). Study the rendering of the Hebrew verb *paratz* in the LXX texts, 2 Sam (2 Kgs, LXX) 13:25, 27 and 2 Kgs (4 Kgs, LXX, acc. to A) 5:23. The Greek word *biazō* was an accepted equivalent.

4. See W. Arndt and F. W. Gingrich, *A Greek-English Lexicon of the New Testament and Other Early Christian Literature* (2d ed.; Chicago: University of Chicago, 1979) 140–41, "intr. makes its way w. triumphant force." See also H. G. Liddell and R. Scott, *A Greek-English Lexicon* (Oxford: Clarendon, 1976) 314, "having broken through all these restraints" or "may sail out by forcing their way" and the discussion of G. Schrenk in *TDNT,* 1.609–14. Unfortunately, something of the anti-Jewish spirit from the age of Nazi Germany impacts some of Schrenk's discussion. He accepts a passive meaning. However, Schrenk calls attention to the view of Melanchthon, F. C. Baur, Zahn, and Harnack when he observed, "A first possibility . . . is to take βιάζεται in the sense of an intr. mid.: 'the rule of God breaks in with power, with force and impetus' " (p. 610). From the study of the linguistic evidence and the original Jewish context of the saying in the ministry of Jesus, this first possibility has much to commend itself. It should be rendered, "The kingdom of heaven breaks forth."

5. See also R. L. Lindsey, *The Jesus Sources* (Tulsa: HaKesher, 1990) 77–81.

6. Flusser, 38–40 [Ger.], 40 [ET]. Without Flusser's insights, these passages would not be properly understood. He writes, "In Jesus' view, John was a prophet, if you like, the one who was preparing the way of God at the end of time, the Elijah who was to return. With John the end-time begins—the decisive eruption into the history of the world."

7. Ibid.

8. See the fine translation of Luke 16:16b in the New American Bible, by the Catholic Biblical Association of America, "and people of every sort are forcing their way in."

9. See Lindsey, *Jesus Sources*, 75–83, and his *Jesus, Rabbi and Lord: The Hebrew Story of Jesus behind our Gospels* (Oak Creek, Wis.: Cornerstone, 1990) 101–4. I appreciate the insights I have received from Lindsey from private conversations we have had concerning this passage. David Flusser has explained the verse's linguistic background and its sources in early Jewish thought. Lindsey has suggested a Hebrew reconstruction of Matt 11:12a and Luke 16:16b.

10. See the Dead Sea Scrolls and especially the recently published Hebrew texts with the words *rodfe daat* "pursue knowledge" (Ben Zion Wacholder and Martin G. Abegg, *A Preliminary Edition of the Unpublished Dead Sea Scrolls* [Washington, D.C.: Biblical Archaeological Society, 1991–92]). See now especially 4Q418, 4Q424, and 4Q299. Cf. also the Manual of Discipline 10:18 (J. Licht, 219) and compare Isa 51:1; Ps 38:21–22; Prov 16:9; 21:21. A beautiful homily about Abraham as the model for the person who earnestly pursues righteousness appears in Gen Rabbah 58:9 (Albeck, 629).

11. John the Baptist probably attacked the morally deficient Herod Antipas so strongly because he felt that the end was very near. John was motivated in part by his eschatology. Surely he felt let down by Jesus, who did not live up to his expectations.

12. See Enoch 69:27–29, M. Black, *The Book of Enoch* (Leiden: Brill, 1985) 66.

13. See the account in Josephus, *Ant.* 18.116–119. It is important to point out a historical note made by David Flusser. He suggested that the mention of Machaerus was probably a mistake made by Josephus. Josephus mentioned Machaerus because of the context in which he wrote: "Machaerus, which was on the boundary between the territory of Aretas and that of Herod" (*Ant.* 18.111). According to Flusser's approach, John the Baptist most probably was held in custody in Tiberias where he would have been executed.

14. The great diversification of views on the messianic task cannot be underestimated. See the work of Joseph Klausner for a survey.

The research he began is far from complete. See Klausner, *The Messianic Idea in Israel* and Charlesworth, *The Messiah*.

15. See b. *Sanh.* 99a; b. *Ber.* 34b; and b. *Shab.* 63a. See also David Flusser, *Die rabbinischen Gleichnisse und der Gleichniserzähler Jesus* (Bern: Peter Lang, 1981) 270f. and Brad Young and David Flusser, "Messianic Blessings in Jewish and Christian Texts," in Flusser, *Judaism and the Origins of Christianity*, 294.

16. Pesikta Rabbati 35; see the English translation by W. Braude, *Pesikta Rabbati* (New Haven: Yale University, 1968) 2.674–75. In Hebrew, see the classic edition of Meir Friedmann, 161a.

17. See note 2 above. Ladd believes that the saying describes the presence of the kingdom in the world regardless of a passive or middle voice. The kingdom has been realized as the future realm of the divine rule which is brought into the present experience. See G. E. Ladd, *Jesus and the Kingdom: The Eschatology of Biblical Realism* (London: SPCK, 1966) 197, n. 18. Ladd revised his work on the kingdom in *The Presence of the Future* (Grand Rapids: Eerdmans, 1980). Ladd writes, "The Kingdom of God means that God is King and acts in history to bring history to a divinely directed goal" (Ibid., 331). For Ladd, the kingdom is primarily the presence of the future rule rather than reality in the present. He writes, "If God has acted in history in this Kingdom, he will bring history to his Kingdom" (p. 332).

18. See Radak's commentary on Mic 2:13 in *Mikraot Gedalot* (New York: Schocken, 1938) 417b.

19. Flusser, *Jesus*, 38–40 [Ger.], 40 [ET]. While it is possible that Radak was referring to Pesikta Rabbati 35, it seems highly unlikely. He appears to be quoting an earlier source.

20. Edward Pococke, *A Commentary on the Prophecy of Micah* (Oxford: Oxford University, 1676) 22–25. I am grateful to my friend Doug Hill, who called my attention to Pococke's commentary. After hearing a lecture which I gave on the relationship between Matt 11:12 and Mic 2:13, Hill examined Pococke's commentary and discovered that the seventeenth-century Hebrew scholar understood the implications of early Jewish exposition of Mic 2:13 and Matt 11:12. Later one of my students, James Thacker, wrote a fine M.A. thesis on this text and also discovered a hint to the tradition in John Calvin. Apparently Calvin may have become familiar with the Jewish teaching through his contact with one of the rabbis in the learned family of Abarbanel. It would be difficult to identify who is referred to as a certain Rabbi Barbinel because of more than one rabbi with the same name. In any case, it is clear that Calvin was not able to comprehend the significance of the teaching in the same way that Edward Pococke grasped the implication of Mic 2:13 and Matt 11:12. See John Calvin, *Commentary on Micah* (trans. T. Parker; Edinburgh: T. & T. Clark, 1986) 210–11 and the

discussion by James Thacker, "The Kingdom of Heaven is Breaking Forth: A Study of the Relationships between Matt 11:12–13, Luke 16:16, and Micah 2:12–13" (M.A. thesis, Graduate School of Theology, Oral Roberts University, 1990) 63–72.

21. Pococke, *A Commentary on the Prophecy of Micah,* 22–25.

22. In the final analysis, Flusser's study of the passage is much more objective.

6
"The Kingdom Is Like . . ."

JESUS DOES NOT GIVE A DICTIONARY DEFINITION OF the kingdom of heaven, but he does tell his listeners what the kingdom is like via simple, yet powerful, parables. Although Jesus used simple word pictures to help his listeners understand, a careful study of the decisive technical term "the kingdom of heaven" in his teachings demonstrates that the original meaning of the kingdom has been routinely misunderstood in modern times. The teaching of Jesus concerning the kingdom of heaven is carefully portrayed in the message of his kingdom parables.[1] That message is being reexamined today perhaps more than ever before.[2]

Is it possible to listen to the parables of Jesus? What is the message of the kingdom parables? Is it possible to recreate the original setting in which they were spoken? Early Jewish sources provide many insights into the original setting of the parables. In fact, unless interpreters possess a knowledge of the parabolic method of the Jewish sages in rabbinic literature, the message of the parables of Jesus can be lost in the multiplicity of modern interpretations and tendentious analyses. The numerous approaches taken by modern commentators to describe the meaning of the kingdom of heaven are confusing at best. Certainly they cannot all be correct.

THE SCHOLARS AND THE KINGDOM

Johannes Weiss, the famous German New Testament scholar, and Albert Schweitzer, the well-known physician and theologian in his footsteps, claimed that the kingdom of heaven is an eschatological (end time) term referring only to the future day of judgment. The views of C. H. Dodd and J. Jeremias also emphasized the future meaning of the kingdom of heaven. In a similar way the dispensationalists claim that the kingdom will not appear until the millennium, at the conclusion of the present church age. In the increasingly prevalent theology of the "kingdom now" movement, the kingdom of heaven is established on earth by human efforts which pave the way for the second coming. Popularly speaking, some Christians believe that the kingdom of heaven refers to life after death. They think that someone must die to enter the kingdom. The famous evangelical New Testament scholar G. E. Ladd taught that the kingdom is "already but not yet." God's reign will be revealed in the future but some vestiges of the divine power are working in the present time according to Ladd's view. In the midst of these competing theories, it is difficult to study the parables of the kingdom. In the parables of the Mustard Seed and the Leaven, however, Jesus described the reign of God as a force in the present world which progressively grows.

Is the kingdom of heaven to be revealed only in the distant future? Are the people of God able to establish his reign on earth by obtaining positions of leadership and power within the present political order? Is the kingdom experienced only at death? In Jesus' teachings, the kingdom of heaven is a powerful force in the world which brings healing and wholeness. Jesus defines the kingdom from his present experience rather than from his view of the end time. He expected his disciples to continue the kingdom's work.

C. H. Dodd was perhaps the most influential writer and New Testament scholar to consider the question of Jesus' use of the term "kingdom of heaven." He thought that the Gospels speak about the reign of God as if it had been realized during a point of time in the ministry of Jesus. Dodd tried to find a solution to the question of how the kingdom can be both present in the ministry of Jesus and yet future. He coined the expression "realized eschatology," which described how the *future* kingdom could be seen in the work of Jesus in an "unprecedented and unrepeatable" fashion. Thus according to Dodd, although the kingdom was still very much a future event, it was operative in advance during the ministry of Jesus. This aspect of the kingdom, however, was only a foretaste of the future reign and could not be repeated. Dodd writes, "It [the kingdom of heaven] represents the ministry of Jesus as 'realized eschatology,' that is to say, as the impact upon this world of the 'powers of the world to come' in a series of events, unprecedented and unrepeatable, now in actual process."[3]

Dodd's statement is incorrect. Moreover, the approaches of Weiss, Schweitzer, the dispensationalists, and those many others who could be discussed are mistaken as well.[4] The mistake is primarily that of Weiss, who sought to interpret Jesus' message only in the context of apocalyptic literature. Here, however, we shall examine two partner parables of Jesus concerning the kingdom, in light of the important contributions of David Flusser and his new approach to the parables of Jesus, as well as R. L. Lindsey's suggestions concerning the relationship of the Synoptic Gospels.[5]

GROWTH IN THE PARABLES

Jesus used word pictures to illustrate his message concerning the kingdom of heaven. What is the kingdom of heaven really like? The twin parables of the Mustard Seed and the Leaven illustrate the basis for Jesus' teaching concerning the kingdom of heaven. They illustrate the progressive growth of the kingdom. Both parables appear in Matthew (13:31–33) and Luke (13:18–21), whereas Mark records only the parable of the Mustard Seed (4:30–32). Mark probably knew both parables and may have abbreviated his Gospel by deleting the parable of the Leaven. He realized, it seems, that both parables illustrate the same message. Here we shall examine the text of Luke, which is more concise than that of Matthew or Mark.[6]

> What is the kingdom of heaven like? And to what shall I compare it? It is like a grain of mustard seed which a man took and sowed in his garden; and it grew and became a tree and the birds of the air made nests in its branches.

> And again he said, "To what shall I compare the kingdom of heaven? It is like leaven which a woman took and hid in three measures of flour, till it was all leavened" (cf. Matt 13:31–33; Luke 13:18–21; Mark 4:30–32).

From the start, the supernatural aspect of this parable should not be overlooked. That a tiny seed can progressively grow into a tree was viewed as nothing less than miraculous. The same must have been true for the action of the leaven in the dough. Growth—this amazing, steady, continuous process—would have been viewed as a true wonder in the eyes of the people.

The major theme of both of these illustrations is this miraculous growth. The idea of a sudden, total reversal of the present situation is not congruous with these parables of progressive growth. Jesus clearly teaches that a day of judgment and recompense is in God's plan, but he never connects the theme of the future judgment with the concept of the steady growth of God's reign. No. The kingdom has deeper implications.

In the land of Israel, the tiny mustard seed is about the size of a grain of salt. It grows into a respectably sized shrub. Certainly birds are able to find rest upon its branches. Moreover, the mustard seed is noted for its ability to take root in rocky, difficult-to-cultivate soil. The seed will grow in between the stones of a building or on a rocky mountainside. The natural growth process of the plant and its roots will literally move huge stones as it grows. The simplicity of the parable helps in creating the deep and powerful mental image which the growth process of the tiny mustard seed conjures.

Nevertheless, one should not fall into the trap of giving a special meaning to every detail of the parable. The parable gives a picture of reality, but it is not that reality. A listener must never try to allegorize every element of the image created by the parable teacher. The one telling the parable must be allowed to communicate. In the present case Jesus appears to be alluding to images from the Hebrew Scriptures, but the images are created in order to communicate his specific theme.[7] Clearly the message of these twin parables concerns a progressive, uninterrupted pattern of growth.

The message of growth in the first parable is reinforced in the second illustration. Jesus depicts a process with which anyone who has baked bread or observed the fermenting property of leaven would be familiar. The action of the leaven entirely permeates the three measures of flour.[8] Again one must take care not to impose meaning upon each component of the picture of the parable. In some contexts leaven is synonymous with the evil within human nature. Hence Paul speaks about how "a little leaven leavens the whole lump" (Gal 5:9). He warns the Corinthians, "Cleanse out the old leaven that you may be a new lump, as you really are unleavened" (1 Cor 5:7). During the Passover celebration all leaven is removed from the home, and even in the Talmud the leaven is understood to be referring to the evil inclination.[9]

THE RABBIS VIEW LEAVEN AS A FORCE

The picture created by the parable of the Leaven in the Gospels, however, is completely positive. The process of fermentation and growth of the leaven is like the growth of the kingdom of heaven. Rabbinic literature demonstrates that a word picture, such as leaven permeating the dough, could be employed not only for a negative image but a positive one as well. In fact, in two different illustrations, the rabbis compared both the strong positive qualities of peace (in Hebrew *shalom*) and occupation with Torah-learning to the permeating action of leaven. In the first case Joshua the son of Levi tells the parable of Peace and Leaven, which calls attention to the power of leaven and the esteemed qualities of *shalom*.

> Great is peace—for as peace is to the earth so is leaven to the dough. Had the Holy One, blessed be He, not given peace to the earth, the sword and the beast would have devastated the world.[10]

Peace is also compared to leaven! Rabbi Joshua ben Levi made a comparison between the great Hebrew concept of *shalom,* which means peace, harmony, and wholeness in every aspect of human experience, and the action of leaven. He has captivated the vivid mental image of leaven permeating the dough. Leaven possesses strong positive attributes in Jewish thought. The permeating power of peace in the world is revealed by the leaven in the dough.

In yet another example from Jewish literature, the inner force of the Torah is compared to the action of leaven. David Flusser has called attention to this important parallel from rabbinic teachings about the study of Torah. The sage Chaya bar Abba[11] taught that even if the people of Israel forsake God, all is not lost, as long as they keep studying the Torah. They may even study Torah for the wrong reasons and abandon observance of God's commands. But if they will just keep themselves involved in studying the Bible, the leaven of the Torah, namely, its inner force and power, will bring the people back to God.[12]

> Rabbi Chaya bar Abba taught, "It is written, 'Because your fathers . . . have forsaken me and have not kept my Torah' (Jer 16:11). If only they had kept observing My Torah! Indeed, even if they forsake me, everything would turn out well provided that they keep studying

my Torah. Because even if they did forsake me, but kept occupying themselves with the study of my Torah, its leaven [inner force], through their engagement with it, would be so powerful as to bring them back to me."

In other words, Torah possesses a compelling or irresistible energy. Even if the people forsake God, when they study the Torah, its innate strength will influence them to return to God. They might study the law without the proper motivation. Moreover, though they have studied it, they may in error forsake its practice. Despite these scenarios, as long as the people do study the law of God, its leaven-like inner force will bring them back to the Lord. Learning Torah affords a great strength. The Torah has an inner force which is referred to as leaven. The leaven of the Torah will bring the people to the Lord. Thus, the same imagery that Rabbi Chaya bar Abba uses to illustrate a certain miraculous process occurring when an individual studies Torah, Jesus uses to illustrate another supernatural process that occurs when his followers submit their wills to God and allow him to spread redemption through them.

Modern interpreters have sometimes missed the message of the kingdom of heaven. It is not about the future age. The kingdom is not heaven in the sense that someone dies to enter in. It is neither the church nor a denomination. It is not given over to human leaders for their custodial care. Jesus did not view the kingdom as a political ideology or program. The kingdom is a process which cannot be imposed upon others through political activism. The kingdom comes by God alone. It is a divine force in the world that brings healing to suffering humanity. Hence, Jesus did not define the kingdom in terms of the future. He viewed the reign of God from his experience in the present. The kingdom has precedent. When God worked the miracle of the exodus, the people sang that his reign is forever and ever (Exod 15:19). The miracles of the Bible reveal the sovereignty of God. In the mind of Jesus, the kingdom is repeatable because he taught his disciples to continue his work of mending the world. For Jesus and his early followers, the kingdom of heaven was a strong force in their personal lives which is experienced in the present age.

According to the Gospels, Jesus teaches that the kingdom is (1) God's reign among people who have chosen to obey God's commands (e.g., Matt 6:33); (2) God's power as manifest in his redemptive purpose of healing and salvation (e.g., Luke 11:20); and (3) the people who have become disciples of Jesus in the movement to bring God's redemption into the world (e.g., Matt 5:3ff.). Each individual chooses God's rule and accepts his authority. God moves dramatically in supernatural redemptive acts. His kingdom is seen at the miraculous deliverance of the people of Israel from Egypt. For Jesus, moreover, the reign of God is manifested in his miracle-working power as well as in the activities of his followers when they continue his work and put his teachings into practice.

Jesus taught that the "poor in spirit" make up the kingdom of heaven. Jesus' followers are those who mourn. They are meek. They hunger and thirst for God's righteousness and long for his salvation. They are merciful and are pure in heart. According to Jesus, the members of the kingdom are the peacemakers. Jesus taught that his followers must turn the other cheek and must go the second mile (Matt 5:38–42). The greatest in the kingdom is the one who serves others and who is willing to suffer in the interim in order to see God's higher purposes achieved. Jesus believed that redemption was possible as each person submits to the divine will and accepts his yoke. When someone who is hated by others loves in return, when someone who is persecuted learns to forgive from his or her heart, then the inner force of the kingdom is released. Indeed such power is able to work the miracles of healing and redemption in a needy world.

Jesus taught about God's reign in parables. Jesus vividly illustrates through parables the progressive growth of the kingdom as it is compared to the mysterious power of a mustard seed and the unfathomable fermenting properties of the leaven in the dough. God's kingdom is not delivered into the hands of select leaders in order to control the lives of others. It cannot be viewed only as a future event reserved for the day of judgment. The kingdom is a present reality for those people who choose to obey the teachings of Jesus, to accept God's redemptive power in their lives, and to exemplify the qualities of discipleship and servanthood in a hurting and needy world. The kingdom is here! It is like a mustard seed that grows into a tree. It is like leaven that permeates the entire loaf.

NOTES

1. See my *Jesus and His Jewish Parables*, 189–235, for a much more extensive study of the teaching of Jesus concerning the kingdom of God in the Gospel parables.

2. Ibid. For some limited discussions of the current scholarly debate, see Gösta Lundström, *The Kingdom of God in the Teachings of Jesus* (Richmond: John Knox, 1963); W. Kissinger, *The Parables of Jesus: A History of Interpretation and Bibliography* (Metuchen, N.J.: Scarecrow Press, 1979); N. Perrin, *Jesus and the Language of the Kingdom* (Philadelphia: Fortress, 1976); and W. Willis, *The Kingdom of God in 20th-Century Interpretation* (Peabody, Mass.: Hendrickson, 1987).

3. C. H. Dodd, *The Parables of the Kingdom*, (Glasgow: Collins, 1961) 41; and see also Jeremias, *Parables of Jesus,* 230.

4. The very significant work of G. E. Ladd and his theory of "already but not yet" concerning the kingdom of heaven teaching in the Gospels closely resembles Dodd's efforts. See Ladd, *Jesus and the Kingdom*, and also G. R. Beasley-Murray, *Jesus and the Kingdom of God* (Grand Rapids: Eerdmans, 1987). Beasley-Murray tends to push the meaning of the kingdom farther into the future than does Ladd. Dodd's realized eschatology senses the presence of the rule of God in the ministry of Jesus more fully than either Ladd or Beasley-Murray.

5. See Flusser, *Die rabbinischen Gleichnisse;* Lindsey, *A Hebrew Translation of the Gospel of Mark;* and Lindsey's introductory essay in his *Comparative Greek Concordance of the Synoptic Gospels* (3 vols.; Jerusalem: Dugith, 1985).

6. Study the similarities and differences between the synoptic parallels, Matt 13:31–33; Luke 13:18–21; and Mark 4:30–32. Mark and Matthew show similarities with each other against Luke in the parable of the Mustard Seed. Mark does not contain the parable of the Leaven. Matthew and Luke show striking verbal identity in the parable of the Leaven. Mark has influenced the wording of Matthew. Most probably Mark has abbreviated his source and thus has not retained the parable of the Leaven. See Lindsey, *Hebrew Translation of the Gospel of Mark*, 19–22, and Lindsey's introduction in his *Comparative Greek Concordance of the Synoptic Gospels*.

7. See Ezek 17:23 and Dan 4:12, 21.

8. See the exact same amount mentioned in Gen 18:6.

9. See b. *Ber.* 17a; and see also Matt 16:6, 12; Mark 8:15; and Luke 12:1.

10. M. Higger, *The Treatises Derech Eretz*, 2.248, 84. See also I. Abrahams, *Studies in Pharisaism* (reprint, New York: KTAV, 1967) series 1, 51ff. I have discussed the parables of the Mustard Seed and the Leaven

in light of their Jewish background more extensively in my *Jesus and His Jewish Parables*, 205–12. See also Flusser, *Die rabbinischen Gleichnisse*, 206ff. and 228, n. 31. Perhaps here it is worth noting that while some editors have taken leaven *(seor)* in Hebrew to be light *(or)*, no doubt the more difficult reading, leaven, must be original. On Joshua ben Levi, see the *Encyclopaedia Judaica* (Jerusalem: Keter, 1978) vol. 10, col. 282f.

11. Concerning the amoraic sage Chaya bar Abba, see W. Bacher, *Die Agada der palästinesischen Amoräer* (Strassburg: Karl Trübner, 1892–99) 2.174–204 and "Ḥiyya bar Abba" in the *Encyclopaedia Judaica*, vol. 8, col. 796. Though he was born in Babylon, he immigrated to Israel where he was able to become acquainted with eminent sages such as R. Joshua ben Levi cited above.

12. Pesikta Derav Kahana 15:5 (Mandelbaum's edition of the Hebrew text, 1.254; see the English translation of W. G. Braude and I. Kapstein, *Pesikta de-Rab Kahana* (Philadelphia: Jewish Publication Society, 1975) 279. See the parallel in j. *Chagigah* 76c, chap. 1, hal. 7.

13. See Matt 5:3ff. and Luke 6:20ff. and also the chapter in the present work, "Blessed Are the Peacemakers."

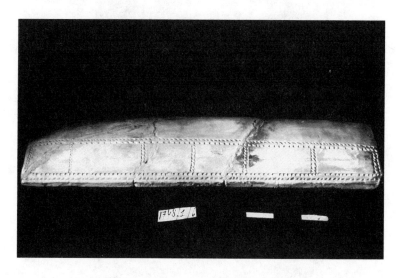

Lid to the "Joseph son of Caiaphas" sarcophagus
Photo Courtesy of the Israel Antiquities Authority.

Ossuary (bone box sarcophagus) of "Joseph
son of Caiaphas" the High Priest.
Photo courtesy of the Israel Antiquities Authority.

"Caiaphas" family member ossuary
Photo courtesy of the Israel Antiquities Authority.

7

"Blessed Are the Peacemakers . . ."

JESUS SAID, "BLESSED ARE THE PEACEMAKERS FOR they shall be called the sons of God" (Matt 5:9).[1] Too often these words of Jesus have become so well known and well worn that they have lost their meaning. Jesus reveals a defined approach to life in this dynamic Gospel text. In fact, the sayings of Jesus in the Beatitudes quite probably portray the major thrust of his entire message (Matt 5:3–13 and Luke 6:20–23). The passage describes the singular lifestyle of Jesus' disciples, which is modeled upon his own example. In the present study we will examine the meaning of one of the blessings from the words of Jesus in its Jewish context (Matt 5:9). Studying the Scriptures which Jesus quoted, the Hebrew language, the Dead Sea Scrolls, and rabbinic literature provides rich insight into the original meaning of his message. In their world, with its harsh realities of war, broken families, and estranged friendships, the disciples of Jesus are challenged: "Blessed are the peacemakers, for they shall be called the sons of God" (Matt 5:9).[2]

Jesus directed the attention of his listeners to the word "peace" when he said, "Blessed are the peacemakers . . ." The Greek word for peace, *eirēnē*, usually means the absence of war.[3] The Hebrew word for peace, *shalom*, however, has a much greater range of meanings. It is derived from the three-letter root *sh-l-m* (ש, ל, מ), which means "to make complete or whole." In the Bible when someone inquires concerning another person's well-being, he or she simply asks, "How is your peace?" The word refers to a person's health, spiritual state, or even his or her prosperity. In essence it includes every aspect of an individual's well-being and inner strength. "Peace" in Hebrew means wholeness or completeness. In certain ways it denotes a person's healing or salvation. Someone who is saved from life's difficulties experiences the peace of God through the wholeness which comes by divine grace and favor. The Hebrew term *shalom* also can refer to the absence of war, the alleviation of strife, or the resolution of a conflict. But more often it refers to an individual's spiritual and physical well-being as an integrated person.[4]

In rabbinic literature, Hillel (20 B.C.E.) describes Aaron, the brother of Moses and the priest of the people, as pursuing peace. Hillel said, "Be of the disciples of Aaron, loving peace and pursuing peace, loving others, and drawing them near to the Torah" (m. *Avot* 1:12).[5] Hence according to early Jewish thought, Aaron desired wholeness for the people. This passage from the Mishnah is extremely important as background for the teachings of Jesus. It portrays the Jewish ideal of harmony among God's people. Not only does Hillel mention Aaron as a model for those who pursue peace, he also teaches that others should follow Aaron's example. Aaron not only loved peace, he pursued it earnestly. The implication is that peace must be pursued and that sometimes one must be willing to pay a high price in order to obtain it.

The saying attributed to Hillel speaks about Aaron's disciples. In Matthew 5:1, the blessings of the Beatitudes are likewise addressed to disciples—Jesus'. So Aaron's disciples are instructed to pursue peace just as their master did, and the disciples of Jesus are taught to be peacemakers. The Dead Sea Scrolls have further defined the audience with the term "poor in spirit" (Matt 5:3), an expression that has recently been shown to possess a clear social context.[6]

The Dead Sea community referred to its members or disciples as "poor in spirit." Clearly Jesus also designated his own followers in the same terms, "Blessed are the *poor in spirit*, for from them is the kingdom of heaven."[7] The term "poor in spirit" reminded the disciples of a whole network of Scriptures from the Old Testament, such as Isaiah 61:1, "the LORD has anointed me to bring good tidings to the poor," or even Isaiah 66:2, "But this is the man to whom I will look, he that is poor and contrite in spirit, and trembles at my word." On a personal level, the disciples could identify with the texts of Scripture where words like "the poor" or "the meek" are mentioned (e.g., Zeph 2:3).[8] These biblical phrases were viewed as describing the characteristics of the followers of Jesus.

As a result of the discovery of the Dead Sea Scrolls, we have strong evidence that Jesus also designated his disciples with this term, "poor in spirit." These words alluded to a rich biblical heritage which possessed profound significance for Jesus' Jewish disciples. The social context of the Beatitudes then may be identified in Jesus' disciples. They are blessed. They possess divine approval and affirmation. But they must strive to live up to their description. They are the "poor in spirit," they are the "meek," and, yes, they are the "peacemakers." God himself is described in Scripture as making peace "in his high heaven" (Job 25:2). Jesus says that the peacemakers will be called the "sons of God." In Hebrew the term "son of" often refers to the disciple of a person. The disciple imitates his master and becomes like him. To be a disciple of Aaron means to be like Aaron and to promote peace through reconciliation. The great Jewish teacher Hillel encourages the people to be among Aaron's disciples by pursuing peace and following Aaron's example. In English the phrase has developed, "Like father—like son." The Hebrew understanding is somewhat similar. "Like mother—like daughter." The children resemble their parents not only in appearance but especially in behavior. To be a child of God, men and women must be like him. The peacemakers will be called his children.

In the Jewish mind it is natural to think of Aaron as a peacemaker. He was commanded by God to bless the children of Israel with the powerful words "you [Aaron] shall say to them, The LORD bless you and keep you: The LORD make his face to shine upon you, and be gracious to you: The LORD lift up his countenance upon you, and give you peace" (Num 6:23–26). The concluding phrase, "and give you peace," refers more to spiritual wholeness and well-being than to an end of war. At least this is the way the rabbis understood it. The context in Numbers, moreover, refers to God's divine favor and spiritual blessing. Aaron and his followers pursued peace. As priests they were mediators not only between God and his people but also between individuals who had broken relationships. According to the rabbis, the priests tried to heal family wounds. They restored peace between a disputing husband and wife. We know this from an early rabbinic text, Avot deRabbi Nathan, which adds the qualification to the saying of Hillel, "Be of the disciples of Aaron, loving peace and pursuing peace, *promoting peace between man and wife.*"[9] In other words, the rabbis viewed Hillel's remarks as promoting peace in the family. Aaron and his disciples mediated the disputes. Husbands and wives must live in peace one with the other.

Thus in the Jewish context, promoting peace and harmony is given high priority. The rabbis tell a story to illustrate the way Aaron worked to establish peace.

> Similarly when two men had quarreled one with the other, Aaron would go and sit with one of them and say, "My son, see what your companion is doing! He beats his breast and rends his garments, exclaiming, 'Woe is me! How can I lift my eyes and look my companion in the face? I am ashamed before him since it is I who offended him.' " Aaron would sit with him until he had removed all enmity from his heart. Then Aaron would go and sit with the other and say likewise, "My son, see what your companion is doing! He beats his breast and rends his garments, exclaiming, 'Woe is me! How can I lift my eyes and look my companion in the face? I am ashamed before him since it was I who offended him.' " Aaron would sit with him until he had removed all enmity from his heart. Later when the two met, they embraced and kissed each other.[10]

Aaron took it upon himself to mediate problems even when reconciliation seemed impossible.

As a priest, Aaron was considered a mediator between God and the people when he functioned in his sacred service. He served to establish peace between God and the people. In a similar way, he is described as making peace between individuals. To be a son of Aaron, one of his disciples, one must pursue peace. Peace must be established between God and the individual as well as between neighbors who have offended one another. So often the greatest disputes arise between family and friends—that is, people who have a close relationship.

The Greek wording of Matthew 5:9, "Blessed are the peacemakers for they shall be called the sons of God," and its meaning in Hebrew involve complex linguistic questions. Does one "pursue peace," or does one "make peace"? Both verbs are similar in meaning and imply exerted effort. On the strength of the rabbinic parallel where Aaron is said to pursue *(rodef)* peace and Psalm 34:14, "Depart from evil, and do good; seek peace, and pursue *(rodef)* it," one might argue that Jesus said, "Blessed are those who pursue peace," instead of the traditional translation, "Blessed are the peacemakers." The case for this reconstruction could be strengthened by Matthew 5:10, "Blessed are those who are persecuted [pursued] for righteousness" *(nirdafei tzedakah),* which might better be interpreted, "Blessed are those who diligently pursue righteousness."[11] On the other hand, the Greek word "peacemaker" is unknown outside the Greek translation of the Old Testament, where it appears as a Hebrew idiom, and the New Testament, where Semitisms are frequent.[12] In Hebrew the phrase "to make peace" describes the intensive effort portrayed in the imagery of the blessing. It would be strange for a Greek translator of the Gospel saying to use an unusual word in Greek unless the Hebrew undertext mentioned "peacemakers." Nonetheless the word play between "to pursue peace" (v. 9) and "to pursue righteousness" or "to be pursued by an intense desire for righteousness" (v. 10) must be carefully weighed.[13]

In any case the meaning of the phrase in the Beatitudes is clear. To make peace or to seek diligently and pursue peace requires effort. It costs something to make peace. In the cause of peace, one should be willing to compromise for the sake of another. One may need to sacrifice personal dignity in order to make peace. The price of peace with a neighbor is of great significance because wholeness and inner strength for each individual are linked to the individual's relationship with God. The blessing and divine approval which are given to the peacemaker come from God. To make peace with God implies that a person has been able to make matters right with others. To be whole in the Hebrew meaning of *shalom* includes accepting oneself, loving others, and entering into a right relationship with God.

JEWISH BLESSINGS OF PEACE

In Jewish literature another remarkable parallel to the Beatitudes appears. In and of itself, the teaching places a premium upon peace *(shalom)*. The passage's structure and message are reminiscent of the words of Jesus to his disciples. The sages of Israel pronounce a blessing of peace upon those who fulfill specific passages of Scripture in their personal lives as an expression of their pious devotion to God.

> Great is the peace which is given to those who study Torah, as was said, "All your sons shall be taught by the LORD, and great shall be the peace of your sons" (Isa 54:13).

> Great is the peace which is given to the meek, as was said, "But the meek shall inherit the earth and delight themselves in the abundance of peace" (Ps 37:11).

> Great is the peace which is given to those who work righteousness, as was said, "And the work of righteousness will be peace" (Isa 32:17).[14]

The structure of the rabbinic blessing, "Great is the peace which is given to," is like the sayings of Jesus, "Blessed are the . . ." Both are followed by a description of the special quality of a disciple, such as "those who work righteousness" in the rabbinic text or "peacemakers" in the Beatitudes. Those who work righteousness will have great peace, just as the peacemakers will be blessed. Jesus' disciples who pursue peace receive divine acceptance and will be called the children of God. Moreover, the rabbinic blessing follows the teaching with a corresponding affirmation or proof from the Bible. The Jewish disciples who work righteousness will possess great peace because the Bible teaches, "And the work of righteousness will be peace" (Isa 32:17). The potency of the rabbinic blessing for peace is affirmed by Israel's sages because of the words from the prophet Isaiah.

Jesus also often alludes to biblical passages to uphold the blessing for his disciples. The rabbis, however, quote directly whole verses of Scripture, whereas Jesus hints at snippets of a verse and expects his listeners to fill in the rest. Like the rabbis, Jesus in one Beatitude quotes a whole verse from Psalm 37:14, "Blessed are the meek for they shall inherit the earth." More often, Jesus alludes to the Hebrew thought in the Scriptures by using terms such as the "poor in spirit" or words filled with rich meaning like "righteousness." When he said, "Blessed are the pure in heart for they shall see God," many would have understood an allusion to Psalm 24:3–4, "Who shall ascend to the hill of the LORD? . . . He who has clean hands and a pure heart." The same structure appears in the teachings of Israel's sages. The rabbis teach, "Great is the peace which is given to those who study Torah, as was said, 'All your sons shall be taught by the LORD, and great shall be the peace of your sons' " (Isa 54:13). The blessing of peace is promised to the students of Torah because of the proof in Isaiah 54:13. Jesus pronounces a blessedness upon the pure in heart. They shall see God because of the corresponding affirmation alluded to in Psalm 24:3–4. The structure and the method of teaching are very similar between the rabbinic literature and the Gospels. The Beatitudes are Jewish. The rich imagery of the language captures the imagination of the Hebrew mind. The peacemakers are blessed because they are like God and will be called the children of God. Jesus taught a way of living in peace with God and with others.

True peace *(shalom)* is not easy to attain. The teachings of Jesus give insight into the way of life that produces spiritual wholeness and well-being. It requires decisive effort. By referring to the "peacemakers," Jesus places a high value upon a full and meaningful life which is lived in peace and harmony with God and other people. The rabbinic literature, moreover, preserves a plethora of sources which elucidate the background of pursuing peace in the community of faith. The saying of Jesus from the Beatitudes is understood properly only in light of its rich Jewish heritage. The gospel of Jesus is a message for living. Like Jesus, the rabbis promoted the pursuit of peace between God and all humanity and between each person and his or her neighbor. As Jesus taught, "You, therefore, must be perfect as your Father in heaven is perfect" (Matt 5:48), he also told his disciples that they must pursue peace to be like God. God is a peacemaker. The children resemble their parents. The disciples of Jesus should be like him and seek to bring healing and wholeness in a world which has such a great need for genuine *shalom*. By pursuing peace they will be like God. "Blessed are the peacemakers, for they shall be called the sons of God."

NOTES

1. Today the term "happy" is often used to translate the Beatitudes instead of the word "blessed." In my opinion this translation is unfortunate and has little foundation. The Hebrew term *ashrei* (which is translated into Greek by *makarios*) "blessed" should not be rendered as "happy." Happiness is not the same as joy. But the word *ashrei* comes from a root that refers to affirmation, acceptance, or favor which is often accompanied by joy and happiness as well as physical well-being and material blessing. Probably the term would be better understood as denoting divine affirmation or approval. It has a spiritual meaning that goes beyond modern views of happiness. A man or a woman who is "blessed" possesses the well-being which accompanies God's favor. He or she has received divine acceptance and blessing. One possesses a sense of belonging to God as well as his affirmation. I much prefer the translation "blessed." For the rich Hebrew background of the word "blessed," consider the use of the term in the context of the Psalms or the story of utter joy associated with the divine favor given at the birth of a child (e.g., Gen 30:13).

2. Clearly the disciples who follow Jesus should be known as peacemakers. Peacemaking is a lifestyle which they pursue. But the deeper meaning of these words is embedded in Hebrew thought and culture.

The study of Hebrew enlightens the original meaning of the words of Jesus in the Beatitudes. As David Flusser has pointed out, the complex of ideas in the Beatitudes is deeply rooted in Jewish concepts. The blessings possess similarity to the Psalms and the Dead Sea Scrolls. See David Flusser, "Blessed Are the Poor in Spirit," *Israel Exploration Journal* 10 (1960) 1–10; the revised text in *Judaism and the Origins of Christianity,* 102–13; and "Some Notes on the Beatitudes," *Immanuel* 8 (1978) 37–47, revised in *Judaism and the Origins of Christianity,* 115–25. Flusser writes, "Jesus' Beatitudes and Woes are Jewish, and in their specific content, their concepts and terms and their antithetic literary character, they are part of a broader complex" (ibid., 119 [*Immanuel,* 41]).

3. See Liddell and Scott, *A Greek-English Lexicon,* 490. See also P. Lapide, *The Sermon on the Mount* (New York: Orbis, 1986) 34.

4. See also F. Brown, *The New Brown-Driver-Briggs-Gesenius Hebrew and English Lexicon* (1906, reprint; Peabody, Mass.: Hendrickson, 1979) 1022–24. Compare also J. Levy, *Neuhebräisches und Chaldaisches Wörterbuch über die Talmudim und Midraschim* (Leipzig: Brodshaus, 1876–89) 4.564; M. Jastrow, *A Dictionary of the Targumim, the Talmud Babli and Yerushalmi, and the Midrashic Literature* (Jerusalem reprint, 1978) 1585–86; and M. Sokoloff, *A Dictionary of Jewish Palestinian Aramaic* (Ramat Gan, Israel: Bar Ilan University, 1990) 554.

5. See J. Hertz, *The Authorised Daily Prayer Book* (New York: Bloch, 1959) 622–23, and Philip Birnbaum, *Daily Prayer Book* (New York: Hebrew Publishing, 1949) 481.

6. See Flusser, "Blessed Are the Poor in Spirit," 11, where he discusses the difference between Matthew and Luke. He notes, "The most important difference is that Luke speaks about the 'poor' while Matthew has the 'poor in spirit.' The current opinion among scholars is that here, as in the next Beatitude (Luke vi, 21), the version of Luke emphasizes the social note of Jesus' message, while Matthew stresses the spiritual side. But we have already tried to show that Matthew's 'poor in spirit' also has a social context." One cannot easily claim that the Hebraism "poor in spirit" was made up by Matthew.

7. In Matt 5:3, the first of the Beatitudes should be translated as a partitive genitive rather than a possessive. It is better to translate, "Blessed are the poor in spirit, for from them is the kingdom of heaven." This is the partitive genitive idea. The possessive genitive translation is more widely used, "Blessed are the poor in spirit, for theirs is the kingdom of heaven." But the poor in spirit do not own or possess the kingdom. They make up the kingdom. The disciples of Jesus comprise the movement spearheading the force of the divine rule in the lives of people experiencing God's favor. See also the discussion in my *Jesus and His Jewish Parables,* 203–5. This approach is taken in the

commentary of W. F. Albright and C. S. Mann, *The Gospel according to Matthew* (AB 26; New York: Doubleday, 1981) 46. Albright and Mann observe, "The best sense here is 'the Kingdom will consist of such as these' " (ibid.).

8. It should be remembered that the Hebrew words for "meek" and "poor" are differentiated from one another only by one letter in Hebrew. They are spelled the same, except for the last letters, *vav* for meek and *yod* for poor. Moreover the letters *vav* and *yod,* which look similar in Hebrew script, were not infrequently confused one with the other by scribes, so that in the manuscript tradition sometimes the poor become meek and the meek become poor.

9. *'Abot de Rabbi Nathan,* version A, chap. 12 (my emphasis). See the edition of S. Schechter, 24b and the variant readings for version A. Compare the references to the meek from Zeph 3:2 and Ps 37:11 in version B, chap. 24.

10. *'Abot de Rabbi Nathan,* version A, chap. 12, and see the English translation in A. Cohen, I. Brodie, *Minor Tractates of the Talmud* (London: Soncino, 1971) 1.72. See also the insightful works of David Wolpe, *The Healer of Shattered Hearts: A Jewish View of God* (New York: Henry Holt, 1990) and *In Speech and Silence: The Jewish Quest for God* (New York: Henry Holt, 1992). One's view of the character of God, as Wolpe shows in his sensitive and scholarly writings, influences one's whole life and all interpersonal relationships.

11. Thus Flusser writes, "The probability that this was the Hebrew wording becomes even greater because, as it seems, there was a play on words in Hebrew which connected 'those who pursue peace' *(rodfei shalom)* in Matt 5:9 with 'those who are persecuted for righteousness' sake' *(nirdefei zedek)* of the following verse (Matt 5:10)" ("Some Notes on the Beatitudes," 122–23 [*Immanuel*, 44–45]). A similar Hebrew construction appears in the Dead Sea Scrolls, 1QH 5:20–25, Hymn 9 (J. Licht, *Megilat Hahodayot* [Jerusalem: Mosad Bialik, 1957] 104, see notes, in Hebrew). G. Vermes translates, "yet [hast Thou done marvels] among the humble [*anavim* or meek] in the mire underfoot, and among those eager for righteousness *[nimharei tzedek],* causing all the well-loved poor to rise up together from the trampling" (my additions in square brackets; see Vermes, *Dead Sea Scrolls in English,* 179). The beauty of this passage in Hebrew and its importance for the Beatitudes are difficult to convey in any English translation. Dupont-Sommer translates "eager for righteousness" *(nimharei tzedek)* with "quick unto righteousness" and "well-loved poor" *(evyonei chesed)* with "poor of grace" (A. Dupont-Sommer, *The Essene Writings from Qumran* [Gloucester, Mass.: Peter Smith, 1973] 216). The members of the community are described as eager or quick to do righteousness and as the poor of grace. They are consumed by a desire for righteousness.

12. See the discussion in Davies and Allison, *Matthew,* 1.457f.

13. See the insightful discussion of Flusser. He observes, "Thus, Jesus' words about the persecuted was [sic] also a deep play on words: those who long for God's righteousness and seek it in their daily life, shall reach it" ("Some Notes on the Beatitudes," 126 [*Immanuel,* 46]).

14. Sifre Numbers 42 (Horovitz, 47).

8
Controversy and Children

HOW COULD CHILDREN[*] BE RELATED TO A MAJOR ruckus in an event from the life of Jesus (Matt 19:13–15; Mark 10:13–16; Luke 18:15–17)? The disciples' actions are actually to blame and not the behavior of the children! Controversy surrounded Jesus' life, but sometimes it is forgotten that even the disciples of Jesus were involved in conflicts with their master. They prevented children from coming to Jesus. They sometimes argued over who would be the greatest or leader among them.[1] It is seldom noticed that a major controversy in the Gospels surrounded the attitude of Jesus' disciples. Jesus criticizes his own on a number of occasions.

When it came to their attitude toward children, the disciples were put down strongly by their master. When they sought to keep the little children from troubling their master, Jesus seized the opportunity to teach them a deeper message concerning the kingdom of heaven. The Gospel picture of Jesus cannot be properly understood apart from understanding the Jewish life setting of first-century Israel and Judaism as it was practiced by his people.

The story is remarkable in and of itself. Other stories about children from the time of Jesus aid in understanding this unusual incident in Jesus' ministry. Unfortunately, they are rare. Stories about children do not appear in the Dead Sea Scrolls, and children are not spoken of in a similar way in the writings of this time period—either in the pseudepigrapha or in the apocrypha—or in Josephus or in Philo. In fact, only a few stories about children that could be studied as parallels appear in rabbinic literature. The talmudic literature and the Gospels, however, report incidents between children and learned spiritual leaders.

---

[*] Dedicated to my son, Matthew David Young.

Rabbinic stories reveal a number of details about the life setting of Jesus' teaching and especially Jesus' relationship with other teachers of this period. What can be known about children and rabbis during the time of Jesus? An interesting story is told about Chanan Hanechba and children. Chanan Hanechba was a pious man, well known for the miraculous answers he received to his prayers. He was at times called Abba (father), which was a title of honor that showed respect for his learning and also his image as a family person. During the period others also had received this name as a sign of honor. Chanan Hanechba was better known for his pious works, deeds of loving-kindness, and miracles of answered prayer than for his scholastic and intellectual ability, though he certainly would have been quite knowledgeable in Torah learning. His name, Hanechba (the hiding one), probably indicates his humility and reluctance to make a show of his pious acts and powerful prayer life.[2] Other teachers tended to be more scholastic and to emphasize Torah learning in preference to actions of good for others and personal spiritual piety. While Chanan Hanechba gave the greatest emphasis to action and spiritual development, he did not neglect learning for doing's sake.[3]

Because he was known for his prayer life and for the dramatic way that God responded to his childlike approach to God in faith, the more scholastic rabbis looked to him in times of need. This may also explain why the name Hanechba (the hiding one) seems to refer to his tendency to maintain a low profile. An interesting story in talmudic literature describes an episode in the life of Chanan Hanechba and his relationship with children. In many ways, it throws light upon the life setting of the Gospels.

During a severe drought the more scholastic rabbis sent children to Chanan Hanechba to ask him to pray for rain. The fact that children were sent as mediators between the more scholastic teachers and Chanan Hanechba may indicate that tension existed between them. His grandfather, Choni the Circle Drawer, also had conflicts with the intelligentsia of his day, as represented by the religious leader Simeon ben Shetach. The friction arose because Choni dared to pray for rain by drawing a circle in the dirt and telling God that he would not move until rain came. What nerve he showed to heaven! Simeon ben Shetach said if it were not for the devout lifestyle of Choni, he would have called for excommunication because of his audacity. Choni was known for the way his prayers were answered miraculously, and friction developed between him and the spiritual leaders who took a more academic and intellectual approach to life.[4] The children, in any case, had access to this group of devout, saintly people of prayer who lived during the time of Jesus before the destruction of the temple. The religious leaders, however, seem to be removed from them to a certain degree. When no rain fell and the nation faced a severe crisis, the more scholastic and intellectual religious leaders of the community knew that they could send children to Chanan Hanechba, the grandson of Choni the Circle Drawer.

Chanan Hanechba was known for his godliness. He had a close relationship to God, and it seems that he was at home in the company of children. The scholastic teachers of the law sent children to him to ask him to pray for rain. The children grabbed his cloak and said to him, "Abba, Abba"—that is, "father, father"—"give us rain!" Chanan Hanechba was moved by their request and realized that these little ones had faith in him. But he also recognized that he was not a father who could give rain. He looked up into heaven and prayed,

> Master of the Universe, for the sake of these [little ones] who cannot distinguish between a father who cannot make it rain and a Father who can make it rain—give us rain (b. *Ta'anit* 23b).

The children had approached him in childlike wonder and faith. God answered the prayer. The rain came!

In the Gospels the disciples of Jesus prevented the children from being brought before Jesus for his blessing. Many Bible students would like to know why the disciples behaved in this way. But their reasons for preventing the children were never even mentioned. Whatever motivated them to stop the children, it is not considered significant or worthy of comment. Jesus called for the children to be brought before him. The conflict and controversy involved the disciples themselves.

The custom of blessing children is referred to in the Old Testament (Gen 9:26–27; 27:28–29; 49), and its importance is emphasized in the literature of the Second Temple period (Sir 3:9). Even today in a Jewish home the father often will lay his hand upon his child's head and say a blessing over him. The occasion may be on the eve of a Sabbath or a holiday, or prior to the child's wedding, or even at the deathbed of the parent. In the Jewish prayer book the blessing of family is described by quoting from Psalm 128. The psalm is recited for a family bless-

ing, and the custom is practiced in many Jewish homes where
the child is dedicated to the Lord at the beginning of the week
at the conclusion of the Sabbath.

While the custom is not fully attested in all the early sources,
the Gospels give us an account where children were brought to
Jesus for his blessing. Today a father will place his hand upon
the head of his son and pray that he would be like the sons of
Joseph and ask the Lord to bless him with the blessing of Aaron
(see Gen 48:20; Num 6:24–26). Likewise, he will bless his
daughter, praying that she should be like Sarah, Rebekah, Ra-
chel, and Leah and be preserved in the peace and grace of the
Lord. Jesus was asked to bless the children. He desired to bless
them. But the disciples tried to stop the children from coming.
Perhaps it was on the occasion of a Sabbath in which Jesus had
taught in the synagogue and was weary. He would have been
tired after a day of ministry. The close of the Sabbath might
have been a proper occasion for the blessing of children, but
one cannot be certain of the time. The picture of parents, the
children, the extended members of families, friends, the disciples, and Jesus creates a vivid scene full of activity, but the
children were stopped by the disciples.

Jesus used the opportunity of conflict with his inner circle of
followers to teach his higher message of the kingdom. Jesus
said, "Let the children come to me. . . ." He wanted to make a
point about coming into the kingdom. To come into the kingdom means to join in the flow of God's reign among his people.
He continues, ". . . do not hinder them for to such as these is the
kingdom of heaven" (Matt 19:14). Jesus recognized the qualities
and the characteristics of the children as being the desired approach to life for his disciples. He relates the kingdom to his
disciples.

CHILDREN AND WONDER

What qualities did Jesus see in the children? Perhaps the story
of Chanan Hanechba and the children assists in some measure
to answer this question. The children were filled with wonder
and were full of faith in God's goodness. The great modern
Jewish philosopher and Judaic scholar Abraham Joshua Heschel
was said to have had a dream like Solomon. In a dream Solomon was offered anything he wanted from God. He did not ask

for wealth but instead asked for wisdom. Heschel also had a dream. But he did not ask for either wealth or wisdom. He asked for wonder.[5]

Wonder, or radical amazement, was the foundation of faith in Heschel's teachings. Perhaps Jesus saw the wonder in the eyes of children when he taught about the reign of God.[6] Like Heschel, Jesus realized that true faith in God originates in a sense of wonder and amazement which is driven from the adult world of perceived reality. Heschel believed that the patriarch Abraham's faith began with a sense of wonder and awe in God's presence: "All Abraham could achieve by his own power was wonder and amazement; the knowledge that there is a living God was given him by God."[7] Wonder and amazement are the first steps to entering the kingdom of heaven. The word of faith in the Bible is comprehended through the wonder of God's presence. Heschel observes,

> His [God's] light may shine upon us, and we may fail to sense it. Devoid of wonder, we remain deaf to the sublime. We cannot sense His presence in the Bible except by being responsive to it. Only living with its words, only sympathy to its pathos, will open our ear to its voice. Biblical words are like musical signs of a divine harmony which only the finest chords of the soul can utter. It is the sense of the holy that perceives the presence of God in the Bible.[8]

The wonder of God's presence, however, must be translated into action. True faith leads to active involvement. "We must keep alive the sense of wonder," Heschel proclaims, "through deeds of wonder."[9] The deeds of wonder are related to vigorous obedience which brings wholeness to others in need.

Perhaps this is a key to discipleship in the kingdom. Children are filled with wonder. They possess faith and trust. The children who came to Chanan Hanechba believed that he could give rain. They possessed childlike faith. Their eyes were filled with wonder. When the children grabbed his cloak and asked him for rain, Chanan Hanechba was touched by their childlike wonder and mysterious faith. What qualities was Jesus looking for in his disciples? He told them that the kingdom of heaven is made up of the childlike ones. He does not explain or elaborate. To understand one must look into the faces of children. One must become like a child to enter the kingdom.

Both the Gospels and rabbinic literature preserve stories about children and spiritual leaders. Obviously Jesus is closely related

to the world of the Jewish people during the days of the Second
Temple and especially to the spiritual background of teachers
and devout people of prayer like Chanan Hanechba. Nonetheless, the focus of the story of Jesus and the children is fixed
upon his message concerning the kingdom of heaven. God's
reign in saving power among his people is for those who are like
children. Enter into the kingdom. Receive God's power as a
disciple. Be like a child. Accept God's authority in childlike
trust. Life in the kingdom is filled with the wonder of God's
goodness and grace. In order to experience the reign of God in
saving grace and healing power, one must become like a child
and participate in Jesus' movement. The disciples brought controversy and conflict because Jesus did not approve of their
actions. He invited the children to come, but he also explained
what he expected from his disciples. Jesus stressed the meaning
of his message: "Truly, I say unto you, whoever does not receive
the kingdom of God like a child shall not enter it" (Luke 18:17).
By a parabolic action Jesus tells his disciples that they have a lot
to learn from children. Children are still able to teach adults
what it means to enter God's reign.

NOTES

1. Controversy over the issue of who should be greatest among the
disciples or who will lead the movement after Jesus is found in Luke
9:46–48, Mark 9:33–37, and Matt 18:1–5 (cf. Luke 22:24–30, Mark
10:41–45, and Matt 20:24–28). In Jesus' teaching the greatest is the
servant of all. One must become like a child to enter the kingdom.

2. One cannot be entirely certain how the name developed. Here we
are relying in part upon the suggestions of the great Jewish interpreter
Rashi.

3. Perhaps one of the finest studies of Jewish life and individuals such
as Chanan Hanechba during this period was written by Adolf Büchler,
Types of Jewish-Palestinian Piety (London: Jews' College, 1922). See
also the important article by S. Safrai, "Teaching of Pietists in Mishnaic
Literature," *Journal of Jewish Studies* 16 (1965) 15–33. See also the
chapter here, "Miracles, Proclamation, and Healing Faith."

4. Many scholars and Bible students fail to understand the essence of
Jesus' controversial ministry. Jesus' conflict with his contemporaries
was not so much over the doctrines of the Pharisees, with which he was
for the most part in agreement, but primarily over the understanding of
his mission. He did sharply criticize hypocrites—that is, people who say
the right things but do not practice what they teach (Matt 23:1–3). As

has been pointed out by R. L. Lindsey and David Flusser, the tension in the Gospels between Jesus and some of the religious leaders of the day is similar to that expressed in the stories of Jewish wonderworkers like Choni the Circle Drawer and Chanan Hanechba. Jesus was ready to provide compelling evidence to support his approach to Jewish law pertaining to matters of *halakhah*.

5. See Abraham Joshua Heschel, *Man Is Not Alone* (New York: Farrar, Straus & Giroux, 1991) 11: "Wonder or radical amazement, the state of maladjustment to words and notions, is, therefore, a prerequisite for an authentic awareness of that which is. Standing eye to eye with being as being, we realize that we are able to look at the world with two faculties—with reason and with wonder. Through the first we try to explain or to adapt the world to our concepts, through the second we seek to adapt our minds to the world. Wonder rather than doubt is the root of knowledge."

6. I deeply appreciate the insight of David Flusser who called my attention to Matt 21:15b–16. At the triumphal entry, the children's praise and excitement over the wonderful things that Jesus did was defended because of their childlike amazement: "And Jesus said to them, 'Yes; have you never read, "Out of the mouth of babes and sucklings thou hast brought perfect praise"?' " The children's sense of awe and wonder is portrayed in these descriptive elements from Matthew's version of the episode. Consider the story of the distinguished Torah sage Rabbi Joshua ben Korha, who is described as playing horse with his son. Rabbi Joshua was asked to solve a halakhic dispute related to a will. A man stipulated that his son could not receive his inheritance until he learned to act foolishly. Rabbi Joshua explained that after the son has children, he will learn to act foolish just like the sage himself, who played horse with his son (Midrash on Psalm 92:13). See L. Ginzberg, *Students, Scholars and Saints* (New York: Meridian Books, 1958) 145.

7. Abraham Joshua Heschel, *God in Search of Man* (New York: Farrar, Straus & Giroux, 1955) 152.

8. Ibid., 252.

9. Ibid., 349.

Elbow keys from the time of Bar Kochba (ca. 132–135 C.E.).
Compare Matthew 23:2, the "keys of the kingdom."
Photo courtesy of the Israel Antiquities Authority.

9

Jesus, the Sabbath, and the Jewish Law

JESUS' ATTITUDE TOWARDS THE OBSERVANCE OF THE Jewish day of rest and the law of Moses has been hotly debated for centuries. The lack of consensus is in large measure due to the fact that the Jewish customs and practices during the time of Jesus have been largely ignored or misunderstood. How was the Jewish Sabbath observed? Deficiencies in this area of learning inevitably give rise to a number of misunderstandings, and consequently the message of Jesus is distorted. In order to rediscover the depth of Jesus' teaching, we must journey through time and reenter the historical environment in which Jesus lived and taught. Three questions are debated: Did Jesus violate the law? Did he teach others to disobey the divine commands? What was his approach to the oral tradition? For an investigation of these issues, we must go into the grain fields with Jesus. This episode from the life of Jesus occurred on the Sabbath as Jesus and his disciples passed through grain fields.[1]

The controversy over Jesus' observance of the Sabbath will be seen in light of early Jewish custom and interpretation. But this Gospel story gives clear direction for proper answers to the three questions: Jesus did not break the Sabbath. He never taught anyone to disobey the commandments. Moreover, Jesus affirms the legitimacy of Jewish oral tradition in his discussion of the Sabbath. In fact, Jesus reveals a profound awareness of the Jewish view of God, humanity, and the higher purpose of the created world when he proclaims, "The Sabbath was made for man, not man for the Sabbath."

The reality of the entire episode is illustrated by the childhood memories of Abraham Mitrie Rihbany, who vividly recalls walking through the grain fields of the Holy Land and eating wheat. As a boy at the turn of the century, Rihbany was fond of eating the ripe grain from the stalks of wheat to satisfy his hunger.

> When a boy it was a great delight to me to wander in the wheatfields when the grain had just passed the "milk stage" and had begun to mature and harden. It is then called *fereek*, and is delicious to eat, either raw or roasted. I could subsist a whole day by plucking the heads of wheat, rubbing them in my hand and eating the fat, soft, fragrant grain. From time immemorial wayfarers in the East have been allowed to trespass in this manner, provided they carried no more grain away than that which they ate.[2]

According to the teachings of Torah, walking through the fields and eating grain was unquestionably permitted: "When you go into your neighbor's standing grain, you may pluck the ears with your hand, but you shall not put a sickle to your neighbor's standing grain" (Deut 23:15). The issue in the Gospels surrounds the time of plucking the grain. Does such plucking of the grain constitute work forbidden on the Sabbath? The sanctity of the Sabbath is one of the Ten Commandments. Such an issue involving obedience to God's law requires serious consideration. We must enter the wheat fields with Jesus on the Sabbath day to understand more clearly the question of those who criticized the actions of his disciples.

THE QUESTION

Jesus himself did not pick the heads of grain. When, however, his disciples became hungry, *they* picked and ate them. Luke's Gospel retains the important detail that the disciples rubbed the grain in their hands (Luke 6:1), an action which was accepted by a number of legal authorities as permissible on the Sabbath.[3] The Sabbath day should be different from the six common days. It was a day of rest and refreshment during which work was not permitted as on other days. Picking grains in large quantities, for example, was forbidden, but during the Sabbath rest you could take a small amount of the grains and rub them in your hands, according to some interpreters. In any case, the custom, like many interpretations of the Bible, was open for debate; and *some* of the Pharisees thought the action violated the Sabbath law. No one should minimize the importance of the question. After all, the command to observe the seventh day of rest is already prescribed in the Ten Commandments and is given by divine decree.

The question of some Pharisees concerning the action of Jesus' disciples was a legitimate concern for everyone who wanted to obey the teachings of the Bible during the time of Jesus. The Ten Commandments should be obeyed. But the proper interpretation of the Bible is needed for the people to respond with a positive attitude to God's will. The Jewish people, in an effort to remain true to the biblical faith, have endeavored to interpret the commandment of the Sabbath rest with the Oral Torah, a body of orally transmitted traditions which were believed to have been given by God to Moses on Mount Sinai in conjunction with the written Torah. The Oral Torah clarified obscure points in the written Torah, thus enabling the people to satisfy its requirements. If the Scriptures prohibit work on the Sabbath, one must interpret and define the meaning of work in order to fulfill the divine will. Why is there a need for an oral law? The answer is quite simple: Because we have a written one. The written record of the Bible should be interpreted properly by the Oral Torah in order to give it fresh life and meaning in daily practice.

Jesus did not treat the question with contempt. His attitude is quite significant. To the contrary, he responded to the legal issue raised by the question of some Pharisees in kind, with an acceptable technical argument. Jesus' specialized discussion was based upon the Jewish interpretive principle of *halakhah*. *Halakhah* refers to the way a person should walk. It is the legal system in Judaism, including the various 613 commandments of the Torah and all of the legal rulings of the rabbis found in the oral law. It is not necessary to deal with all the intricacies of Jesus' brilliant answer here, but it should be observed that he demonstrated a considerable depth of understanding and an intimate knowledge of the oral law. Moreover, it should be remembered that the Oral Torah was not a rigid legalistic code dominated by one single interpretation. The oral tradition allowed a certain amount of latitude and flexibility. In fact, the open forum of the Oral Torah invited vigorous debate and even encouraged diversity of thought and imaginative creativity. Clearly some legal authorities were more strict than others, but all recognized that the Sabbath had to be observed.

JESUS AND THE ORAL LAW

The oral law served to alleviate some of these difficult questions, spawned at times by the written law itself. For instance, cutting was forbidden on the Sabbath because it constituted work. Circumcision, which was performed on the eighth day after a child's birth, requires an incision. Cutting, such as an incision, is, of course, strictly forbidden on the Sabbath. Thus, one faces a dilemma: In order to fulfill the requirements of the law to circumcise a child on the eighth day, one might be forced to transgress the Sabbath if the two days coincide. In such a case, if one observes the Sabbath, one transgresses the law of circumcision. If one fulfills circumcision, however, one violates the Sabbath. When the two days coincide, one cannot observe both commandments of the Bible. What can one do? To fulfill one commandment means that a person will have to violate the other. While the written law does not deal with the question directly, the Jewish Oral Torah resolves the conflict. The *halakhah* determined that the law of circumcision takes precedence over the Sabbath. Hence a child should be circumcised on the eighth day, even if it happens to be the Sabbath, and even though cutting is strictly forbidden.[4] The halakhic decision concerning circumcision on the Sabbath day is already mentioned in John 7:22–23, where Jesus himself quotes the Oral Torah: "on the Sabbath a man receives circumcision, so that the law of Moses may not be broken." The ancient sources of the oral tradition should always be carefully studied.

When questioned by some of the Pharisees concerning the picking of grain on the Sabbath, Jesus develops his discussion upon the foundation of Jewish oral teachings. In addition to other points of his discussion, here Jesus reminds his listeners of more legal principles which would be similar to his argument in John concerning circumcision taking precedence over the Sabbath observance. He defends his more lenient position concerning the Sabbath rest with a similar proof. He mentions the famous episode from the life of King David when he tried to escape the death plot of King Saul. David and his men ate the bread of the presence which according to Jewish law was forbidden for them to eat. These points are clear from the words of Jesus in the Gospel story concerning the Sabbath controversy.

The Jewish oral tradition gives Jesus' argument definitive force. According to traditional Jewish interpretations of the

incident in King David's life, the bread of the presence was
always baked on the Sabbath (Lev 24:5). The fact that this event
in David's life happened on the Sabbath made it so much more
pertinent to the question concerning Jesus and his disciples. So
not only did the incident occur on the Sabbath, but also according to Jewish commentary on the biblical passage, David and his
men's lives were at risk because of their great hunger. Their
life-threatening hunger is crucial because of the legal rulings in
the Oral Torah.

The Jewish oral tradition places great emphasis on the preservation of life. All commandments of the Bible must be suspended to save a human life. The Pharisees emphasized saving
life at all costs. The only exceptions to this rule are idolatry,
incest, and murder. One should choose death rather than commit idolatry, incest, or murder. Nonetheless, the preservation of
life takes precedence over Sabbath observance. David and his
men were being pursued by Saul. They were so hungry, according to Jewish traditional interpretation, that their lives were
at risk. All the commandments of the Bible must be suspended
to save their lives. They were hungry and so they ate the bread
of the presence from the house of God. The written account of
David's dramatic escape from Saul's death plot does not refer
to the serious hunger of David and his men, but the hunger is
described in the oral tradition as being life-threatening. Food
is necessary to sustain life, and sometimes hunger is overwhelming. The oral law recognized this extreme hunger as a common
frailty of human experience. In any case, without sufficient
nourishment David and his men would never have the strength
for their dangerous getaway.

In a humorous observation the Jewish commentary remarks
that because of his great hunger, David ate an excessive amount
of bread on that day![5] According to this vivid description of the
incident in David's life, the Jewish commentary explains, "because he found only the bread of the presence there [in the
house of God], David said to him, 'Give me some to eat, so that
we will not die of hunger. The preservation of life takes precedence over the Sabbath.' " Jesus and his listeners probably knew
more about the story of David than is reflected in the Gospel
account. In Jewish oral tradition, the episode about David's
escape refers to the Sabbath and eating food to preserve life.
Jesus hints at the oral tradition to promote a deeper appreciation of the meaning of the Sabbath.

Moreover, Jesus directly refers to the oral tradition concerning the priests and the requirements of the Sabbath. He notes that the priests perform their tasks in the temple on the Sabbath, even though these activities constitute work and would be forbidden without a proper interpretation of the Oral Torah. The same argument is a recognized case in Jewish oral tradition. In the Gospels this ruling is described with precision in the same way it appears in later Jewish sources.[6] The priests perform their work in the temple on the Sabbath because their sacred duties take precedence over the laws pertaining to the day of rest. Jesus employs the oral tradition to address those who questioned the actions of his disciples. He possesses an intimate acquaintance with the Oral Torah and does not betray any interest in violating either the written law or its traditional Jewish interpretations. The Oral Torah gives the written letter of the Bible its true force.

GOD'S WORLD IS FOR HIS PEOPLE

Jesus' answer rises above a purely judicial ruling and reaches beyond into Israel's past to create a dynamic approach to Sabbath observance. In fact, the words of Jesus concerning the Sabbath and every human being are closely paralleled in the rabbinic literature. As Christians we have sometimes been taught that the teaching of Jesus was so revolutionary that it has no parallels. Jesus and his Jewish theology have deep roots, however, in the ancient Hebrew heritage of his people who looked for God's sovereignty in every aspect of the created world. When we put the words of Jesus side by side with the words of the rabbis, we often discover significant theological ties between Jesus and other Jewish teachers. Sometimes the sayings of the ancient Jewish rabbis are quite similar to the Gospel teachings of Jesus. For example, the words of Mark's Gospel are almost identical to the teaching of a Jewish sage, Rabbi Simeon ben Menasya, concerning Sabbath day observance. According to Mark's Gospel, the listeners are challenged by these words upon the lips of Jesus.

The Sabbath was made for man, not man for the Sabbath, so the Son of man is lord even of the Sabbath (Mark 2:27–28).

A strikingly analogous statement is attributed to Simeon ben Menasya.[7] The saying appears to be taken from an independent source which is probably common to both the Gospels and rabbinic literature. Here the Jewish understanding of God and the love and care God has for every human being created in the divine image is portrayed in a description of the higher purpose of the Sabbath. The Sabbath is given to people for their benefit. In rabbinic literature we hear Simeon ben Menasya speak about the meaning of the Sabbath in the creation of the world.

The Sabbath was given to you and not you to the Sabbath.[8]

The words of Jesus and Simeon ben Menasya represent a common stream of Jewish thought, characteristic of a unique approach to the law and religious life. The language of Simeon ben Menasya emphasizes the idea of a gift. The tradition of the Sabbath is "given to" (in Hebrew, *masorah*) or "passed on" to God's people as a special custom for their blessing and benefit. But, as David Flusser pointed out to me, the saying of Jesus has a deeper meaning.

The deeper meaning is tied to the Jewish teaching concerning the creation of the world. As is well known, the Ten Commandments themselves and the seven days of creation are closely linked because God himself created the world in six days but rested on the seventh. The divine order is reflected in the Decalogue by the injunction to observe the Sabbath as a day of rest. Flusser observed that the Greek word *ginomai*, translated as, "The Sabbath *was made* . . . ," is the accepted translation in the Septuagint for the Hebrew word *bara*, "to create." Perhaps it would be preferable to translate our Gospel passage, "The Sabbath *was created* . . . ," in an effort to represent more accurately the Hebrew saying of Jesus, which is an implicit allusion to God's creative activity in the Genesis account.

According to Jewish traditional teaching, the world was created for all humanity. Moreover, God created humankind on the sixth day right before the beginning of the first Sabbath. The beauty of creation was fashioned as the domain and individual sphere of human beings, who are created in the divine image. In order to drive home the deeper meaning of the world's design, the rabbis describe the creation in parabolic language. Their view of the creation of the world is based upon Jewish interpretations of the Bible. By wisdom (Prov 8–9) God created the world. But he fashioned the world for humanity in the same way that a king prepares a banquet for his invited guests. In the same way: Carefully, with the guests in mind, the Holy One designed the world with every person in mind. God created the world and prepared everything so that humankind would be created on the eve of the Sabbath and thus enter directly into observance of God's commandments. Indeed Adam, representative of all human beings, was created on the eve of the Sabbath, and hence he was directed to rest on the Sabbath day as a response to God's command. He was given the finest work of the greatest master designer, who sanctioned it with a day of rest that represented humanity's obedience to God. Humankind was created on the eve of the Sabbath and the Sabbath was created for every human being.

> Man was created on the eve of the Sabbath so that first and foremost he could enter into the observance of the commandments. Furthermore in another interpretation, it is explained, "Why was man created last?" A parable illustrates the matter. It may be compared to a king who prepared a banquet. After everything is ready for the banquet, only then does he invite the guests. Thus the Bible teaches, "Wisdom has built her house" (Prov 9:1). This refers to the Holy One Blessed be He who built the world through wisdom, as it is written, "The LORD by wisdom founded the earth. . . ." Thus also [by wisdom] He "has set up her [the world's] seven pillars" (Prov 3:19, 9:1). These seven pillars refer to the seven days in which God created the world. Moreover, it is written, "She [wisdom] has slaughtered her beasts, she has mixed her wine" (Prov 9:2). This passage refers to the lakes and rivers as well as all the needs of the world. Consider also the passage, "Whoever is simple, let him turn in here!" (Prov 9:4, 16). This Scripture refers to Adam and Eve.[9]

Quite probably, Jesus referred to a similar, familiar Jewish interpretation of Scripture. After all, people are the invited guests. God's beautiful creation is for all humanity. The Sabbath is intended to be a joy as people observe it out of love for God. The Sabbath was created for the good of people. It is a day of rest which is described in vivid detail in the story of the creation of the world in Genesis. The world was designed for the people God created in his own image. Hence the Sabbath is for them. After all, humankind was created on the eve of the Sabbath. While Jesus did not abrogate the Sabbath, he did take a more lenient approach which humanized the Jewish halakhic observance. Moreover, it is clear that this approach would be accepted by many Jewish rabbis like Simeon ben Menasya. Hence, the Son of man—in this case, every human being—is lord also of the Sabbath. Though Jesus often employs the term "Son of man" *(ben adam, bar anash)* as meaning a supernatural figure, as in Jewish interpretations of Daniel 7:13,[10] he also uses the generic meaning in a number of passages.[11] Here Jesus is teaching a humanizing approach to the individual's life of faith and one's struggle to obey God's commands fully.

Jesus accepted the challenge of those who questioned the action of his disciples and their Sabbath observance. He employed accepted Jewish halakhic discussion and interpretation to respond to the legal aspects of the issue. The words of Jesus, when translated into their historical Jewish context, ring with a dynamic authenticity and the magnetic originality of the teacher from Nazareth. In a most eloquent manner Jesus exploited this opportunity afforded to him by the Pharisees' question to speak about God's creative activity and the divine order. But the divine presence meets each person on the human level with his or her basic needs, for "The Sabbath was created for man and not man for the Sabbath."

NOTES

1. Matthew 12:1–8, Mark 2:23–28, Luke 6:1–5. Sadly, these fascinating questions cannot be answered in great depth in this brief study. See also the crucial article of M. Kister, "Plucking on the Sabbath and Christian-Jewish Polemic," *Immanuel* 24/25 (1990) 35–51.

2. Abraham Mitrie Rihbany, *The Syrian Christ* (New York: Houghton Mifflin, 1916) 290–91.

3. Flusser, *Jesus,* 46 [ET], notes p. 140; cf. b. *Shab.* 128a.

4. See b. *Yoma* 85b and parallels.

5. See the Yalkut Shimeoni II, 130 on 1 Sam 21:5. See the discussion of J. N. Epstein, *Introduction to the Tannaitic Literature* (Jerusalem: Magnes, 1957) 281 (Hebrew).

6. E.g., Matt 12:5 and t. *Shab.* 15, b. *Yoma* 85b, and parallels.

7. On the R. Simeon ben Menasya, see the *Encyclopaedia Judaica*, vol. 14, col. 1561, and W. Bacher, *Die Agada der Tannaiten* (Strassburg: Karl Tübner, 1890) 2.489ff.

8. See the Mechilta de Rabbi Yishmael on Exodus 31:3 (Horovitz, 34) and parallels.

9. See j. *Sanh.* 22c, chap. 4, end, b. *Sanh.* 38a, and parallels.

10. See, e.g., Matt 25:31ff. The Son of man is the Redeemer who performs the task of the eschatological judge. The high view of the

Redeemer is probably the most prominent use of the term Son of man in the teachings of Jesus. For a fine discussion of the term, see W. Horbury, "The Messianic Associations of the 'the Son of man,' " *Journal of Theological Studies* 36 (1985) 35–55.

11. See, e.g., Matt 12:31–37, Mark 3:18–30, and Luke 12:10 where the one who speaks against the Son of man is forgiven but not someone who speaks against the Holy Spirit. Here the generic meaning, i.e., every human being, is most probably intended.

10

Divorce and Adultery in Light of the Words of Jesus

MANY INTERPRETERS HAVE BEEN PUZZLED BY THE words of the Gospels concerning divorce.[1] Did Jesus permit divorce? Was remarriage after divorce prohibited by the teaching of Jesus? As is well known, many Christian denominations permit divorce or annulment only under strict circumstances and prohibit remarriage after divorce.[2]

The issue has been debated and discussed for centuries, but a careful analysis of the sayings of Jesus in light of early Jewish thought throws fresh light upon the question: Did Jesus equate divorce with adultery?

Perhaps the most well-known case where the issue of interpretation had far-reaching consequences was that concerning Henry VIII (1491–1547) and Catherine of Aragon.[3] Although the question was debated by the Reformers, Catholic theologians, and many concerned politicians, the issue was never satisfactorily resolved. On a more personal level closer to everyday life, many families, friends, and children of loved ones are confronted with the breakup of the family unit. Many pastors face this question in the ministry. The breakdown of the family has made the question of divorce and remarriage of great concern.

The Jewish sources are seldom consulted when the question is considered. Here we will examine only one of the contexts in the Gospels where Jesus speaks about divorce, adultery, and remarriage (Luke 16:18 and parallels) and suggest a new translation that may shed light on the issue. The Jewish background and rabbinic literature can be of great aid in understanding the original meaning of Jesus. Because the Gospel of Luke is often neglected in the study of the interrelationships of the Synoptic Gospels, many interpreters miss the meaning of this saying of Jesus. Here we will study the saying of Jesus from Luke 16:18 in

light of early Jewish sources.[4] According to this context in Luke
16:18, Jesus says, "Every one who divorces his wife and marries
another commits adultery, and he who marries a woman divorced from her husband commits adultery."

Before one can study divorce, it must be recognized that in
many ways marriage and the family were the primary focus of
Judaism during the time of Jesus. The home was a place of love
and togetherness. The man, the wife, and their children formed
a family unit where the study of Scripture, prayers, and blessings provided a solid foundation for home life. The Jewish faith
and piety of the period emphasized peace in the home (shalom
bayit) and the oneness of God who sanctioned the marriage
relationship. Nonetheless, the Scriptures clearly teach that divorce
was possible under certain circumstances (Deut 24:1–2). In the
ancient Near East, the woman could have suffered greatly when
the family unit was broken. Originally, the law of the Hebrew
Scriptures from Deuteronomy 24:1–2 was designed to preserve
the unity of the family and to discourage divorce. The Gospels
indicate that Jesus desired to strengthen the position of the wife
in the event of divorce.

Here attention will be focused upon Jesus' teaching in Luke
16:18 where the words "divorce" and "adultery" are often misunderstood. Not infrequently Christian clergy and laypeople
have thought that Jesus made divorce synonymous with adultery. Nothing could be further from the truth; it is clear that
divorce and remarriage were permitted in Jewish law. Did he
abolish the laws which refer to divorce and remarriage? Jesus
did not come to destroy the law. He came to place it upon a
firmer foundation by proper interpretation. Prohibiting divorce
would abrogate the Torah passage in Deuteronomy 24:1–2. Jesus
was intent on interpreting the Torah properly, but he did not
want to destroy it. How could a spouse be protected in the event
of the divorce? How could the family be preserved? Divorce
was discouraged by the Jewish teachers of the time, and the
family unit was so sacred that it was seldom broken.

The husband and wife were thought to have been brought
together by divine appointment, and the foundation of the family
goes back to the creation of the world. In the custom of the
period, arranged marriages were the accepted practice, and people
were wed at a young age. In Proverbs we read that a "prudent
wife is from the LORD" (19:14). God receives credit for the
match between Isaac and Rebekah in Genesis 24:50.

Jesus did not prohibit divorce; however, in Luke 16:18 we discover a saying which deals with a specific situation: "Every one who divorces his wife and marries another commits adultery." Is divorce synonymous with adultery? When we understand the Jewish background of the saying, its meaning becomes clear. In the Mishnah (*Sotah* 5.1) we discover that a woman who is divorced because of an adulterous relationship is not permitted to marry her paramour.[5] In this Gospel passage did Jesus seek to prevent injustice and to set limits on the interpretation of the biblical law which might encourage divorce for the sake of remarriage? As is often the case, divorce can be employed as a convenience for a man to divorce the wife of his youth in order to remarry a younger, more attractive woman. While the Mishnah deals with the case of a married woman who commits adultery, Jesus addresses a somewhat similar case. What if a man divorces his wife in order to marry someone else? Actually Jesus seems to be addressing this specific case. Divorce used to marry another is the same as adultery.

In Luke both verbs "divorce" and "marry" are in the present tense. The parallel in Mark 10:11 puts them in the subjunctive mood.[6] In Hebrew the force of the expression would have linked the two actions together in continuous motion: *kol hasholeach et eshto venose acheret noef*, "Every one who divorces and marries another commits adultery." Perhaps in English one could better capture the meaning of the saying by translating it, "Every one who divorces his wife [in order] to marry another commits adultery." This suggested new translation makes the saying of Jesus clear.

The second part of the verse must be understood in a similar fashion. In light of the Mishnah passage in *Sotah,* if a man marries a woman who obtained a divorce merely for the sake of her second marriage, then it is considered adultery. Divorce is not adultery. However, one can obtain a divorce for the sake of remarriage and thereby break the sacred trust of marriage fidelity.

The approach of the saying concerning divorce and adultery adopted here clarifies a number of problems. First it would seem that Jesus did not desire to abrogate the teaching of the Hebrew Scriptures concerning marriage, divorce, and remarriage. However, he did desire to set limits to its application. If a man divorces his wife because he desires to marry someone else, it is adultery. Even if such an action preserves the letter of the law, it violates its spirit. Probably a large number of divorces may be attributed to infidelity when one mate decides to find someone new instead of opening communication at home and dealing with the problems. Many of these marriages could be saved. When a man breaks the marriage bond through infidelity and divorces his wife to marry someone else, he has abused the laws of the Hebrew Scripture concerning divorce and remarriage. It is the same as adultery.

In essence, Jesus says that when one divorces his wife in order to marry the other woman, it is wrong. The sages had a high view of marriage. Rabbi Eleazar said that even the altar weeps tears when a man divorces the wife of his youth (b. *Git.* 90b). Many marriages that end in divorce could be saved. Restoring peace between partners was considered meritorious. The importance of resolving conflicts in the family unit and making peace where bitterness and hatred separate family members must be the goal of all involved parties.

Here in this brief discussion of one saying of Jesus, we have not been able to solve all of the problems surrounding Jesus' teaching concerning divorce. However, by studying one passage in light of its Jewish parallels, it is hoped that the entire issue is clarified. Jesus did not abrogate the Old Testament law concerning marriage, divorce, and remarriage. But the Torah must be interpreted properly to protect all parties involved in the vulnerable position of the sacred experience of marriage. *Divorce is not adultery.* Remarriage after divorce is not adultery. However, divorce can be employed to commit adultery. The Torah should be interpreted in such a way as to protect two vulnerable individuals trying to make a marriage work.

When the legal system is used to abuse one partner of the marriage contract by seeking a new relationship, the meaning of the higher purpose of the law is annulled. No one should attempt to lessen the force of a powerful saying of Jesus. When a man abuses the law and divorces his wife in order to marry someone new—it is the same as adultery.

NOTES

1. Two contexts in the Synoptic Gospels preserve the words of Jesus pertaining to marriage, divorce, and remarriage (Matt 19:3–12, 5:32; Mark 10:11–12; Luke 16:18). The first context is found in Matt

5:31–32, Mark 10:10–12, and Luke 16:18, with a doublet parallel to Matt 5:31–32 in Matt 19:9. Here the first context for the saying will be examined which deals with a specific application of the legal aspects of divorce. The second context is contained in Matt 19:3–9 and Mark 10:2–9 where the grounds of divorce are discussed. It is impossible to deal with all the issues of both contexts of the Gospels in this section, but on the second context in the Gospels one may refer to G. Vermes, "Sectarian Matrimonial Halakhah in the Damascus Rule," *Journal of Semitic Studies* 25 (1974) 197ff. Here the first context will be examined where the version of Luke's Gospel has often been ignored.

2. See the fine overview and treatment of the sources by Theodore Mackin, *Divorce and Remarriage* (Mahwah, N.J.: Paulist, 1984).

3. As will be remembered, this controversy did not give King Henry VIII a child and heir to the throne, but it did aid in giving birth to the Church of England. It is noteworthy that the great biblical scholars and theologians of the time such as Erasmus of Rotterdam and Martin Luther wanted to allow Henry a second marriage in order to provide opportunity for an heir. See Mackin, *Divorce and Remarriage*.

4. On the synoptic problem, see also my *Jesus and His Jewish Parables*, 129–63.

5. See Abrahams, *Studies in Pharisaism and the Gospels,* 66–81, esp. 74. Here I am greatly indebted to Abrahams' insights without which the present study would not have been written. I appreciate being able to discuss this text with R. L. Lindsey and David Bivin in Jerusalem.

6. The subjunctive mood in Greek sometimes carries with it the sense of purpose. This is the case when it is used with the *hina* clause. While no *hina* clause appears here, it is possible that Mark thought of the purpose in using the subjunctive. The Markan parallel would also be rendered by, "Whoever divorces his wife in order to marry another commits adultery against her" (Mark 10:11). The same idea, therefore, is carried over in the next verse: The divorced person is one who obtained the divorce in order to remarry. Often adultery leads to divorce. The marriage bond should be maintained without an extramarital affair. The specific situation dealt with by this saying, however, would not treat the issue of remarriage after divorce under different circumstances. The Torah does allow remarriage, but divorce must not be used as a convenience to consummate adultery.

"To the place of the trumpeting" inscription, from the temple.
Photo courtesy of the Israel Antiquities Authority.

Signet ring (cf. Luke 15:22).
Photo courtesy of the Israel Antiquities Authority.

11

Giving Thanks—a Way of Life

WONDER, AWE, AND AMAZEMENT ARE THE PILLARS that support a firm foundation for giving thanks to God as a way of life. True faith is rooted in a profound awareness of the utter majesty of God. The awe of God became the basis of the Jewish theology of giving thanks. Everything comes from God. The Jewish people wonder at his noble sovereignty in an awe-inspiring world created according to his design. It was natural for the rabbis to connect the sovereignty of God to prayers of thanksgiving. Rabbi Zeira and Rabbi Judah wanted to emphasize the significance of God as king in their prayers. They taught: "A blessing wherein the kingdom of heaven is not mentioned is no blessing, for it is said, 'I will extol thee, my God O King' (Ps 145:1)."[1]

Like Rabbis Zeira and Judah, another famous rabbi from Nazareth also placed great importance upon the kingdom of heaven in his disciples' prayer life. He taught them to pray, "Thy kingdom come." In the example of Jesus and his disciples, the theology of giving thanks comes to life in a deep and meaningful way. The actions of Jesus and his disciples regarding prayer have deep roots in the Jewish customs and practices of the Second Temple period.

Already in the daily life of Jesus and his disciples, thanksgiving and blessing were an integral part of their everyday experience and customary practice. For instance, pronouncing a blessing to God before eating was the common practice of Jesus and his circle of followers. Reflected both in early Jewish literature and in the liturgy of the synagogue, from Bible times to the present, it is a fact that the Jewish people have made giving thanks a significant part of every aspect of daily life. In Jewish theology no tasks should be considered mundane, because God sanctifies every facet of human experience in the life that he gives.

The concept of blessing and giving thanks is not only reflected in the Gospel story of the life of Jesus, it is also seen clearly in the Pauline epistles. Here we will examine the Jewish sources and the New Testament evidence in order to gain deeper insights into the early Jewish approach to giving thanks.

The Scriptures were the source book of Judaism during the time of Jesus. The precepts and lifestyle taught in the sacred pages of Scripture and their interpretation by Israel's sages formed the basis of Jewish life and practice. The Jewish people were and continue to be the people of the Book. The five books of Moses were carefully studied in order to understand the way of life God desired from his people. Not surprisingly, the Jewish people developed an approach to life which emphasized God's lordship and sovereignty over all that he created. They emphasized God's goodness, his genuine concern for each individual, and his creation, which he designed and intended for humankind's enjoyment and fulfillment.

The rabbis viewed all people as stewards of God's benevolence. Each person is created in God's image. Every one is given responsibility to obey God in God's domain and to care for the beautiful world that God designed for his people. The foundation of the Jewish understanding of thanksgiving and blessing was the belief in God's goodness and his creation. The people were taught to give thanks to God for his goodness. The sages developed a radical approach to life which encouraged a person to bless God and give thanks for every benefit received from God's creation. Hence, at every meal a person should give thanks to God, who provided the food. The written word of the Bible itself formed the basis for this approach to God's provision.

Deuteronomy 8:10 is the basis of the Jewish concept of giving thanks to God in the form of a blessing for a meal: "You shall eat and be full, and you shall bless the LORD your God for the good land he has given you." The foundation of blessing God for his goodness is derived from the Torah. The phrase "and you shall bless the LORD your God," was understood, in part, as a way of giving thanks to God for the grace he gives to all people. Note that one blesses the LORD himself and not any material object. In reality, the concept of blessing goes much deeper than mere praise because, in essence, blessing God is a full recognition of his lordship and sovereignty. One could say that one is actually acknowledging the kingdom of God, his rule, and his reign as sovereign Lord of his creation. Often it has been asked: How can a human being bless God? The Hebrew term *barakh,* in this context (Deut 8:10), does not mean to provide a blessing but rather means to worship God by acknowledging his kingdom and his authority, an action which also influences a person's conduct in daily life.

The Hebrew theology of blessing recognizes the innate goodness of God's creation. Unlike the gnostic or Greek religions, which often viewed the material universe as being inherently evil, the Jewish version of creation in Genesis proclaims that God made the world and that it is *good.* The failure to bless God for benefit received from the world is to deny his goodness and his authority over all that he has created.

The Jewish people have developed blessings to be recited in praise of God for specific occasions. When one eats bread, one says, "Blessed art thou O Lord, King of the Universe who brings forth bread from the earth." God has created the world from which people receive his benefit. An equally suitable blessing is recited over wine, "Blessed art thou O Lord, King of the Universe who brings forth fruit from the vine." Such blessings are used during meals.[2] Certainly Jesus would have employed these same blessings with his disciples, not only during the Passover but as a standard practice. A special blessing is recited when one comes to a place where God has worked a miracle, when one sees a king, or even when one performs natural body functions.[3] One entire tractate of the Jewish oral tradition reflected in the Mishnah, *Berakhot,* is dedicated to the subject of blessings. Both the Jerusalem and the Babylonian Talmuds comment extensively on this tractate of the Mishnah. Blessings and prayers were integral to everyday experiences of the people.

The rabbis developed a theology of blessing God for every aspect of a person's life. Each individual is required to acknowledge God's sovereignty and to live in a God-consciousness whatever one's occupation or circumstances might be. God's presence is to be recognized in everything. The rabbis taught that a person should give thanks to God for the good in life as well as the bad. The teachings of the Jewish oral tradition link giving thanks in all matters both good and bad with the commandment to love God with all one's heart. The rabbis stressed, "A person is bound to bless [God] for the evil even as he blesses God for the good, for it is written, 'And thou shalt love the

LORD thy God with all thy heart and with all thy soul and with all thy might' [Deut 6:5]."[4]

One famous rabbi was well known for his joyful heart. He gave thanks for all things, whatever his lot in real life experience. His name was Rabbi Nahum Eish Gam Zo (Gimzo). The words Gam Zo in his name probably are derived originally from the name of a town close to Lod called Gimzo, where Rabbi Nahum Eish Gam Zo grew up. Because of his cheerful attitude, Rabbi Nahum's colleagues made a word play in Hebrew based on his reputation for giving thanks as a way of life and the name of his home town. In Hebrew, the words *gam zo* are translated literally as "this also." Rabbi Nahum became famous for his spirit of optimism even in the midst of terrible adversity. No matter what happened, he would always say, "This also is for the best."[5] He always looked for the bright side. In Hebrew the saying contained his name, *gam zo letovah*, "This also is for the best." As a result his friends began to call him Nahum Eish Gam Zo rather than Gimzo. He gave thanks for everything and always managed to find a blessing in hard times. Rabbi Nahum Eish Gam Zo's thankful heart demonstrates the Jewish concept of giving praise to God for the good as well as for the difficult experiences in life.

The Jewish sages based their theology of thanksgiving to God upon Psalm 24:1. An illuminating passage from the Talmud drives home the message of the biblical text: "To enjoy anything of this world without a blessing of thanks is like making personal use of things consecrated to heaven, since it says, 'The earth is the LORD's and the fullness thereof' (Ps 24:1)."[6] Interestingly, another Jewish teacher, a student of the eminent Rabban Gamaliel, also employs Psalm 24:1 when he discusses the pastoral problem of food and drink in the mixed congregation of Jews and Gentiles in Corinth. With some stipulations Paul advises them to accept what is set before them with thanks, because, "The earth is the LORD's and the fullness thereof" (1 Cor 10:26). Paul's Jewish upbringing and training in the Scriptures influenced his choice of proof text and his approach to the issue at hand. The earth is the LORD's, and hence, whenever a person benefits in any way from God's created world, that person must give thanks and praise to God—the one who has made it.

Strangely enough, in Christian practice, often the custom at mealtime is to ask God to bless the food to the nourishment of the body. This phrase in prayer, although employed in many religious contexts, actually reflects a basic misunderstanding of blessing. One does not bless the created object. No, one blesses the source of all creation—the Lord himself who made it! The mistake of blessing objects instead of God who gives all good things in this world is probably a result not only of a misunderstanding of the Jewish custom in Jesus' time, but also of a wrong reading of the Gospels. Modern translations mention that Jesus blessed, broke, and gave bread to his disciples. In the miracle of the multiplication or in the Last Supper he blesses, breaks, and gives. The image of blessing God before one partakes of food is familiar in Jewish sources. For example, the famous Rabbi Akiva taught, "A person is forbidden to taste anything before saying a blessing over it."[7] Before eating, Jesus surely would have said a blessing. Jewish readers would have understood that the blessing was praise to God for the food. Then the bread was broken and given to the disciples. At an early period Christians somehow developed the idea of blessing the food instead of God. As was pointed out to me by David Flusser, in one important Greek manuscript of Luke 9:16, there is a distinct reference to a reading which may describe how Jesus blessed God for the food.

The usual version of the saying from Luke 9:16 reads, "And He took the five loaves and the two fish, and looking up to heaven, He blessed them and broke *them* . . ." (Luke 9:16, NASB). From the translation "He blessed them" many have adopted the practice of blessing the food before a meal. However, in a few manuscripts, including the uncial Codex Bezae, Flusser discovered a significant textual variant. Instead of blessing "them," these texts insert a preposition before the direct object, "them," so that the text reads, "He said a blessing *over* them *(ep' autous)*." In other words, some better Greek manuscripts preserve the image of the original Jewish practice of giving thanks to God, the provider.[8] Jesus said a blessing to God over the food. This makes the miracle of Jesus more meaningful. He gave thanks to God for his provision, and the five loaves and the two fish were miraculously multiplied to feed the five thousand. It is a miracle of God. Even the leftovers of twelve baskets far exceeded the original small meal given to Jesus. Jesus' custom of blessing God before tasting anything demonstrates an approach to life that was based upon the Jewish understanding of God's goodness and grace. One may bless children and give them to the Lord for God's service. Even possessions or other material assets may be dedicated for the kingdom of God. The practice of blessing food, however, is based upon a misunderstanding of the New Testament. God who has provided well for people created in the divine image should be blessed for his benevolence. God is the source of everything. The Gospels and the rest of the New Testament reflect the early Jewish practice of reciting a blessing in praise and honor of God for his unmerited favor.

Why should God be blessed? The foundation of ancient Jewish thought and faith is "Hear O Israel! The LORD is our God, the LORD is one" (Deut 6:4). The acknowledgement of the "Hear O Israel" affirmation of faith and commitment was understood as one's total denial of other gods and sincere acceptance of God's authority. God's reign and lordship are manifested when people acknowledge that, indeed, he alone is God. God created this world and the source of all life comes from God. The sanctity of the life God has given is too often obscured by mundane worries and concerns. God is exiled from the experience of life. True faith acknowledges God's presence in every dimension of human existence. Giving God praise and blessing for all benefit derived from his creation is a way in which the believer sanctifies life and receives the kingdom into all parts of his or her daily experience, the dreary routines as well as the spiritual highs. Awareness of God's grace and presence gives deeper meaning to the mystery of life. Faith is rooted in the human sense of wonder, awe, and amazement over all that is known and unknown about God.

NOTES

1. See Midrash Psalms 16:8 and b. *Ber.* 12a, 49a. Consider also the mention of God's kingdom in the frequent blessing "Blessed is his honorable name, his kingdom is for ever and ever" (Genesis Rabbah 98:3).

2. See Hertz, *The Authorised Daily Prayer Book,* 964ff.

3. See Flusser, *Judaism and the Origins of Christianity,* 535–42.

4. See m. *Ber.* 9:5 and parallels.

5. See b. *Ta᷄anit* 21a and parallels. Rabbi Nahum Eish Gam Zo was the teacher of Rabbi Akiva. His influence went beyond his own years in the work of his influential disciples.

6. See b. *Ber.* 35a and parallels.

7. Ibid. Cf. also b. *Ber.* 28b, 47a; b. *Shab.* 9b and b. *Git.* 62a.

8. The preposition is mainly added in Western readings, D, it, sy[(s).c]; Mcion (See NTG, Luke 1, 146). Codex Bezae, however, is thought to preserve Semitisms which might give evidence of Gospel sources. At an early time, the preposition *epi* may have been deleted because of stylistic concerns. On the other hand, the external evidence is weak and one may observe a tendency to add prepositions in later texts. In reality, to recite a blessing "over" them seems awkward in Greek and does preserve the original Hebrew idiom. Metzger observes that the Semitic background of Jesus' teachings must be considered in weighing the textual evidence, (*Textual Commentary,* 28). Could this be original?

Fragments of a Hebrew Epistle among the Dead Sea Scrolls 4QMMT.
"A Summary of the Works of the Law."
Photo courtesy of the Israel Antiquities Authority.

Qumran, Cave 4. Photo Brad Young.

PART 3

THE JEWISH THEOLOGY IN JESUS' PARABLES

Many modern theologians increasingly attempt to define the message of Jesus over against Judaism. Jesus is said to have taught something quite different, something original, unacceptable to the other Jews. The strong Jewish opposition to Jesus' proclamation is emphasized. . . . Even though he gave his own personal bent to Jewish ideas, selected from among them, purged and reinterpreted them, I cannot honestly find a single word of Jesus that could seriously exasperate a well-intentioned Jew.

—David Flusser

12

Jewish Grace in Jesus' Parables

A JEWISH THEOLOGIAN TEACHES ABOUT GOD through real-life stories that illustrate the divine nature. The pictorial world of story parables illustrates the way God loves people. Perhaps more than any other parable, the illustration of Jesus concerning the Laborers in the Vineyard teaches us about the character of God (Matt 20:1–16).[1] In fact, the Jewish view of God's grace is described in the vivid imagery of Jesus' story. This parable lays the foundation for all the parables. How do people come to understand God? The parables of Jesus focus on the proper understanding of the divine nature. Is God like an employer who pays a wage? Is he like someone who holds a gun to a person's head demanding certain actions or else? The parable beautifully portrays the grace of God, a concept so integral to Jewish thought during the time of Jesus and yet very difficult to grasp. Without a proper understanding of Judaism during the days of the Second Temple, however, we will never fully comprehend the depth of Jesus' message concerning the divine character.

As Christians we tend to view God apart from the Jewish background of Jesus' teachings. Even fine biblical scholars fall victim to this error. In the case of this parable, they sometimes teach that the story is attacking the Jewish view of God.[2] Some have wrongly assumed that Jesus was hostile to his contemporaries when he preached divine grace for human need. Such an incorrect assumption demonstrates well that the parables of Jesus must be viewed in their original Hebraic environment. The Jewish concept of God permeates the parables of Jesus. In the world of Jewish *agada* (storytelling to illustrate a message), Jesus creates striking word pictures so that everyone can understand what God is like. The Jewish roots of his teachings allow us to rediscover the life setting of the parable of the Laborers in the Vineyard. Actually, the Jewish concept of God was not different from Jesus'. Here we must explore the deeper meaning of the story in its Jewish background.

The situation for the parable of the Laborers in the Vineyard was familiar to the original audience.[3] The setting assumes the difficult economic conditions of first-century Israel. Many day laborers are standing in the market hoping to be hired for a day job. The original audience could readily identify with these workers and their real-life situation. They understood how the day workers felt because many of them had similar experiences. Day laborers were on the bottom end of the economic structure. They received minimal wages for sporadic work. As the primary wage earners, they had to support their families by the odd jobs they could acquire for day service. During the time of harvest, the situation improved as landowners needed additional day laborers to harvest the crops on time.

The pay for a day's work was one denarius. This minimum wage was required to meet the daily needs of each laborer's family. The payment was given to the worker at the conclusion of each day's labor (see Lev 19:13).

The conflict of the story is a wage dispute. Jesus used the issue of finance to capture the attention of the people. The questions concerning a fair wage and the sharp disagreement about money invited the listeners to become involved in the resolution of the conflict. The laborers in the parable are angry at the householder. He hired workers early in the morning, but probably because of the demands of the harvest, he hired additional day laborers later in the day. He even took on new laborers at the eleventh hour, near the end of the work period. The work of the harvest determines the need for additional man power.

At the end of the day, the wealthy landowner had to pay the laborers for the work they had done. Payment was made on a daily basis. As the parable tells us, the landowner hired the latecomers with a promise to give them what was fair. The color of the story emerges as the landowner commanded his steward to pay them from the last to the first. This dramatic element builds the interest of the listeners. The anticipation of the laborers who worked all day long cannot escape the audience. These workers expect more money. When they saw the latecomers receive full pay, they wanted more. After all, they had endured the burning heat of the afternoon sun. Contrary to all their expectations, however, the laborers who worked the entire day in the vineyard receive only one denarius, a full day's wage. Immense tension fills the story as the stage is set for a major wage dispute.

By most standards of fairness, the householder was unjust. Reason and equity would dictate one of two actions. Either he should pay the workers who withstood the heat of the day in the difficult work of the vineyard more than a denarius, or he should pay the others less money because they came to the job later in the day. When the first workers saw that the latecomers received a full day's pay, they began hoping that they would receive bonus compensation. This, however, was not the case. The landowner paid everyone the same. The paradox and irony of the parable are seen in the fact that the landowner is fair. He gives everyone what is just. This shock element of the parable challenges all reason. The justice in the story flies in the face of propriety. Many would want to argue with Jesus whether the landowner is just and fair in his dealings.

Not surprisingly the workers who labored the entire day complain. On what grounds can the landowner justify giving the same wage to all? These men had anticipated additional compensation when they saw how the latecomers were paid so well. But when their turn came, they were disappointed.

In the context prior to the parable in Matthew, Jesus says, "But many that are first will be last, and the last first" (Matt 19:30). This is one of the difficult sayings of Jesus which puzzles many students of the Gospels. In the conclusion of the parable of the Laborers in the Vineyard (Matt 20:16), the saying is repeated: "So the last will be first, and the first last." When one studies the context, the saying's meaning is clear. If the first are last and the last are first, everyone receives the same wage. All are equal before the Lord.

In the difficult economy of the period, the laborers who had been fortunate enough to receive work in the morning should have rejoiced at the generosity of the landowner. After all, the workers who stood idle in the market hoping to obtain a job had the same financial responsibilities for their families. A denarius would meet their needs. Instead of identifying with their need and the landowner's noble generosity, their own greed made them want more compensation than they had agreed upon at the beginning of the day. The landowner was fair—but not according to accepted standards.

In the rabbinic literature we discover a number of important
parallels to this parable.[4] By comparing them, we are able to
understand the message of Jesus more clearly.

Once, at a funeral, a rabbi tells a similar parable, "the Industrious Laborer," to comfort the bereaved. A dedicated scholar
of Scripture had died at a young age. How can a God of goodness and love, according to the Jewish view of the divine character, allow a scholar to die at the young age of twenty-eight?
The parable of the Industrious Laborer can provide insight. The
Jewish view of God's compassion and grace must be defended.
Despite such a tragedy, the goodness of God should be searched
out. The rabbinic parable told on this occasion contains similar
imagery to Jesus' illustration. The young man had accomplished
as much in his short lifetime as other distinguished scholars who
are precise in all matters pertaining to the study of the Scripture
would do in a longer period.[5]

The rabbinic parable praises the industrious work of the man
who died so very young. The story deals with his reward. Like
the king, God will give a reward. The amount of the reward is
based upon the grace of the king, who represents God.

> To what may Rabbi Bun bar Chaya be compared? To a king who
> hired many laborers. One of them was extremely industrious in his
> work. What did the king do? He took him and walked with him the
> lengths and breadths [of the field]. In the evening the laborers came
> to take their wages. But [to the one with whom he had walked—the
> king] gave a full day's wage. The laborers murmured and complained,
> "We worked all day long, but [the king] has given this one who only
> worked two hours a full wage like us." The king answered them, "He
> has done more in two hours than what you did for the entire day!"
> Thus though R. Bun labored only twenty-eight years, he did more
> than a learned scholar could have studied in a hundred.[6]

At the funeral the family received comfort from the praise
given in memory of their twenty-eight-year-old son who had
died so young. The king in his grace recognized the laborer's
special merit. He wanted to walk across the lengths and breadths
of his field with the industrious laborer. The other workers
should not complain because of the king's grace. The young
man worked hard during his time in the field. No one would
believe that he was able to do a day's work in two hours. He is
paid on the basis of the king's grace and compassion. The other
laborers should have rejoiced in the good fortune of their

co-worker who received special individual attention from the king. The rabbinic parable cannot be understood to teach a "save yourself" or "earn your own way" religious faith. The towering image of the king overwhelms the vivid word pictures created by the parable. He is gracious and full of compassion. One must search for his goodness even when a personal tragedy strikes a family and takes the life of a young man in the prime of life. God's grace is found in the reward which he gives to the young industrious laborer regardless of the amount of time he spent on the job.

During the Second Temple period, a religious revolution in Jewish thought transpired. The new sensitivity in Judaism influenced the Christian message.[7] The strong emphasis on divine grace, that is, serving God from the primary motive of love, emerged from the thinking of Israel's sages. What is more important, love or fear? The Jewish sage Antigonus of Socho, who lived about 150 B.C.E., taught, "Be not like servants who serve the master for the sake of receiving a reward, but be like servants who serve the master not on condition of receiving a reward. And let the fear of heaven be upon you" (m. *Avot* 1:3). All the ingredients of a parable appear in this wisdom saying. The servants serve their master, but not for a reward. God is not to be viewed as an employer who writes the paycheck. He is filled with grace and compassion.

Likewise the parable of Jesus illustrates the grace and the wage the landowner will give. Study the grace of the king in the rabbinic parable of the industrious worker. The parallel in the word picture is remarkable. As in the Gospel parable, one discovers sharp complaints from the other workers. The realistic setting of the workplace creates an action-packed drama with which it is easy to identify. After all, many people have heard laborers complain about their wages and express anger at the good fortune of their co-workers.

In yet another rabbinic parable, "the King and the Lazy Workers," the Jewish view of God's grace is clearly expressed in a commentary on the book of Psalms. God does not deal with a person only on the basis of good deeds. A person cannot earn acceptance, in the Jewish view. God's grace is unmerited. The theology of Judaism expressed in the parable emphasizes divine grace. The midrash on Psalms colorfully drives home the point:

Solomon said to the Holy One blessed be He: Master of the Universe! When a king hires good laborers who perform their work well and he pays them their wage—what praise does he merit? When does he merit praise? When he hires lazy laborers but still pays them their full wage![8]

Divine grace is revealed as the king pays the lazy workers their full wage. They receive their compensation even though they have not merited the king's benevolence. Judaism is not a "salvation by works" religion. The need for God's mercy and grace is strongly felt in Jewish thought. While obedience to God is never minimized to invite immoral conduct, the human condition presents a need for divine compassion and mercy. In the theology of the rabbis, parables helped to create a mental picture of God's grace and mercy.

In another rabbinic parallel, "Grace or Works," the same imagery is exploited to illustrate the message of grace. David Flusser noted how this illustration gives deeper meaning to the parable of Jesus.[9] Both examples use similar word pictures and are imbued with the force of divine mercy for the human condition. The workers and their wages are prominent. God rewards someone not only on the basis of the work accomplished but also because of divine love.

According to Jewish tradition, Samuel the prophet only served the people of Israel for 52 years. The ministry of Moses, on the other hand, extended for more than double that of Samuel. He labored in the vineyard of the Lord for 120 years. Nonetheless, according to the rabbis, God's grace is given to both Samuel and Moses in equal measure.

How do the righteous come [into the world]? Through love, because they uphold the world through their good deeds. How do they depart—also through love. Rabbi Simeon ben Eleazar told a parable. To what may the matter be compared? To a king who hired two workers. The first worked all day and received one denarius. The second worked only one hour and yet he also received a denarius. Which one was more beloved? Not the one who worked one hour and received a denarius! Thus Moses our teacher served Israel one hundred and twenty years and Samuel [served them] only fifty-two. Nevertheless both are equal before the Omnipresent! As it is said, "Then the LORD said to me, 'Though Moses and Samuel stood before me'" (Jer 15:1); and thus He said, "Moses and Aaron were among his priests, Samuel also was among those who called on his name" (Ps 99:6); concerning them and others like them He says, "Sweet is the sleep of the laborer whether he eats little or much" (Eccl 5:12).[10]

This parable is especially insightful for the Jewish theology of grace. Love is vital. Both workers in the rabbinic parable receive a denarius, that is, a day's wage. The first worked all day; the second, only one hour. Moses served the people in his divine call 120 years. Samuel the prophet labored in his ministry for only 52 years; yet both merit the same reward according to the rabbinic illustration. The parable exclaims, "Both are equal before the Omnipresent One!" In other words, the last are first and the first are last.

The message of Jesus' parable of the Laborers in the Vineyard teaches us that God does not deal with us according to what we earn. He is not like an employer who pays his workers merely on the basis of their merit. One cannot earn divine grace. No one can make God love more than he does. Nor is he like someone with a gun who threatens retaliation if people do not do what he wants. He is full of grace. His love is so much greater. The workers who went to the vineyard at the eleventh hour are paid a fair wage in the eyes of Jesus.

How can one describe God? What is his grace like? Jesus and the rabbis employed colorful word pictures to illustrate the Jewish view of the divine character. This contrasts with some modern discussions about the divine nature, which tend to reach theological heights far-removed from the life experiences of the common people and are, therefore, difficult to understand. People cannot identify with a God so far-removed from everyday life. Jesus and the rabbis used Jewish *agada*, that is, story illustrations, with a higher didactic purpose. *Agada* is designed to teach God's unlimited love. When Jesus says that God is like a noble landowner who is characterized by magnanimous generosity, the people could gain greater insight into God's nature. No Jewish teacher would claim that God is the landowner. But the wealthy landowner who is full of grace is like God, and he offers us a glimpse of the divine character. Divine grace is embodied in Jewish theology. The earthly world possesses a natural affinity with the spiritual dimension. The physical world in which we live and interact with others mirrors God's ways and reveals his concern for humanity. We are like the workers in the vineyard. He is like the generous landowner.

HEBREW WORD PLAY

The words of the landowner are very significant at the end of the parable. It is quite possible that a word play in Hebrew stands behind the conclusion of the argument which the landowner carries on with the disgruntled workers. When the workers who labored all day complain, the noble landowner says, "Take what belongs to you, and go; I choose to give to this last as I give to you. Am I not allowed to do what I choose with what belongs to me? Or do you begrudge my generosity? [literally, an evil eye is opposed to one who is good] (Matt 20:14–15)." The last verse contrasts the generous spirit of the landowner with the miserly selfish attitude of the angry workers: "Or is your eye evil while I am good?" The saying of the magnanimous landowner alludes to the Hebrew expressions "evil eye" and "good eye" which suggested the sharp contrast between a generous person full of kindness and a stingy, selfish individual. The generous person with a "good eye" is driven by a concern to help others and to see their needs met. The selfish person is consumed by one interest: what belongs to him or her.

Not only is there a hint of the Hebrew idiom "good eye," which means "generosity,"[11] but also Hebrew-speaking listeners might have discerned a play on the similar sounding words "mine" *shele* and "yours" *shelkha*. Perhaps it would be something like the equivalent English phrases "mine" and "thine." At least when I read a similar saying in Jewish literature about the four kinds of people, it seemed that a form of this saying stood behind the Hebrew word play in the parable. What is God like? In the Jewish view he is greater than any human being in his infinite grace. However, to understand him one must draw a comparison between known human qualities and the unknowable, incomprehensible, divine character. Both the rabbis and Jesus drew upon comparison and contrast to help people understand: "He is like . . ." God may be compared to a gracious king or a noble landowner. Kings possess magnanimous generosity and care for people under their charge. At times a contrast is made by the rabbis. An earthly king behaves in such a way, but not so concerning the Holy One, blessed be he. God's grace and compassion far exceed that of any earthly monarch.

In human terms the rabbis spoke about four different types of individuals. Their rich humor is illustrated by this well-known saying:

Four characters of people:

He who says, what is mine *[shele]* is mine and what is thine *[shelkha]* is thine. This is the average type. [Some say it is the character of Sodom.]

He who says, What is mine is thine and what is thine is mine. He is ignorant.

He who says, What is mine is thine and what is thine is thine. He is a saint *[chasid]*.

He who says, What is thine is mine and what is mine is mine. He is wicked.[12]

The landowner in the parable speaks about what is his, which he gave generously to all the laborers. He also spoke about what belonged to the first workers, who vigorously complained about the landowner's generosity. The landowner is concerned about others. The disgruntled workers are only concerned about themselves. The function of the word play is ingenious and very creative in the Hebrew language, as it contrasts the two words, "thine" *shelkha* and "mine" *shele*. What is God like? He is not like three of the well-known four types of people. Rather, he is like the saint *[chasid]* who says, "What is mine is thine and what is thine is thine." The divine character is described in human terms that the people could comprehend in the rich world of Jewish parabolic teaching.

God's generosity far exceeds that of any noble landowner. He does not give us what we deserve. He deals with people according to his grace. The divine character is mirrored in the noble actions of the generous landowner of the parable. But the landowner of the parable is not like the reasonable businessmen who carefully calculate labor costs into their profit projections! Usually such businessmen are most concerned with how much profit they are able to pocket. Above all else they desire to eliminate the labor costs as much as possible. Unlike them, God is full of grace and compassion. Above all else, like the generous landowner in the parable, God desires to bless his people by meeting their needs.

The intricacies of parabolic teachings are revealed in the sophisticated way that the listener suddenly sees himself in
the story. Most Hebrew speakers who first listened to the
story, like many people today, would feel that the laborers
who complained about the latecomers possessed just cause in
their argument. As a result, the original listeners almost unintentionally find themselves becoming involved in the wage
dispute. Suddenly they step upon the stage to settle the
argument as they become a part of the story. We are like
the laborers who worked all day long and complained about
the landowner's generosity. Hence, it is not unusual to find
embedded in the narrative of the story parable two parallel
themes. It is a double-edged sword. Not only has God's nature
of grace and his character of love been revealed in a dramatic
story, but also the difficulty we have in receiving those latecomers is illustrated. The story illustrates God's grace and the
problem we face as we struggle to accept it. His just mercy is
extended for the latecomers as well as for those who labored
all day.

The faithful sometimes have difficulty receiving the wayward
into the family of God with love and acceptance. The latecomers are often rejected. The divine image is imprinted into
each individual regardless of race, ethnic heritage, or sordid
past. Every person is of inestimable value. Listeners discover
something about the divine character from the actions of the
landowner. But they are also challenged to be godlike in their
relationships with others. The divine image is revealed in the
parable on one edge of the sword. But the second edge calls
upon the disciples of Jesus to imitate those godlike qualities of
grace, compassion, and acceptance of the outcast.

The character of God is generous. He is like the person who
says, "What is thine is thine and what is mine is thine," in a
powerful Hebrew word play. The first group of laborers, however, wants more wages than they agreed to work for and begrudge the generosity of the landowner. Such an approach to
other people is unacceptable. The parable gives a solemn warning against this dangerous attitude. Especially in times of economic hardship, the laborers who were fortunate enough to
have worked all day are expected to rejoice because their co-
workers have received enough pay to feed their families. The
stern warning in such a parable must not be overlooked.

Other parables of Jesus address similar issues. The parable of the Pharisee and the Tax Collector and the parable of the Two Sons teach similar messages (Luke 18:9–14, Matt 21:28–32). People must love, forgive, and accept the outcast in the same way that God extends his grace, so undeserved and unmerited, to everyone who comes to him.

As a Jewish theologian, Jesus uses pictorial illustrations and metaphorical images to teach about God and his compassion. The word pictures make people think in concrete terms. For the Eastern mind theology should not be so philosophical that it misses the heart of the people. The stories of Jewish *agada* inspired the listeners to view God and his relationship to each individual created in the divine image in a fresh way. *Agada* engages the intellect but pushes beyond the mind to reach the heart and the imagination. Often the parables of Jesus made the people laugh. They are rich in Jewish theology from the creative thought of the Second Temple period. We must not overlook the Jewish theology in the stories which Jesus tells. After all, over one-third of his teachings are in parables. When we miss the parables in the richness of their Jewish culture, we miss Jesus and his powerful message.

God's grace is unfathomable. How can one grasp it? Jesus shows the way. He tells stories which shock and surprise us. When understood in the context of their original Jewish theology, the parables of Jesus sometimes make us laugh. His dramatic stories always manage to capture our attention as they illustrate the nature of God as well as our relationship with him and other people. We must be astonished at the parables once again in the same way the first audience was astonished. The Jewish setting allows us to experience the didactic humor and the shock element embedded in the plot of the story. The parables can help us love the way God loves because they show the essence of the divine character.

The grace of God is given to all in equal measure.

NOTES

1. See my extensive treatment of this parable in *Jesus and His Jewish Parables,* 259–66.

2. See the discussion of J. Jeremias, *Parables of Jesus,* 136ff. Jeremias claims that the parable shows the difference between two entirely

different worlds—that of Judaism and that of Christianity. He discusses "the difference between two worlds: the world of merit, and the world of grace; the law contrasted with the gospel." Even a great mind like that of Jeremias is sometimes prejudiced against seeing the grace in Jewish theology. Jeremias has not properly understood the rabbinic parable or its relationship to the parables of Jesus.

3. On the daily life of the worker see the fine work of M. Ayali, *Poalim Veomanim* (Jerusalem: Yad Letalmud, 1987), in Hebrew.

4. The best study of these texts appears in the work of David Flusser. See Flusser, *Die rabbinischen Gleichnisse,* 97f., and *Yahadut Umekorot Hanatzrut* (Tel Aviv: Sifriyat Hapoalim, 1979) 175–77. I have discussed these rabbinic parallels in *Jesus and His Jewish Parables*.

5. For readers interested in Hebrew philology, it is of interest to note the meaning of the term *vatik,* which is usually translated as meaning, "distinguished" (see the parable of the Industrious Laborer). On a recent trip to Jerusalem, David Flusser pointed out to me that the Hebrew term actually means one who is precise and is sharp to give attention to each detail. Perhaps the best lexicon which alludes to this meaning is Levy, *Wörterbuch über die Talmudim und Midraschim,* 1.506.

6. See Rabbi Zeira, j. *Ber.* 5c, chap. 2, hal. 8.

7. See the important article of David Flusser, "A New Sensitivity in Judaism and the Christian Message," republished from *Harvard Theological Review* 61 (1968) 107–27, in a revised form, in Flusser, *Judaism and the Origins of Christianity,* 469–89. This is a foundational work of supreme value in the study of early Christianity and its Jewish roots.

8. Midrash Psalm 26:3.

9. See Flusser, note 4 above.

10. Semachot de Rabbi Chiyah 3:2.

11. See Deut 15:8–9 and Matt 6:23. The expression "evil eye" appears in the wording of the parable, and the master implies that he is good, meaning that he possesses a "good eye." Dale Allison and W. D. Davies point out, "What is involved is the antithesis of generosity: selfishness, covetousness, an evil and envious disposition, hatred of others. Compare Matt 20:15: 'Am I not allowed to do what I chose with what belongs to me? Or is your eye evil because I am good?' This last means, as the RSV translates, 'Or do you begrudge my generosity?' Matt 6:23a–b, accordingly, tells us that just as a 'good eye,' a proper disposition towards others, is an effect of the light within, so similarly is a bad eye, that is, a selfish, ungenerous, miserly spirit, the companion of inner darkness. Or to put it another way, while inner light leads to loving one's neighbour, inner darkness leads to illiberality and niggardliness." See Davies and Allison, *Matthew,* 1.640.

12. M. *Avot* 5:13. I have learned from my friends in Korea and especially from the insights of Sarah Ahn that a similar word play

occurs in Korean. It probably has other parallels in late antiquity as well as in other languages. The word play is worthy of further research. Certainly in the Hebrew language the clever word play is particularly striking. The humor of the parables of Jesus, while difficult to appreciate fully because of language and cultural differences, often emerges clearly in his creative ways of illustrating his message. Humor is a forceful characteristic in the teachings of Jesus.

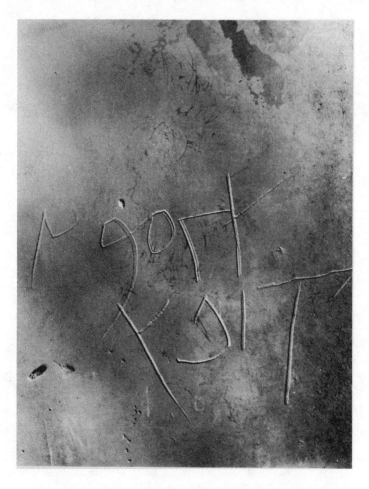

Close-up of the inscription, "Joseph son of Caiaphas."
Photo courtesy of the Israel Antiquities Authority.

Rosette decorations on the side of the "Joseph son of Caiaphas" ossuary. Photo courtesy of the Israel Antiquities Authority.

Close-up view of the rear [?] Joseph son of Caiaphas inscription. Photo Courtesy of the Israel Antiquities Authority.

13

The Compassionate Father and His Two Lost Sons

IN LUKE 15:11–32 JESUS TELLS A PARABLE ABOUT A FA-
ther and his two sons. Tradition has named this story
the parable of the Prodigal Son. It might be better
titled "the Compassionate Father and His Two Lost Sons." The
younger son is the prodigal who wastes his father's wealth.[1] He
asks for his share of the inheritance before his father dies,
converts it into cash, and departs for a far country where he
squanders the money. The elder son stays at home and works.
The compassionate father is portrayed as a helpless parent who
loves his sons. Although his two children make bad decisions,
he stands behind them with love when they need him.

When this parable is studied in its original Jewish context, the
traditional title, "the Prodigal Son," becomes misleading. Actually, the title that we know so well distorts the story's true
meaning. It is a story with three key actors, the father and his
two sons. The listener must pay close attention to each one of
these performers and ask questions about the story's setting in
life. Three questions need to be asked: What did the father
think when his younger son asked for his inheritance? How
should the elder brother have responded to the family crisis?
What laws governed inheritance? Here we must begin with the
cultural setting of the story and note some of the mistaken ideas
that have hidden the message of Jesus.

The parables of Jesus are a slice from the reality of life. By
means of characters, images, and settings which are familiar to
the audience, they teach a message concerning the nature of
God and the needs of human beings. After all, Jesus is a Jewish
theologian. He is a master at telling captivating illustrations.
Like so many of Jesus' other parables, this story about a father
and his two sons communicates a profound awareness of the

divine character. Sadly, however, this message is severely distorted when the parable is studied without sensitivity to its
original Jewish context. With colorful word pictures, Jesus illustrates his message of God's unlimited compassion and the great
need of every individual. Jesus teaches his theology by telling
parables. It is a Jewish way of teaching. These attention-holding
stories tell his listeners what God is like. They call each person
to make a decision. God's love is for everyone. God's deep love
is illustrated in the word picture of a father. People created in
the divine image are challenged to reach out, one to the other,
with the same kind of Godlike compassion.

THE FATHER AND HIS TWO SONS

Note carefully the first words of the parable, "There was a
man who had two sons" (Luke 15:11). Jesus tells a story about
a man and his two sons. The story deals with relationships
within a family circle. Not only does the parable teach about the
love of the father, it addresses the relationship between two
brothers. The behavior of the younger son, who becomes the
prodigal, is only a symptom of the real crisis. Even though the
father has great compassion, the family problems portrayed in
the parable are immense. Neither of the brothers understands
his father's love. Nor does one brother possess love in his heart
for the other.

Jesus emphasizes the connection between the brothers. He is
teaching about God's compassion and how people respond to it.
Jesus is not making a veiled attack against the Pharisees. Such
an approach, which criticizes the Pharisees, claims that they
opposed repentance and the acceptance of the outcast. New
Testament interpreters who make claims of this sort not only
misrepresent the core of the teachings of the Pharisees, they
completely miss the message of Jesus as well. They divorce his
teachings from their original setting.

The Pharisees emphasized the love of God. They taught that
God would receive with great compassion anyone who truly
repents. The rabbis, who were the spiritual heirs of the Pharisees, said that if a person would just take the first step toward
repentance, by making an opening as small as an eye of a
needle, God would take the initiative and receive that individual in love. For example, Rabbi Jose talks about God's great

compassion for the sinner who repents. He tried to describe divine love in vivid terms to drive home the message.

> By the verse, "Open to me" (Song Sol 5:2), the Holy One means, "Make for me an opening as big as the eye of a needle and I will make the opening so wide that wagons full of soldiers and siege battlements can go through it."[2]

Like Jesus the Pharisees believed that God was compassionate and desired to receive each individual who makes the first step. Divine grace is given to the sinner who repents and returns to God.

A reader looking for an attack upon the Pharisees in this parable will miss the point. Jesus intended each person to see himself or herself in this story. Each person who hears this story looks into a mirror. Jesus wants his followers to see themselves. When interpreters see the Pharisees, they miss the point of the story. Will one see the image of the father? Will one recognize his or her behavior in the actions of one of the two brothers? Each individual must carefully examine his or her image in the mirror of this parable. In the end the parable calls for a decision from the audience.

THE INHERITANCE

What did the father think when his younger son asked for his inheritance before his death? In reality, the younger son was asking his father to die. The strong element of shock and dismay felt by the original audience often is lost for the modern reader. The father in Jesus' story would have said to himself, "My son wants me dead." When the younger son asked to receive his inheritance early, his father understood what he was saying, as would any father in an Oriental cultural setting. A father would have been shocked and would have realized that his own son preferred his death to his life.

Both brothers, however, misunderstand their father. The younger wants to see him dead. The elder serves his father like a servant who desires eventually to receive a reward. Both brothers have a distorted view of their father. They see him as someone who pays a wage but has no generosity or grace. As a result neither of the brothers has a proper relationship with his father or his brother.

Many people want to live their lives without God. They want their inheritance but reject their relationship with God, the one who created them. They desire to be free of the Father's care. They are like the younger son who asks for his inheritance. He desires a life free of his father and without his brother. The parable communicates to these individuals who are found in every audience of the story.

The reality behind this dramatic story introduces the listener to God's incomprehensible compassion in the actions of the father.[3] When people reject a relationship with their Creator as the younger son in the parable did, they are saying that they wish God to be dead. They want to travel into a faraway country and live their lives as if God did not even exist. They do not comprehend the love and mercy that God gives to everyone who accepts his love.

In his book *Poet and Peasant* Kenneth Bailey has recorded one occasion in the Middle East where a son asked his father for his inheritance before his father died. The father was a physician and in good health. Bailey writes, "in great anguish the father reported to his pastor, Vilen Galoustian of Iran, 'My son wants me to die!' The concerned pastor discovered that the son had broached the question of the inheritance. Three months later the father . . . died. The mother said, 'He died that night!' meaning that night the son dared ask his father for the inheritance."[4] The shock element of Jesus' parable is extremely effective upon the audience. A son wants his father to die.

The Elder Brother

How should the elder brother have responded when his brother asked his father to drop dead so that the inheritance could be divided prematurely? In Jesus' story, it must be pointed out, the father actually divided his living between *them*, that is, between both brothers (Luke 15:12). The elder brother received his share of the inheritance along with his younger brother. But the older brother remains silent. He does nothing. The elder brother should have helped heal the broken relationship in the family. Within the cultural setting of the story, as elder brother, he had a strong responsibility to act as mediator in such a family crisis. Instead he gladly takes his share of the inheritance, which is twice as much as the younger brother's portion of the estate. His silence in the whole affair communicated a clear message to the original audience.

What were the laws of inheritance in such a situation? In Jewish law, as recorded in the Mishnah, the father was able to make a will before his death. He could take the initiative and divide the estate. In the case of the parable, the younger son initiates the process by asking his father to divide the inheritance, which would have included property, land, and all other family assets in the estate. The Mishnah specifically deals with the situation of the parable when a father divides the inheritance while he is still alive. His estate must be divided between both sons.

In such a case, however, the sons could not take possession of the property until the father's death. Hence the father was able to live off the estate's income until he died. The income could be invested into the estate and would be realized for the sons at the father's death. The sons could sell the property, but the buyer would not be able to take possession of the land until the father died. The son would have the right to ownership. The father could not sell the land, except for the limited period remaining in his life. So in essence, if the father sold the land, it would be as if the buyer were leasing it until the father died. The buyer could have possession of the land only as long as the father who sold him the property was still living. Moreover, the sons were also allowed by the law to sell the property, but with similar restrictions. Though the younger son is able to sell the property, the buyer could not take possession until the father died. Everything depended upon the death of the father. Transactions could be made. Money could change hands. The younger son could sell the property of the estate, but no land changed hands until his father's death. The Jewish law of inheritance from the Mishnah describes the situation in the parable of Jesus with precision.

> If a man assigned his goods to his son to be his after his death, the father cannot sell them since they are assigned to his son, and the son cannot sell them because they are in the father's possession. If his father sold them, they are sold [only] until he dies; if the son sold them, the buyer has no claim on them until the father dies. The father may pluck up the crop of a field which he has so assigned and give to eat to whom he will, and if he left anything already plucked up, it belongs to all his heirs.[5]

Joachim Jeremias, the noted New Testament scholar and authority on the parables of Jesus, summarizes the implications of the Jewish law in the Mishnah: "(a) the son obtains the right of possession (the land in question, for example, cannot be sold by the father), (b) but he does not acquire the right of disposal (if the son sells the property, the purchaser can take possession only upon the death of the father), and (c) he does not acquire the usufruct which remains in the father's unrestricted possession until his death."[6]

The conditions set forth by this law are reflected exactly in the details of the parable. The property remains like a trust for the father. He is able to give orders to the servants and maintain limited control over the estate (Luke 15:22–24, 31). The father has divided the inheritance between both sons, but the law of the Mishnah gives him a measure of control over the estate's assets until he dies. However, in the parable the younger son is able to realize the value of his share of the estate before his father's death. He probably sold the estate at a considerable loss because the buyer would have to wait until the father died in order to take possession of the property. The people hearing the story understand that the younger son is taking a third of the family's accumulated wealth, selling it at a low price, and running away from his father and his family's heritage (see Deut 21:17).[7]

The father allows his two sons to take advantage of their inheritance before his death. He is apparently in good health. He is victimized by his sons whom he loves. His heart is broken. He is a helpless parent. As a father he was able to provide love and guidance for his children, but his two sons possess freedom to make their own choices in life whether good or bad. Both sons are lost to their father but in different ways. The younger son leaves. The elder son is silent.

THE YOUNGER SON

The younger son wastes his inheritance. He goes to a far country. The story depicts the son as going as far away from his father and his brother as possible, just as many people try to run away from their Father in heaven. They travel to their own faraway country and seek to be completely free from the loving care of their Creator.

In the faraway country, the young man becomes desperate. A great famine sweeps across the country, causing extreme hunger and human suffering. Having expended all his resources, the younger son is forced to rely upon the benevolence of a non-Jewish foreigner. This man probably intends to run off the Jewish youth by telling him to feed pigs. As a Jew who humiliates himself by tending to the swine, the younger son probably expected some food from the foreigner who assigned him the unpleasant task. He was so hungry that he wanted to eat the pigs' food. No one will give him anything.

The younger son makes a decision. He decides to return to his father. Because of his enormous need, he is willing to do whatever is required. He is willing to pay back everything he has wasted by becoming a hired hand in his father's house (Luke 15:18). When he says, "I will arise and go to my father," he was saying, "I repent." He decides that he will return to his father's house. He realized that he had sinned against heaven, that is, God himself, as well as his father. In Jewish theology, the concept of repentance centers on the idea of return. The person who repents is restored by his or her return to the God who loves his people. The younger son changes directions. Instead of going into a far country away from home, he intends to return to his father's house. At this point, the son still does not comprehend the depth of his father's love and continues to view him as an employer. The father changes all this.

When his father sees him, he runs to receive him with great compassion. The father demonstrates his love and grace by running out to greet his lost son. The younger son does not have an opportunity to make a deal with his employer because the compassionate father completely restores him without condition. The lost son who has returned to his father must accept his position as a full member of the household. The clothes he receives indicate his restoration, and the ring the father gives him guarantees his position and his access to the father's support. The younger son is restored completely to the father's love. Because of the self-sacrificing compassion of the father, the son is restored. The broken relationship is healed. The father does not allow him to become a hired servant who receives his wages according to the work done, but he restores him completely into the household as his son.

When the elder brother hears that his younger brother has returned, however, he refuses to join the joyous celebration. He does not even enter the house. The elder brother resents his father's great joy concerning his brother's return. He has served his father faithfully and feels that his brother is unworthy to receive anything. The elder son has the same problem because he, like his younger brother, viewed his father as the employer who pays the wage. According to the custom of the period, he would have been expected at least to pretend that he shared his father's joy. Again the father expresses his compassion when his elder son humiliates himself in front of everyone. He goes out to the courtyard to discuss the matter with his angry elder son. But how does the story end?

The compassionate father and the unforgiving elder brother stand in the courtyard. The elder brother shouts, "Lo, these many years I have served you, and I never disobeyed your command; yet you never gave me a kid, that I might make merry with my friends! But when this son of yours came, who has devoured your living with harlots, you killed for him the fatted calf!" (Luke 15:29–30). The elder brother fails to comprehend his father's love. He thinks of his father as a man who has the money to pay his hired servants. There is no hint of family love in his words. He does not even accept the prodigal as his brother but calls him the son of his father. He doesn't really know about the activities of his brother, but he is quick to accuse. Characteristically the compassionate father again reasons with his elder son. The elder son was lost, too. The only difference is that his separation from his father's love is more difficult to recognize. The story does not conclude but is left open-ended. Perhaps that is the reason most commentators concentrate on the younger son and ignore the other lost son. No one likes a story without a clear ending.

THE MESSAGE OF LOVE

Jesus, the master storyteller, is reaching out to everyone who hears the parable. There is a drama. There is a stage. There are characters and an exciting plot. What will be the end of all this? Jesus wants the listeners to step up on the stage and determine the story's conclusion by their own response. Jesus has adeptly placed the mirror in front of his listeners. They see themselves and decide what will happen. In essence, Jesus is saying that the decision belongs to the hearer of the parable.

The listeners will decide whether the elder son will accept the father's love and demonstrate similar compassion to his lost brother.

The parable teaches God's grace. What is God like? He is full of compassion and grace. He allows his children to make their own decisions. In this respect he is like a helpless parent. No matter what terrible wrong they may work, however, the love of God is never limited. The grace of God is freely offered to both lost sons. The younger son was a rebel who needed the love, forgiveness, and acceptance of his father whom he spurned. The elder son was a dutiful son who had the same needs, even though he continued to live under his father's roof. Both had a distorted view of their father. A father's grace and acceptance are needed by every individual whether he or she realizes it or not. The elder son tried to earn the acceptance. The younger son rebelled against the father's love. But in each case the father's favor cannot be earned. The sons simply must receive the compassion of their father, and the elder one must forgive his younger brother. He is concerned about himself but not his brother. The father's love is a challenge. He is the model for his children. They must forgive one another in the same way that they have been forgiven.

THE JEWISH THEOLOGY OF GRACE

The Pharisees emphasized the magnitude of God's grace for receiving everyone who comes to him in repentance. In the parable of Jesus the loving father is the word picture describing the nature of God. This glimpse of the divine character has many parallels in Jewish thought. While the father plays the leading role, the actions of his two sons describe the problems of two different types of people. Both brothers need God's forgiveness. Neither is able to earn the father's compassion. But in the beginning both sons view their loving father as an employer who pays his workers for the job they do. As has been seen, the rabbis also emphasize the grace of God. The Jewish literature provides modern readers of the parables a window to the wider background of Jesus' teachings. God will welcome his wayward child who returns home. If people will crack open the door of repentance, God will do the rest.[8]

God's grace is given to all who will receive the Father's compassion. One should not serve God in an effort to win his approval. No one is able to do anything to make God love them more than he already loves them. No one is able to do anything to make him love them less. This is a major theme in Jesus' parable of the Compassionate Father and His Two Lost Sons. One can never earn God's love. In the Jewish literature a similar parable is told. The parable of "the Loving King and His Evil Son" illustrates the theme of repentance and God's desire for his children to return to him. The theology of the rabbinic parable of Rabbi Meir illustrates the approach of the Pharisees who believed that God forgives the sinner.

> "You will return to the LORD thy God . . . ," Rabbi Samuel Pargrita [perhaps of Phrygia] said in the name of Rabbi Meir: The matter can be compared to the son of a king who took to evil ways. The king sent a tutor to him who appealed to him saying, "Repent, my son." The son, however, sent him back to his father [with the message], "How can I have the effrontery to return? I am ashamed to come before you." Thereupon his father sent back word, "My son, is a son ever ashamed to return to his father? And is it not to your father that you will be returning?" Thus the Holy One, blessed be He, sent Jeremiah to Israel when they sinned, and said to him: "Go, say to My children, Return."[9]

The message of a father to his beloved son is clear. The son must not allow his shame to prevent him from receiving the unmerited grace of his father's compassion. The father pleads with his evil son, "Please return, my son, and I will forgive you for everything."

A parable teaches a message in concrete terms. The rabbinic parable of Rabbi Meir illustrates God's compassion for his people. The magnitude of his grace is so vast that he longs for the evil child to return home. In Jesus' parable, his Jewish theology portrays God's compassion to disobedient children in the image of a father and his two lost sons. The younger son wanted to live without the father. Many desire to go to a land far away from God because they misunderstand his true nature. Others try to earn his approval and can never receive an outcast with genuine love, forgiveness, and acceptance. Both lost sons need to experience the father's compassion in order to love one another.

THE COMPASSIONATE FATHER AND HIS TWO LOST SONS

The so-called parable of the Prodigal Son should be named the parable of the Compassionate Father and His Two Lost Sons. In many ways it illustrates the relationship of every type of person to his or her Father in heaven. The younger son is like so many people who do not want to be near religious faith. They choose their own way in rebellion. They run away from God and his compassion. On the other hand, the elder son is like so many who try to serve God in religious practice but misunderstand his great love. Rather than accepting God's unmerited grace and fostering a close relationship of trust, they try to earn divine favor. In Jesus' story the compassionate father is the key player and leading actor throughout the drama. He loves the rebel who plays the role of a sinner despised by all. But the father also loves the saintly son who is every bit as much a sinner as his rebellious brother. He is a respectable sinner, but surprisingly, his needs turn out to be very similar to those of his brother. Whether one has deep religious convictions or rejects faith in God altogether, the divine compassion is the same. The needs of both lost sons are met by the compassion of the father. He is without power when his sons make the wrong decision to reject his love. In spite of rejection, the father is waiting to receive his sons when they come to themselves and realize their need for fellowship with him. In their weakness the two lost sons look at their father more as an employer whom they must please rather than as a parent with whom they are able to develop a relationship of love and trust. Jesus tells his listeners what God is like and makes them see themselves in his ingenious illustration. The story has no conclusion. Each person must decide for himself how the parable will end. In the same way that God shows compassion for his children, they in turn must demonstrate love for one another.

NOTES

1. The word "prodigal" in the traditional title of the parable comes from the Latin adjective *prodigus* which means "extravagant" or "wasteful." The younger son wastes the inheritance he received from his father.

2. See Pesikta Derav Kahana 24:12.

3. Flusser has demonstrated this fact in *Die rabbinischen Gleichisse,* 57f.

4. Bailey, *Poet and Peasant*, 162, n. 73. Bailey's point is well taken. He has shed fresh light upon the cultural background of the parable, but unfortunately he allegorizes the parable to the extreme, somewhat like the church fathers. In spite of his contributions, Bailey does not understand the faith and piety of the Jewish people during the time of Jesus.

5. See m. *B. Bat.* 8:7, ET H. Danby, *The Mishnah* (New York: Oxford University, 1977) 377. See also the following note.

6. Jeremias, *Parables of Jesus*, 128–29. Compare the law of inheritance in the Mishnah according to Philip Blackman's translation: "This is the view of Rabbi Judah. Rabbi Jose says, It is not necessary. If one assigns in writing his estate to his son [to become his] after his death, the father cannot sell it since it is conveyed to his son, and the son can not sell it because it is under the father's control. If the father sold it, it is sold until he dies; if the son sold it, the purchaser has no claim therein until the father dies. The father may pluck up [produce] and feed it to whomsoever he pleases, but whatever he left plucked up belongs to his heirs" (m. *B. Bat.* 8:7; Blackman's edition, 4.212; and see b. *B. Bat.* 136a).

7. "In this case, since there were only two sons, the elder would receive two thirds and the younger one third of the property" (Fitzmyer, *Luke*, 2.1087).

8. Already in the second century B.C.E. we learn that Antigonus of Socho taught that one must not serve God in order to receive a reward. He said, "Be not like servants who serve the master for the sake of receiving a reward, but be like servants who serve the master not for the sake of receiving a reward" (m. *Avot* 1:2).

9. See Deut. Rabbah 2:24, ET, Soncino edition, 7.53. The rabbinic parable is based upon the biblical background of the prophet Jeremiah's words concerning the fatherhood of God and his desire for the people to return unto him (Jer 31:9, 20; cf. 3:12).

14

The Old Wine Is Better!

LUKE 5:33–39, SOMETIMES TITLED "THE QUESTION about Fasting," does not really deal very much with fasting. While it is true that Jesus is questioned concerning the additional fasts introduced to the Jewish liturgical calendar by John the Baptist and the Pharisees, Jesus does not answer the question directly. Should we concentrate on the question or on the answer? The answer possesses greater value. A deeper meaning of the story is to be found in Jesus' reply. Why does Jesus respond to a question about fasting by telling them that the bridegroom will be taken away? Why does he speak about the patch of new cloth in an old garment and new wine in old wineskins? Jesus evokes images of life, from the wedding scene to pouring new wine into old wine skins. What is the central point of Jesus' illustration? Jesus leads his listeners on a path of discovery. No one who has drunk old wine will desire new. The main focus of the teaching emerges in Luke's version when Jesus says, "The old wine is better" (v. 39).

In spite of the traditional title, fasting is not the major issue here. Although Jesus was asked about fasting, he wanted to say something more. He explained his own mission in terms the Jewish people of the first century could understand. When asked a question about fasting, Jesus took the opportunity to teach a deeper message. The message of Jesus was intimately related to his task and to his desire for the people's salvation.

FASTS—NEW AND OLD

Is fasting the issue? Many Bible students tend to overlook the final words of Jesus in Luke 5:39, "And no one after drinking old wine desires new; for he says, 'The old is better.' "[1] The Jewish liturgical year included a number of specified fast days for the entire nation. On Yom Kippur, the Jewish Day of

Atonement, for example, all the people afflict themselves and
fast, asking for God's mercy and forgiveness. The Pharisees
desired spiritual renewal. They wanted the people to be close to
God all the time. Also the movement of John the Baptist was
characterized by its urgency for spiritual revival.[2] This passage
indicates that both the Pharisees and John the Baptist instituted
new fasts to intensify the spiritual awareness of the people.

What did Jesus think? Jesus was spearheading a renewal
movement within the Judaism of his day. His approach to reform was much less radical than the Pharisees or John the
Baptist, though all of them desired a return to the people's
spiritual heritage. The fasting of John's disciples and the Pharisees was one way to call for revival. The disciples of Jesus
apparently did not observe these additional fasts. Jesus answers
the question about fasting with two parables. The form of these
two parables and their Hebrew background are firmly rooted in
the teaching of Jesus.[3] The structure of these parables of the old
garment and the wineskins, moreover, leads up to Luke's conclusion and forceful application in Luke 5:39 when Jesus declares that the old wine is better. The emphasis on the old wine
indicates that all the talk about fasting may not be the answer
for the true spiritual renewal. In modern times, however, Jesus'
saying about the old wine has been overlooked and sometimes
emphasis has wrongly been focused on the new wine.[4] No one
should forget that when it comes to wine, the old is better than
the new. Jesus seems to speak about the rich Hebrew heritage
of Judaism in his day with the highest esteem.

THE OLD WINE

The old wine refers to the ancient faith and practices of the
Jewish people. Then the question of fasting is related more to
these additional fast days, which were called by John the Baptist
and the Pharisees, and certainly not to the recognized fasts of
the Jewish holy days, which would be observed by everyone.
New fast days were used sometimes for encouraging members
of a particular religious order to express their identification
with their movement. These new fasts were being called in
addition to the accepted practice. The new fasts may be compared to new wine while the old wine is closer to the accepted
practices of the ancient faith. For genuine spiritual renewal,

according to Jesus, the people must return to the best of the old wine.

The purpose of Jesus was to revitalize the people spiritually by a revival through the old wine. He did not teach that Judaism should be abolished. Rather he compared the Judaism of his day to an old garment which needs mending or to old wineskins. Jesus was saying that the spiritual condition was not ideal. But certainly he did not desire to put away the noble traditions of the ancient faith. On the contrary, when he says that the old wine is better, he is upholding the finest contributions of ancient Judaism and seeking wholehearted reform from within. The old wine is the Judaism of his time. It is best.

Jesus wanted people to revitalize their faith in God. New fast days may not be the best way to pursue the path leading back to the old wine. He wanted to see fresh wineskins for old wine. The truth and grace of the ancient faith must be renewed for all the people. Men and women must embrace the ancient faith with their whole hearts and receive God's salvation.

The old wine is good. It teaches the way of life according to the faith in the one and only God of ancient Israel. But the old wine needs new wineskins. Men and women of God must be renewed in order to hold the old wine. Jesus points the people to the truth of God's love and grace on the basis of the best in the old wine. But fresh skins are required for the old wine!

In his study of these sayings of Jesus, David Flusser has rightly understood this meaning in Jesus' words.[5] While many New Testament scholars would deny the truth of Luke 5:39, "The old wine is better," Flusser has shown the clear authenticity of the saying in his careful study of the Gospels. Flusser notes, "The best opinion of Jesus' opinion about Judaism in his days would probably have been, if Jesus had said: 'Fresh skins for old wine!' "[6]

Sometimes almost unintentionally Mark's Gospel is studied without examining the sayings of Jesus in Luke. Since it is taught that Luke copied from Mark as his best source for Jesus' life and teachings, there is supposedly no reason to read Luke's version. Because of the accepted theory of Gospel origins, sayings of Jesus recorded only in Luke are not considered authentic. Luke is wrongly considered to be secondary to Mark in every detail. When we understand the work of R. L. Lindsey, the Gospel of Luke cannot be discounted as a late corruption of Mark's earlier version.[7] Luke's Gospel preserves vital testimony about Jesus that should be admitted as evidence in the study of

Jesus' life. The saying "The old wine is better" (Luke 5:39) cannot be attributed to the later church. In fact, it seems that the heretic Marcion was quick to delete it from his Bible because it spoke about Judaism in a positive way. Jesus was telling the people something about his purpose. He came to bring renewal and redemption through the power of the kingdom of heaven. His purpose was not to destroy the significance of Torah but to fulfill it. The old wine of Torah is best.

When it comes to wine, the rabbis, along with wine connoisseurs, would agree with Jesus. Old wine is better than new. The rabbis related wine to the study of Torah. The more one studies the Scriptures, the more proficient one will become. Knowledge of Scripture will change an individual's life. Concerning old wine and the study of Torah, the rabbis taught:

> One does not feel the taste of the wine at the beginning, but the longer it grows old in the pitcher, the better it becomes; thus also the words of the Torah: the longer they grow old in the body, the better they become (*Soferim* 15:6).

Jesus desired to see new wineskins—that is, a revitalized people—enjoying the best of the old wine. The old wine is best. A spiritual renewal is needed. The new fasts may contribute something toward this goal, but the future of the spiritual renewal will be linked more to Jesus and his disciples as they teach about God's reign than to the new innovative fasts being called for by John the Baptist and the Pharisees.

Jesus was not against the Judaism of his day. The ancient faith is like the old wine. He did not come to destroy the law but to fulfill it. He desired the revitalization of the faith—a renewed people, spiritually prepared for the best of the old wine.

THE BRIDEGROOM

Jesus speaks, moreover, concerning the bridegroom. In fact, the whole passage surrounds the image of the bridegroom. Why do Jesus' disciples not fast? The bridegroom is with them. The day will come when the bridegroom is taken. In Hebrew the term "taken" used in this context is a euphemism clearly understood to refer to death.

The bridegroom is for a wedding, the occasion of supreme joy in Jewish thought and custom. Great joy is reserved for the wedding ceremony. The exact opposite is the case for a funeral. The grief expressed at a funeral is the supreme act of mourning. Jesus combines the two strongest emotions of men and women: the great joy of a wedding and the solemn mourning characteristic of a funeral.

His purpose is to revitalize fresh skins for the best of the old wine. But he also speaks about his redemptive mission. He is the bridegroom! He brings joy which is compared to the happiness associated with the customs of the wedding. On the other hand, he also brings mourning.

When Jesus said, "But when the bridegroom is taken away from them," the people were probably puzzled. The word "is taken away" (in Hebrew *lukach*, in Greek *aparthē*) was another way of saying, "when he dies" or "when he is killed." Why must the bridegroom die? The term "bridegroom" could be associated with the coming of the messianic Redeemer (cf. Matt 25:6). The time will come when he will be taken; then his disciples will fast. In the puzzling saying of Jesus, one sees both joy and sadness interrelated. But how can one associate the joy of a wedding with the death of the bridegroom? Perhaps the answer to this question is related to the messianic task as defined by Jesus himself.

Jesus quite possibly alludes to Isaiah 53:8, where the same Hebrew word refers to the death of the suffering servant.[8] Joy is associated with the coming of the Messiah. But when the messianic idea is connected to the suffering servant in the words of the prophet Isaiah as Jesus taught in his prophecies concerning his death, a reference to the death of the bridegroom is not out of place. Both of the diverse feelings of joy and mourning may be associated with the coming of the messianic figure in the teachings of Jesus. At least in Isaiah 53:8, we read, "*He was taken away* from rule and from judgment. . . . For he was cut off from the land of the living*.*" Is it possible that Jesus makes a veiled mention of his death as the bridegroom?

Probably "The Question about Fasting" is more properly named, "Jesus Speaks Prophetically about His Sufferings." The bridegroom is here. Now is not the time for fasting. He brings renewal. He is fulfilling his mission. Renewed wineskins are being prepared for the finest old wine. But the day will come when the bridegroom will be taken. He will die. This also will be a part of his mission.

ANCIENT JUDAISM AND THE OLD WINE

The twin parables of "the Garment" and "the Old Wine"
make no sense when they are separated from their original
religious setting of the first century. The message of these parables must be heard as a dialogue within Judaism. Some of the
new efforts at reform such as innovative fast days will not
contribute to a deeper level of interaction with the ancient faith.
Jesus is an insider promoting renewal and reform from within
the system.

According to Jesus the old wine is best! We as Christians have
tended to view the Judaism of the time of Jesus in a negative
way. The teachings of Jesus, however, evaluate Judaism posi-
tively. When we prefer new wine, the message of Jesus is distorted. The followers of Jesus should be for Judaism and enjoy
the fine taste from the best of the old wine. A greater understanding of the Jewish roots of early Christianity will enhance
our appreciation of the theological depth of Jesus' message.

NOTES

1. The KJV translates, "The old is better," while the RSV renders the
text, "The old is good" (Luke 5:39). I believe that the comparative
meaning of the verse is the best translation for the context, "The old is
better *(chrēstoteros),*" even if we accept the better manuscript attestation for *chrēstos* "good." Translating *chrēstos* as "better" probably conveys the original meaning of the text more clearly. The old is better
than the new wine.

2. Thus we read, "The disciples of John fast often and offer prayers,
and so do the disciples of the Pharisees, but yours eat and drink" (Luke
5:33).

3. On the Hebrew background of the parables of Jesus, see the
discussion in my *Jesus and His Jewish Parables,* 40–42. On the parables
as traditional literature, see the fine work of David Stern, *Parables in
Midrash* (Cambridge: Harvard University, 1991) 34–37.

4. Luke 5:39, "And no one after drinking old wine desires new; for he
says, 'The old is better.' "

5. David Flusser, "Do You Prefer New Wine?" *Immanuel* 9 (1979)
26ff.

6. Ibid.

7. Lindsey, *Hebrew Translation of the Gospel of Mark.* This book is
much more than a Hebrew translation of Mark. It has a comprehensive

introduction to the Gospels and is vital for a proper understanding of the text.

8. Such an understanding of Isaiah 53:8 seems to be attached to Acts 8:33f., when Philip joined the chariot of the Ethiopian eunuch. The Ethiopian eunuch was a proselyte to Judaism who was reading from Isaiah and asked Philip for help in interpretation. The eunuch probably recognized Philip as a religious Jew or teacher of the law and so he believed that Philip could explain the words of the Hebrew prophet. Philip interpreted Isaiah 53:8 to the eunuch as referring to Jesus who had been killed. This story is deeply rooted in the best sources of Luke–Acts and represents an early understanding of Jesus' sufferings. See also the important work of A. Neubauer and S. R. Driver, *The Fifty-Third Chapter of Isaiah according to Jewish Interpreters* (1877; reprint, New York: KTAV, 1969). Though outdated, the work remains valuable.

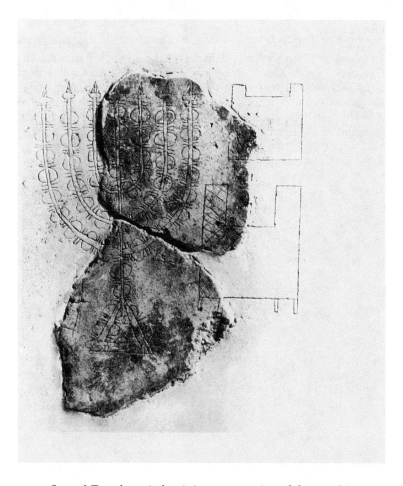

Second Temple period artistic representation of the temple's menorah, altar, and table of showbread.
Photo courtesy of the Israel Antiquities Authority.

15
Friends and Enemies in the Parables

T HE PARABLE OF THE GOOD SAMARITAN IN LUKE 10:29–37 is the classic form of the story parable. Parables are stories which communicate a message. The core message of the story rests upon the foundations of a strong Jewish theology about God and about each human being created in the divine image. As an artistic creation, the parable of the Good Samaritan has a structure which is similar to many story parables. It is a mini-play with members of a cast and a live drama which quickly moves from one scene to the next. The parable drives home a profound theological truth. It introduces the members of the cast, and then it takes the listeners on a journey in which they come into contact with the internal conflict of the drama. The resolution of the conflict communicates the deeper meaning of the story.

Parables teach truth on different levels. Probably the desired response to the parable of the Good Samaritan would be understood by every child. However, there is a deeper theological level of meaning.[1] The Jewish background of the mini-drama provides the key for understanding that deeper level of understanding in the message of Jesus.

The parables of Jesus are Jewish. The Jewish sources provide rich insight into the original meaning of Jesus' story. One must study the parables in light of early Jewish thought of the period in order to appreciate fully their deeper message.

JEWISH AGADA AS THE HEART OF JESUS' PARABLES

The core meaning of Jesus' parables is discovered in the rich heritage of Jewish *agada*, that is, telling an illustration to drive home a higher theological truth. Like the parable of the Good Samaritan, the world of Jewish *agada* often focuses on human existence as a reflection of God's creation. Every person is

important to God because every person is created in the divine
image. An example of Jewish *agada* in the Talmud illustrates
the message of the Bible so much more clearly than a sermon or
a commentary on the biblical account of creation.

The Talmud employs *agada* to communicate a deeper theological message. The story of "the Rabbi and the Exceedingly
Ugly Man" captures the attention of the audience and communicates a powerful theme from the theology of the Jewish
people.

> On one occasion Rabbi Eleazer son of Rabbi Simeon was coming
> from Migdal Gedor, from the house of his teacher. He was riding
> leisurely on his donkey by the riverside and was feeling happy and
> elated because he had studied much Torah. There he chanced to meet
> an exceedingly ugly man who greeted him, "Peace be upon you,
> rabbi." He, however, did not return his greeting but instead said to
> him, "*Raca* ["Empty one" or "Good for nothing"] how ugly you are!
> Is everyone in your town as ugly as you are?" The man replied, "I do
> not know, but go and tell the craftsman who made me, 'How ugly is
> the vessel which you have made.' " When Rabbi Eleazar realized that
> he had sinned, he dismounted from the donkey and prostrated him-
> self before the man and said to him, "I submit myself to you, forgive
> me!"[2]

Rabbi Eleazar son of Rabbi Simeon could not help himself
when he met the exceedingly ugly man. He was so ugly that
Rabbi Eleazar let what he was thinking to himself slip. But
when he comments on the appearance of the exceedingly
ugly man, everyone is shocked. The ugly man is much different
on the inside. The man was probably a day worker who did
not have the privilege of studying at the feet of a learned
teacher of Torah all day long like Rabbi Eleazer. Apparently
he did not have transportation. He walked by the river-
side while Rabbi Eleazer rode leisurely upon his donkey.
Surprisingly, however, the common man with an unseemly
appearance possessed greater Torah wisdom than the learned
rabbi who studied all day long. The day laborer was wiser
than the rabbi! The common people loved a story like this.
Each person could identify with the characters and their
conversation.

Every individual is created in the image of God. Even the
exceedingly ugly man was created according to the divine plan,
and his rich spiritual insight demonstrates his godlike characteristics. In Jewish theology love for each person is based on the

understanding of creation. God's goodness is discovered in the people he created. The story of the Rabbi and the Exceedingly Ugly Man is a fine example of Jewish *agada*. The theology behind the illustration is crucial. The same is true for the parables of Jesus. They are stories based upon the foundations of ancient Jewish theology.

THE THEOLOGIAN'S QUESTION

The parable of the Good Samaritan is an answer to the lawyer's question, "Who is a neighbor?" The lawyer asks a theological question, and it thus might be more appropriate to view him as a student of the Torah (in Hebrew, perhaps *ben Torah*), or in the English language the term "biblical scholar" or "theologian" would be similar in meaning. He is not a lawyer or attorney in the modern sense of the word, but a man devoted to the Scriptures. The theologian asks Jesus the rabbi, who is certainly also a Jewish theologian, this decisive question concerning loving one's neighbor. It is a legitimate question because the Hebrew word for "neighbor" can be translated and interpreted in different ways. In Hebrew, the word "neighbor," *rea*, in its stricter sense, means someone who is near to you. One who is near to you could be a friend but certainly not an enemy. Does Leviticus 19:18 teach, "Love your friends as you love yourself"? It depends on how you translate the word *rea*. Jesus answers the theologian's question with a parable.

THE LEADING ROLES

The three key actors in the story parable, namely, the Levite, the priest, and the Samaritan, all have a function to fulfill. In English when people hear the word "Samaritan," everyone is conditioned to think of a good person who helps others. But in the time of Jesus, no one would have associated goodness with a Samaritan. In the mind of the people, "Samaritan" was anything but good. The Samaritan was understood to be an enemy. Though Samaritans accepted the five books of Moses as authoritative for faith and practice, they rejected the oral law and were not considered to be Jewish. The Samaritans had a place of worship in biblical Shechem. On a number of occasions, historians of the period noted that civil conflicts erupted with Samaritans. Often the disorder resulted from religious issues and disagreements between the Samaritans and the Jewish people.

In contrast to the Samaritan, the Levite and the priest were true members of the Jewish community and served in the temple. Although they were descended from the priestly families, they had one thing in common with the Samaritans. The priestly class from the time of Jesus was almost exclusively composed of Sadducees, and like the Samaritans, the Sadducees rejected the oral law.

The oral law, which was accepted by the Pharisees and the majority of the people during the period, taught that preservation of life supersedes all other laws. The Sadducees, having rejected the oral law, interpreted the Scriptures in a literal fashion. They emphasized religious and ceremonial purity. Unlike the Pharisees who interpreted the law in a way to give it practical application in daily living while preserving its validity, the priests and Levites preferred to adhere to the letter of the law.

In the parable, the Levite and the priest avoid ritual uncleanness and do not give life-sustaining assistance to the man who fell among bandits. They are going down from Jerusalem to Jericho, probably after fulfilling their religious functions in the temple. They do not desire to become ritually unclean and do not wish to go through the process of ceremonial cleansing. They may have reasoned, "If the man is not dead already, he will probably die anyway." He is half-dead.

THE ORAL TORAH

The term "half-dead" probably refers to the Hebrew word *goses* which had a technical meaning in the Jewish oral law. The *goses* is a dying man who is in agony. According to the Jewish oral law, most of these individuals will die (b. *Git.* 28a). The rabbis were concerned that the *goses* would not receive adequate care. They ruled that the *goses*, i.e., dying person, must be treated as a living person in every respect (Semachot 1:1). All means must be used to save his life. He may perform all legal functions in regard to will and testament. Often the deeper meaning of the Jewish oral tradition is misunderstood. Accord-

ing to the oral tradition, every law in the Torah may be broken
if it will extend and save life. In fact, if it is a matter of life and
death, the letter of law *must* be broken in order to observe the
spirit of the law—which is to give life.[3]

What if the Levite and the priest thought that he was dead?
The written law teaches that a priest and a Levite cannot become ritually impure even for a member of their own family
(Lev 21:11). If they discovered a dead corpse in the middle of
the road, they could pass by on the other side, keeping the
proper distance, and thus protect their ritual purity. At least a
literal interpretation of the written law would prohibit a priest
or a Levite from burying an abandoned dead corpse. But this
violated the oral law.

The Pharisees lived by a different code. In the oral law they
have another tradition. The Oral Torah teaches that a person is
required to bury an abandoned corpse (in Hebrew, *met mitzvah*). In fact, they taught that though the high priest himself
may not become ritually impure to bury a member of his own
family, he is *required* to become impure in order to bury an
abandoned body. The Mishnah teaches, "The High Priest and
the Nazir do not become unclean for their relatives, but they do
become unclean for a *met mitzvah*."[4]

In either case, whether the unclothed, beaten man in the
middle of the road was dead or alive, the priest and the Levite
were required to stop. According to the oral law, they either
had to bury the dead or give life-sustaining assistance to someone in need. But they are Sadducees, and they reject the Oral
Torah.

The Samaritan stops. He reverses the actions of the bandits.
The bandits (1) stripped the man, (2) beat him, (3) abandoned
him, (4) and, having robbed him, left him half-dead. The Samaritan (1) bound his wounds by clothing the stripped man,
(2) poured on oil and wine where he had been beaten, (3) took
the man with him to an inn, (4) paid the bills of the man who
had been robbed. He gives healing and life-sustaining help. No
one could discern the identity of the person in need. Is he a
priest? Is he a Pharisee? Is he Jewish? Is he a Samaritan? His
clothes, which could identify him as belonging to a particular
community, had been taken. He was a person in need. Perhaps
the original audience anticipated the third player. They probably expected a Pharisee to play the role of the Samaritan.

After all, they believe in the oral law. Instead an enemy—that is, the Samaritan—appears in the story.[5]

MY ENEMY IS MY NEIGHBOR!

In listening to the story, often it is mistakenly thought that the neighbor is the one who needs help. The parable teaches that the neighbor is not the man in need of life-giving assistance but the enemy. The key for understanding the parable is Matthew 5:43, where Jesus teaches us to love our enemies. How is the word "neighbor" to be defined? How is one to answer the question? Only by assuming the position of one in need is it possible to recognize that a neighbor is actually the enemy. When a person is in need of life-saving assistance, even an enemy who behaves like a friend is welcome. One discovers reciprocity in Jesus' definition of neighbor. In order to understand the term "neighbor" one must be a neighbor. The enemy becomes the neighbor in the story. The Samaritan, who is viewed as an enemy, teaches what is meant by the word neighbor because he acted like a neighbor to someone who needed help.

Many listeners to the parable would have anticipated a different ending to the story. They may have thought that a Pharisee would wind up being the hero. After all, the Pharisees lived according to the oral law. Instead it is the enemy who is the neighbor to the one in need. Not surprisingly, the theologian understood the parable correctly. He was a Bible scholar. When Jesus asked him, "Which one of these three do you think proved neighbor *(rea)* to the man who fell among the robbers?" the student of the Torah answered correctly, "The one who showed mercy." He was saying, "Even my enemy is my neighbor."

One must not miss the connection between the Samaritan and the Sadducean priest and Levite. Not only do the priest and the Levite reject the oral law but also the Samaritans lived only by the written letter of the five books of Moses. From a religious perspective the Samaritan was endangering his ritual purity in the same way that the priest and the Levite may have become ceremonially unclean. The Sadducees were not willing to take the risk, but the Samaritan realized that saving life was the top priority. Moreover, the Samaritan was taking risks to help the man in need. After all, if the injured man died, he could be blamed for his death.

UNCONDITIONAL LOVE

The theologian who asked Jesus the question understood the parable perfectly! Included in the meaning of the biblical command to esteem "thy neighbor" is even one's enemy. The meaning of unconditional love for every human being created in God's image cannot be diminished. The esteem one demonstrates to his or her neighbor is not based upon what a neighbor has done to earn or merit love. Godlike love is for everyone, friend and enemy alike. Divine love is more powerful than human hate. Esteem for others mends the world. Jesus valued other people by word and deed whether they were considered friends or enemies. He taught his disciples to love their enemies (Matt 5:43). This is the main point of this sophisticated story parable. Now is the time to decide about unconditional love. Love demonstrates its force in action. To love one's enemy is to fulfill God's will. This is how one must translate the commandment from Leviticus 19:18, "Love even your enemy as yourself"!

In essence, the parable teaches Jesus' disciples that when one defines the word "neighbor," the message of reciprocity must be heard. In order to understand the meaning of the term "neighbor," first one must learn to behave like a neighbor. One must assume the position of someone in need. Each follower of Jesus must do something for an individual in need. What would we want someone to do for us, if we had the misfortune of being in a difficult position? To know what the word "neighbor" means, one must be a neighbor.

The parable of the Good Samaritan teaches the disciples of Jesus to love their enemies.[6] It is a story parable which reaches the listeners on different levels. The parable communicates its message to the uninitiated, but it also reaches the scholar and the theologian on a deeper level. Everyone should abandon prejudice and love all people—even someone who may be considered to be an enemy. The message of Jesus in the parables seeks a response. Jesus said to the theologian, "Go and do likewise."

NOTES

1. When he discusses complaint and theodicy in the parables, David Stern deals with the multiple themes and the deeper meaning of the story. "With this mashal, one begins to understand how the various

functional rhetorical-thematic categories overlap and coincide—not because the categories are inadequate but because a good mashal [parable], like any true fictional artifact, is more complex than a theoretical category will ever allow" (Stern, *Parables in Midrash,* 151).

2. B. *Ta'an.* 20a–b.

3. The oral law of the Pharisees and their rabbinic heirs placed extreme value on saving human life. The law *pikuach nefesh* (law of life, that is, preservation of life) or *safek nefeshot* (doubt for life, that is, danger of losing life) referred to the responsibility to save a life at all costs. Every law in the Bible must be broken to save a life. While some exceptions apply, see b. *Yoma* 85a and the Mechilta de Rabbi Ishmael on Exodus 31:12 (Horovitz 340–41). Compare also "*Pikku'ah Nefesh,*" in *Encyclopaedia Judaica,* vol. 13, cols. 509–10.

4. See m. *Nazir* 7:1 and compare the fine work of J. Mann, "Jesus and the Sadducean Priests: Luke 10:25–37," *Jewish Quarterly Review* 6 (1914) 415–22. See also E. P. Sanders, *Jewish Law from Jesus to the Mishnah* (Philadelphia: Trinity, 1990) 41ff.

5. See also Flusser, *Die rabbinischen Gleichnisse,* 70ff., and Young, *Jesus and His Jewish Parables,* 239–41.

6. Often the term "enemy" in the Gospels has been used to justify a wrong approach to pacifism. The word "enemy" should be studied in light of David Bivin and Roy Blizzard's *Understanding the Difficult Words of Jesus* (Arcadia: Makor Foundation, 1983) 106–10.

16
Faith as Chutzpah!

MANY CONFUSING DEFINITIONS HAVE BEEN PRO-
posed for the word "faith." Jesus tells stories
about people in everyday situations in order to
illustrate his Jewish theology about prayer and faith in God.
Jesus often surprises his listeners by using humor and colorful
word pictures to describe the higher divine purpose within the
human experience of living in a world which seems to be devoid
of God's presence. The essence of faith, according to Jesus, is
defined in parables. They portray a practical theology of prayer
which focuses on the nature of God and his love for every
person. What do the parables teach about faith and prayer?

Two partner parables of Jesus probe the meaning of faith in
the experience of his followers. The parable of the Importunate
Friend at Midnight (Luke 11:5–8) and the Unjust Judge (Luke
18:1–8), as they are traditionally called, deal with the life of
prayer and the disciple's faith in God. After a study of these
parables in the light of their Jewish background, it becomes
clear that in Hebrew Jesus could make a word play that would
compare faith to a form of the Hebrew term *chutzpah*. The
word *chutzpah* is difficult to define in a single word. It means
headstrong persistence, brazen impudence, unyielding tenacity,
bold determination, or what in current English terms might be
referred to as raw nerve. Can faith be described by the Hebrew
word *chutzpah*?

But the real issue with prayer concerns God. These parables
teach expectancy in prayer.[1] The great Jewish theologian Abraham Heschel noted that the real issue of prayer is how one
understands God.[2] It is not a problem with the words in a
liturgy or the proper formula for prayer. The difficulty of prayer
is the way one views the divine nature. The two partner parables, which I would prefer to name "the Contemptible Friend"
and "the Corrupt Judge," teach headstrong persistence in prayer.

One prays with bold determination because God is good. He is
not like the contemptible friend who would not help his neighbor. He is *not* like the corrupt judge who feared neither God
nor man and refused to help a needy widow. True faith requires
bold perseverance. Sometimes it is expressed by brazen impudence. True faith is committing all one knows about himself or
herself to all he or she knows about God. Faith can be defined
as *chutzpah*.[3] Persevere with unyielding tenacity.

The story in the parable of the Contemptible Friend describes
the actions of two friends. The cultural setting in first-century
Jewish village life is the background. In the Middle East the
obligation of hospitality was highly valued as an essential re-
quirement. At midnight the contemptible friend hears his neighbor's voice outside the house. The neighbor does not knock
because this would cause unnecessary alarm. He is recognized
by his voice. He explains that an unexpected guest has arrived.
By all custom and etiquette the neighbor must offer his guest
traditional hospitality. In many ways, according to the culture,
the visitor is not only the neighbor's guest but the guest of the
entire village. A dinner, including bread, the essential part of
every meal, must be prepared for the visitor. Everyone who
hears the story understands the situation. The time of night
emphasizes the urgency of the emergency. The listeners anticipate the answer of the friend inside the house.

What do the listeners expect? When they hear the story, they
expect the friend to open the door for his neighbor. He recognizes his neighbor's voice. In his kitchen he has what he needs.
Probably he will not only give him the bread but will load him
down with other food items to host the unexpected guest. Instead of providing the anticipated result, however, without even
opening the door, the contemptible friend answers with a feeble
excuse, "Do not bother me, the door is now shut, and my
children are with me in bed. I cannot get up and give you
anything" (Luke 11:7).

The outrage of the audience will be directed toward the unacceptable behavior of this friend. The only acceptable excuse
might be that he does not have any bread, in which case he
would open the door and give him other foods. Instead he
refuses. The children and probably everyone else nearby in the
village could have heard the dialogue in the still silence of
midnight in a small Galilean town. His excuse is totally unacceptable. Everyone hearing the parable will view him with ex-

treme contempt. They will complete the story because they know what the neighbor standing outside the house will do. Shamelessly he will pound on the door with bold tenacity.[4] The humor of Jesus emerges from the parable because he concludes the story by saying, "I tell you that he will not get up and give him anything because he is his friend, yet because of his bold persistence he will rise and give him anything he wants!" Here the Greek word *anaideia* is translated as "bold persistence." It is sometimes translated as "importunity" or understood as referring to boldness. The man outside the house demonstrates his brazen tenacity as he reacts to his friend's contemptible behavior in refusing to answer a simple request in the time of an emergency.

Literally, the Greek term *anaideia* translated here as "bold persistence" means shamelessness. It would appear that behind the Greek word in the Gospels stands a key Hebrew term. In the parable of the Corrupt Judge, the term is parallel to faith. When one studies these parables as twin illustrations, it becomes clear that faith is being defined in a mini-drama in which steadfast perseverance is depicted as the perfect example of true faith in the goodness of God.[5] The Greek word *anaideia* is not easy to translate into the original Hebrew idiom of Jesus' teachings. However, when *anaideia* is studied in light of the Jewish sources, the best parallel term in Hebrew is a form of the word *chutzpah*. Probably the Hebrew form *chatzufo* was the language of the Gospel parable. "Tenacity" or "bold persistence" would be good translations of this key term from the parable. Clearly the man displayed raw nerve or *chutzpah* in his bold persistence.

The widow in the second parable is described by her brazen tenacity. The corrupt judge is not concerned with equitable jurisprudence and fears neither God nor anyone. In the end Jesus says, "Hear what the unjust judge says. . . ." The term "unjust" is the same word used to describe the dishonest steward in Luke 16:8. The Jewish view of a magistrate possessed the highest concern for fairness and just judgment. The judge represented divine authority on earth and was required to make equitable decisions based upon all the evidence (2 Chron 19:6–7). In Sirach God himself is described as the just judge of the widow and the orphan.[6] In Jewish thought God is viewed as being greatly concerned about the well-being of the widow because she is an unprotected, and sometimes forgotten, member of society.

Saying that a judge does not fear God is a most serious charge. Apparently he is more concerned about himself than about others. The widow in the parable is at an extreme disadvantage because she possesses no influence. She cries out, "Vindicate me against my adversary!" Her adversary apparently controls a corrupt court by his powerful influence with an unscrupulous magistrate. Tenacity was the only weapon the widow possessed. She exercised her firm resolve and was tireless in her persistent requests to the corrupt judge. "For a while he refused; but after this he said to himself, 'Though I neither fear God nor regard man because this widow bothers me I will vindicate her or she will wear me out by her continual coming' " (Luke 18:9). Thus the story reaches its climax. The unjust judge passes a righteous judgment. The widow as the outcast is received and the villain magistrate becomes a hero of sorts. The judge does not change his philosophy of jurisprudence. The powerful judge, however, is beaten down by the determined tenacity of the helpless widow. Faith can be defined as bold persistence or raw nerve.

The rabbis possessed a high evaluation of *chutzpah*. When the Jewish literature is examined, a number of striking parallels are found which focus upon *chutzpah* as a valid expression of religious faith. In English raw nerve or bold persistence is not always considered polite. Certainly one should never approach God in such a fashion. Jewish literature, however, is replete with examples of bold persistence in the relationship between the one holy God and humankind. As Abraham argued with God in dialogue, other leaders in Jewish history sometimes employed boldness in their prayers. What is fascinating about the use of a form of the term *chutzpah* in the teachings of Jesus is the fact that a parallel rabbinic parable employs the same terminology.

On one occasion Rabbi Akiva described himself and his prayers for rain by comparing himself to someone who possessed bold persistence or raw nerve. He does this by telling a parable. In the parable we discover a clear parallel to the use of the Greek term *anaideia* "bold persistence" in the Hebrew word *chatzuf,* which is another form of the term *chutzpah*. In Hebrew the term *chutzpah* can describe a positive characteristic. In times of drought both Rabbi Eleazer and Rabbi Akiva prayed for rain by calling a fast. Rain did not come after the fast of Rabbi Eleazer. However, as soon as Rabbi Akiva offered his prayer to

God, the answer came and rain began to fall. The people were in awe of this astounding miracle, which created some tension with Rabbi Eleazer, who was older than Akiva. In fact, Akiva was one of Eleazer's students. How can the student's prayer have more influence in heaven than the petition of his teacher? Before the people became too excited about the miraculous answer to Akiva's prayer, he told them a parable, "It is like a king who had two daughters: one was tenacious (*chatzufa*) and the other was gracious (*kashirah*). . . ." Akiva had captured everyone's attention with his humorous and appealing illustration.[7] Everyone wanted to know about a king with two daughters like that. The word I have translated as tenacious is a form of the Hebrew word *chutzpah,* which is closely related to the Greek term *anaideia* in the Gospels. She possesses bold determination. His other daughter is proper and polite.

Rabbi Akiva explained that whenever the tenacious daughter made a request, the king fulfilled it immediately in order to get rid of her. On the other hand, whenever the gracious daughter appeared before the king with a request, he prolonged his interview with her because he enjoyed listening to her conversation. In his characteristic cleverness Akiva had explained that although his prayer was answered promptly, he is like the tenacious daughter who possessed headstrong persistence. Her father wanted to finish with her in a hurry. Rabbi Eleazer, on the other hand, was like the gracious daughter who possessed all the proper and appealing qualities everyone admired in Rabbi Eleazer. While the parable alleviated the tensions between Rabbi Eleazer and Rabbi Akiva, both daughters of the king possessed good qualities. But the tenacious one received a more prompt reply.

On another occasion when Rabbi Samuel the Short prayed for rain by a fast, the rain came after the fast was completed at sunset. Samuel the Short did not want the people to feel like they had earned God's favor by special merit of the fast. God's grace cannot be earned by merit in the view of the rabbis. He illustrated the point. "I will tell you a parable. To what may the matter be compared? To a servant who requested a reward from his master. [His master] said to them, let him wait until he has languished and grieved himself and then give him [his reward]" (b. *Ta'an.* 25b).[8] The need for perseverance with expectant prayer is the message of the parable of Rabbi Samuel the Short. Sometimes the position of the faithful is one of waiting before God. After fasting and prayer, the rains came. Everything depends upon the goodness of the master. The parable encourages faith in God as one practices perseverance in prayer.

Perhaps one of the greatest examples of bold determination from the rich Jewish heritage of Jesus in the days of the Second Temple occurs in the story of Choni the Circle Drawer. Because of the severe drought, the people approached Choni and asked him to pray for rain. When Choni prayed and no answer came, he took decisive action, which offended some of the religious leaders of his day. Choni had the audacity to draw a circle in the dirt and pray to the Almighty, "I will not move from this circle until You send rain." The miracle happened! The much-needed rain fell. The leader of the Pharisees, Simeon ben Shetach, was deeply offended by such impudent action and sharply criticized Choni. He sent Choni a message declaring that if anyone other than Choni had taken such bold action, he would have excommunicated him. However, because Choni had not violated the law and his prayer was miraculously answered, Simeon merely sent a warning. What could be done to Choni? Choni, Simeon explained, serves God like a child because a son can act with bold tenacity toward his father and have his request granted. He said, "What can I do to you? You act with impudence against the Omnipresent and he performs your will, like a son who acts with impudence against his father and he performs his will!"[9] The talmudic story describes Choni and his raw nerve in a positive manner, even though Simeon ben Shetach criticized his bold initiative. Choni's strong-willed perseverance is a true expression of his devout faith in the goodness of God.

In the Talmud, *chutzpah* is valued as a positive characteristic. Rabbi Nachman observed that "bold persistence *(chutzpah)* even against heaven is of avail." Rabbi Sheshet said, "Bold persistence *(chutzpah)* is a kingdom without a crown" (b. *Sanh.* 105a).[10] The individual must take bold initiative as a response of faith. One asserts him- or herself in an unyielding tenacity. Rabbi Abahu describes Moses in this way. The Bible tells us that when the people of Israel sinned by worshipping the golden calf in the wilderness, God was angry. He declared to Moses that he would destroy the people. Moses pleaded with God to forgive and pardon the people. Rabbi Abahu compared Moses to a man who grabs his fellow by the garments to demand action. Even Moses could use unyielding tenacity in crying out to God with an urgent need. Rabbi Abahu explained, "Were it not explicitly written, it would be impossible to say any such a thing; this teaches that Moses took hold of the Holy One, blessed be He, like a man who seizes his fellow by his garment and said before him: Sovereign of the Universe, I will not let You go until You forgive and pardon them."[11]

In a similar way Jesus of Nazareth teaches that faith is like determined perseverance. In a number of the healing stories in the Gospels, Jesus responds to an individual who has demonstrated strong-willed determination by saying, "Your faith has saved you." When the friends of a paralytic made great efforts to bring their sick friend to Jesus in spite of the crowds, the Gospels say that Jesus saw their faith.[12] They had displayed bold persistence. The woman with a hemorrhage showed firm resolution when she pressed through the crowds around Jesus and touched the hem of his garment, which no doubt referred to his prayer fringe.[13] Jesus said to her, "Your faith has saved you." Luke's Gospel describes the woman who burst into the house of Simeon with a bottle of ointment. She poured it on the feet of Jesus and by her actions gave evidence of her rigid persistence and raw nerve. Her faith, Jesus remarked, had saved her (Luke 7:50). In Matthew's account of the story of the Canaanite woman who steadfastly begged Jesus to heal her child, he described her actions as demonstrating her faith (Matt 15:28). She would not give up. When Jesus said that he was sent only to the lost sheep of the house of Israel, she persisted. When Jesus encountered her unyielding determination, he declared, "Great is your faith!" The example of the blind man in Jericho is very much to the point. When he heard that Jesus was passing by, he began to call out in a loud voice, "Jesus, Son of David, have mercy on me!" The people around him rebuked him and told him to be quiet. He was relentless. He showed brazen tenacity. The blind man shouted out with stubborn persistence and Jesus healed him saying, "Your faith has saved you" (Luke 18:42; Mark 10:52). The firm determination of these individuals who approached Jesus with their needs and Jesus' affirmation of their faith demonstrates the qualities of the Hebrew term *chutzpah.*

The twin parables of the Contemptible Friend and the Corrupt Judge illustrate the need for faithful perseverance in prayer. They betray the use of the Jewish principle of *kal vechomer,* which deals with the light, *kal,* side of an argument, and the weighty, *chomer,* side.[14] The rabbis often expressed this principle by the term *al achat kamah vekamah* "How much more . . . !" On the

light side of the argument, if it is true that a contemptible friend
who will not even assist his neighbor with three loaves of bread
at midnight will be moved to action by the tenacity of the
petitions of his neighbor, how much more, on the weighty side,
will the merciful God be moved by the prayers of his people.
If, on the light side, a corrupt judge will give an equitable
decision in favor of a helpless widow because of her bold persistence, how much more, on the weighty side, will God grant
the steadfast petitions of those who serve him. Clearly Jesus is
employing the well-known principle of *kal vechomer*, that is, the
light and the weighty. God is not like the contemptible friend.
He is not like the unscrupulous magistrate. God is good. He is a
trustworthy friend and a fair judge. Jesus uses irony and humor
to illustrate the nature of God. The issue of prayer is God.
People mistakenly pray as if God is a friend who does not care
or a judge who does not deal justly. By role-playing with the
divine nature, and by using an exaggerated characterization of
what God is not like, Jesus teaches his followers what God is
like. In many ways the theme of these colorful illustrations can
be summarized by saying, "God is your good friend." Because
God is good, perseverance in prayer will receive the answer.
Faith in God is defined as bold persistence.

With their clever use of humor and irony, the parables of
Jesus probe the true essence of faith in the experience of prayer.
When we realize what God is like, we will be able to approach
God in faith. The rabbis such as Simeon ben Shetach offer
valuable warnings about taking the concept too far. Perhaps
even Choni would recognize the limitations of such an approach
when it is divorced from the proper lifestyle of Jewish piety. At
least Choni's faith was evidenced by his holy life. Nonetheless,
according to the parables of Jesus, faithful persistence in prayer
reaches the God who cares about his people. In the metaphorical world of the parables of Jesus, faith may be defined in
Hebrew thought by the word *chutzpah*.

NOTES

1. In modern New Testament scholarship different approaches have
been advanced for these parables. Jeremias, *Parables of Jesus*, 146–60,
emphasized the endurance needed for the final tribulation and regarded eschatology as the theme. The end times is an important mes-

sage in the parables. Bailey, *Poet and Peasant,* 119–41, emphasized the shame-and-honor society of the Middle East. Fitzmyer, *Luke,* 2.909–13, correctly criticized Bailey. By overemphasizing side issues, these modern studies sometimes miss the strong theme of prayer and the divine nature within the context of ancient Judaism. Soon I will publish a longer treatment of these two parables which will deal with these issues. See now the excellent discussion of Flusser, *Die rabbinischen Gleichnisse,* 85ff. In my *Jesus and His Jewish Parables,* 28ff., I have discussed many of these issues. In a future study I plan to publish further documentation for the approach taken here in this concise study. In an oral presentation of this material, I was encouraged by Cyrus Gordon's remarks when he said that the research for the approach taken for these two parables from Luke was compelling and convincing.

2. See A. J. Heschel, *Man's Quest for God: Studies in Prayer and Symbolism* (New York: Scribner's, 1966) 87. Heschel observes, "The issue of prayer is not prayer; the issue of prayer is God." On the Jewish concept of God, see also the significant contribution of David Wolpe, *The Healer of Shattered Hearts: A Jewish View of God.*

3. See Billerbeck, *Kommentar zum Neuen Testament aus Talmud und Midrasch,* 2.187. See Sokoloff, *A Dictionary of Jewish Palestinian Aramaic,* 213. The word *chutzpah* has a number of forms. In its Aramaic form it is written with an *aleph* instead of a *he.* In mishnaic Hebrew also the form *chatzuf* is used. One rabbi is called Rabbi Chutzpit (literally, "Rabbi Tenacity"), and he is considered to be a great scholar.

4. One MS of the Latin Vulgate adds the comment "Yet if he will continue knocking . . ." at the beginning of verse 8. New Testament scholar A. Resch viewed it as an original part of the parable. See his *Die Logia Jesu* (Leipzig: J. C. Hinrichs'sche Buchhandlung, 1898) 75. While the reading is certainly secondary, it does reveal an early interpretation of the parable which is valid.

5. R. L. Lindsey has viewed these parables as being taught on the same occasion. He has convincingly suggested that the original order of the story in the text of Jesus' life may have been Luke 11:1–4, 9–13, 5–8, 18:1–8.

6. See Sir 35[32]:14–18 (for the Hebrew text and a commentary see the fine edition of M. Segal, 220).

7. See L. Finkelstein, *Akiba, Scholar, Saint and Martyr* (New York: Atheneum, 1975) 105f. and the work of S. Safrai, *R. Akiva Ben Yosef* (Jerusalem: Bialik Institute, 1970) 37–38 (Hebrew). The parable of Rabbi Akiva appears in j. *Ta'an.* 66d, chap. 3, hal. 4, and see also b. *Ta'an.* 26b.

8. David Flusser spoke with me about the importance of this rabbinic parable and its relationship to the Gospel texts (private communication). I appreciate his rich insights.

9. See m. *Ta'an.* 3:8 and parallels. See the study of G. Vermes, *Jesus the Jew,* 58–82. Jesus and Choni received similar criticism. This fact makes one read the Gospels with a greater appreciation of the Jewish context. Jesus was not against his people. See the discussion of David Flusser in the foreword to Lindsey, *A Hebrew Translation of the Gospel of Mark,* 5. See also the chapter here, "Miracles, Proclamation, and Healing Faith."

10. The fine English translation of the Talmud published by Soncino Press renders *chutzpah* in this text as "impudence." It is a notoriously difficult term to translate with an exact English equivalent. Here "bold persistence" has been used. Perhaps "strong-willed tenacity" would also convey the idea of the term.

11. See b. *Ber.* 32a and the fine discussion of A. Heschel, *Torah Men Hashamayim,* (New York: Soncino Press, 1972) 1.196.

12. Luke 5:20; Matt 9:2; Mark 2:5. Lindsey has often spoken of faith in this way. I am grateful for his insights into the meaning of faith in the Gospels. Students of the Gospels will benefit from his work *A Comparative Greek Concordance of the Synoptic Gospels.* See especially the entry on the word "faith."

13. This fact has often been brought to the attention of Christians by Roy Blizzard. See the references to faith in Luke 8:48; Matt 9:22; Mark 5:34.

14. See my *Jesus and His Jewish Parables,* 28ff.

17

The Pharisee and the Tax Collector

He also told this parable to some who trusted in themselves that they were righteous and despised others:

"Two men went up into the temple to pray, one a Pharisee and the other a tax collector.

The Pharisee stood and prayed thus with himself, 'God, I thank thee that I am not like other men, extortioners, unjust, adulterers, or even like this tax collector. I fast twice a week, I give tithes of all that I get.'

But the tax collector, standing far off, would not even lift up his eyes to heaven, but beat his breast, saying, 'God be merciful to me a sinner!'

I tell you, this man went down to his house justified!" (Luke 18:9–14).

THE FIRST RESPONSE TO JESUS' STORY ABOUT TWO men who went up to the temple to pray is, "I am certainly glad that we are not like those Pharisees." But that is exactly what the Pharisee said about the tax collector! What did Jesus really desire to communicate when he told this humorous illustration?

The parable of the Pharisee and the Tax Collector frequently is interpreted in a way which vilifies the Pharisees but extols the preeminence of Christianity over Judaism. Is this what Jesus wanted? The original message of Jesus is lost when we as Christians give praise to ourselves that we are not like the Pharisees. The obvious problem with an understanding that sharply contrasts Judaism and Christianity emerges from the drama of the parable itself. As a result, we as Christians ironically behave in a manner nearly identical to the dramatization of the Pharisee in the parable. In Luke's words we trust in ourselves that we are righteous and despise others (Luke 18:9).[1] As a result of our religious bias, we allow the first-century context of the parable to fade from view.

Is it possible to listen to the story apart from the prejudice of the past? I believe that the centuries-old barriers to the original meaning of the parable are not insurmountable, but many difficulties beset a historical study. The first great problem is the strong negative connotations for the term "Pharisee" in English. This problem is foremost in the study of the dramatic story. After all, Pharisaism as found in our dictionaries is defined as a synonym for hypocrisy. The name Pharisee itself evokes a very different image for today's English speaker than it would have for the average first-century person. A Jewish audience of the first century was not oblivious to the shortcomings of some Pharisees; nonetheless, that audience possessed a positive evaluation for the foundations of Pharisee theology and the rich spiritual heritage of a movement that called for the renewal of genuine faith and practice among the people. The Pharisees were respected for their reverence and for their contributions to the spiritual well-being of the nation. By way of sharp contrast, the image of a Pharisee in modern usage is that of a self-righteous person.

Another barrier hindering our understanding of the dramatic story concerns the prominence of the temple in the parable. The role of the temple in the worship of ancient Israel must be carefully studied, since the parable itself assumes a background in the temple. The stage is set for the Pharisee and the tax collector to step into location. Could this parable have been developed after the temple was destroyed? Some New Testament scholars have questioned the authenticity of the parable, claiming that the early church invented the story apart from the teachings of Jesus. Would the early church describe an individual as receiving forgiveness and justification during the sacrificial service in the temple? Perhaps a strong argument for an earlier date of the parable and its place in the Gospel of Luke is discovered here. The later church community would not invent this story and attribute it to Jesus. The realistic character of the parable's background indicates that it possesses deep roots in the historical setting of the people of Israel before the destruction of the temple in 70 C.E.

Even today the careful listener can still sense the keen wit and the strong personality of Jesus in the theme of contrasts. The tables are turned as the seeming villain of a story behaves like a hero. Listeners are astonished when their preconceptions of which character is a good person turn out to be false. An "evil" tax collector humbles himself and sincerely prays to God for forgiveness, whereas a "holy" Pharisee is not as righteous as everyone assumes. The word for tax collector in the parable is sometimes translated as "publican." The tax collector was a public official who gathered the revenues for the government. These publicans collected taxes and were viewed as friends of Rome who made themselves rich by pocketing large amounts of money in excess of what was required by law. The listeners realize that although the publican collected taxes for a hated regime, he recognized his own need for God's mercy. The two individuals, one symbolizing good and the other evil, surprise the listeners by their unexpected behavior. The Pharisee was considered to be holy and righteous in the eyes of the first-century Jewish audience. The story is a live drama accompanied by the rich humor which is so characteristic of Jesus' parables. The artistry of the story would have delighted the original listeners. The bad is good and the good is bad. So while certain problems beset properly understanding the parable in its historical context, the point of challenge within the story remains sharply in focus.

The Gospel teachings of the parables are best viewed in their original Jewish setting. The literature of Israel's sages preserves rich insights for the proper understanding of the Pharisees and the central position of the temple in the religious life of pious Jews before the glorious sanctuary was destroyed by the Romans in 70 C.E. Moreover, our study of the parable will demonstrate that the Jewish teachings concerning the proper attitude of the heart (*kavanah* in Hebrew) are essential background materials for the parable.

THE PHARISEES

The original audience listening to the story did not consider the Pharisee to be a stereotype of the self-righteous hypocrite. On the contrary, the Pharisees were respected for their sincere piety. John Crossan captures the essence of the problem when he suggests a humorous modern equivalent, "A pope and a pimp went into St. Peter's to pray."[2] The contrast between a pope, who is naturally considered holy, and a pimp, who is obviously unholy, drives home the point of just how unexpected the behavior is for the leading roles in this drama. Two men go up to the temple to pray. One is viewed as holy, and the other is wicked. The parable invites parody of the exaggerated actions of the main characters.

A Pharisee in the mind of the people of the period was far different from popular conceptions of a Pharisee in modern times. The widely read book on the parables of Jesus by George Buttrick goes so far as to say that the Pharisee had no God. In order to explain the parable, Buttrick launches a strong assault on Pharisaism by saying:

> Pharisaism has no friends and no friendliness, for it is cursed by the inward-turning eye and looks not on the "things of others" except to feed its own conceit of character. Pharisaism has no hope, for it has already attained. It has no God, for it feels no need of God.[3]

Is Buttrick suggesting that the Christian should be thankful that he or she is not like the Pharisee? Despite all the honor due Buttrick for his rich contributions to biblical studies, on this point I must strongly disagree. Jesus is not attacking the theology of Pharisaism in this parable but addressing the need for sincerity when one directs his or her heart to God in prayer. On the contrary, Jesus never criticized Pharisaism as a religious movement. He did, however, sharply rebuke the hypocritical behavior of some Pharisees. Instead of hearing the message of the parable and its warning against self-righteousness, Buttrick has fallen prey to his own bias against the Pharisees, and thus he has missed the focus of the story.

The image of the Pharisee in early Jewish thought was not primarily one of self-righteous hypocrisy. While Jesus disdained the hypocrisy of some Pharisees, he never attacked the religious and spiritual teachings of Pharisaism. In fact, the sharpest criticisms of the Pharisees in Matthew are introduced by an unmistakable affirmation, "The scribes and Pharisees sit on Moses' seat; so practice and observe whatever they tell you, but not what they do; for they preach, but do not practice" (Matt 23:2–3). The issue at hand is one of practice. The content of the teachings of the scribes and Pharisees was not a problem.

Archaeology and rabbinic literature have clarified the meaning of the term "Moses' seat" from the words of Jesus. A chair carved out of basalt stone has been discovered in excavations of a synagogue in Chorazim, a city in which Jesus preached.[4] The

city is located north of the Sea of Galilee, and although the
synagogue itself in which the chair of Moses was found is not as
early as the first century, archaeologists believe that it is similar
in architecture and structure to the synagogues contemporary
with Jesus. The chair in and of itself is a magnificent discovery.
Because it is fashioned from native stone, the chair seems to
capture something of the geographical surroundings as well as
the essence of the religious experience of the people in this
village of Galilee. The learned religious leaders of the community would sit upon the stone chair and share their teachings
concerning Torah. While the "seat of Moses" is mentioned specifically in the Jewish literature, the archaeological find provides a vivid picture of daily life. The homiletical midrash
Pesikta De Rav Kahana, which preserves so many fine holy day
sermons from the early synagogue, actually refers to the "seat
of Moses" by name.[5]

Moreover, in yet another parallel from rabbinic literature, the
archaeological discovery is brought to life as the ancient Jewish
sources describe the lively discussions among rabbis in the story
of "the Stone Chair and Mount Sinai." The context of this
reference to a stone chair involves the heated arguments between two rabbis. Jewish culture of the period encouraged free
thinking, creativity, and innovative methods of studying the
deep meaning of Torah. In fact, sometimes it is quite surprising
for many who are untutored in the methods of Jewish education
to discover that the rabbis encouraged diversity of opinion and
freedom of expression.

A stone seat is described in rabbinic literature where Rabbi
Eleazer was accustomed to sit and teach. Not everyone in the
community accepted Rabbi Eleazer's message even though he
was an influential spiritual leader. It was common knowledge
that Rabbi Eleazer often had serious disputes with the well-
known and highly esteemed sage Rabbi Joshua. For the record,
their strong disagreements became legendary in rabbinic literature. Rabbi Eleazer and Rabbi Joshua both represented
powerful streams of thought in their respective teachings. They
engaged in fierce debates pertaining to vital issues of Jewish
religious life. The culture of Pharisaism, as well as rabbinic
discussion, fostered creative approaches to the study of the
written and oral law. Often divergent views would emerge
from the scholarly occupation with Torah. Careful debate becomes a way to achieve a greater appreciation of the deep

meaning of the Scriptures. Originality of thought and innova-
tion frequently will invite opposing views. Hence the Jewish
approach to the study of the Scriptures created an atmosphere
which encouraged rich diversity of opinion within a common
framework.

Even though strong opinions were held by leading teachers
who disagreed with one another, a degree of honor was given to
different views. The strong differences of opinion between these
two prominent rabbis must be understood in order to appreciate
Rabbi Joshua's reference to the stone seat upon which Rabbi
Eleazer sat and taught. Since their opposition to each other's
teachings was well known, the story of Rabbi Joshua's actions
adds brilliant color to Jesus' criticism of the Pharisees who sit
on Moses' seat. While Jesus honored the content of the teachings of the Pharisees who were sitting upon the seat of Moses,
he was encouraging greater care in practice.

Rabbi Joshua lived longer than Rabbi Eleazer. After Rabbi
Eleazer's death, Rabbi Joshua would pass by the stone upon
which Rabbi Eleazer sat to teach. One day, Rabbi Joshua honored his colleague with whom he often argued. In the story
which compares the stone chair of Eleazer to Mount Sinai, the
Jewish commentary on the Song of Solomon describes what
Rabbi Joshua did.

> The Bet Hamidrash of Rabbi Eleazer was shaped like an arena.
> There was a stone in it which was specially reserved for him to sit
> upon. Once Rabbi Joshua came in and began kissing this stone and
> said, "This stone is like Mount Sinai and the one which sat upon it
> was like the Ark of the Covenant."[6]

Although Rabbi Joshua sharply disagreed with Rabbi Eleazer
in the interpretation of Torah, he could compare the stone chair
upon which his esteemed colleague Rabbi Eleazer sat to teach
with Mount Sinai. Embracing the chair he began kissing the
stone as he recalled the brilliant contributions to Torah learning
made by Rabbi Eleazer. Comparing the stone to Mount Sinai
was tantamount to comparing Rabbi Eleazer to Moses!

The stone chair discovered at the dig in the village of Chorazim and the rabbinic sources provide a much clearer picture of
the meaning of the words "seat of Moses" in Matthew 23:2.
New significance is given to the words of Jesus. The Gospel text
refers to the place from which the Pharisees taught. The mention of Moses recalls Mount Sinai and the authoritative nature

of the divine revelation contained in Torah. The teachings must be recognized as valid even when the lifestyle of the teachers fails to measure up to the Torah's high standard of holiness.

The rabbis offered nearly identical criticisms against those who teach but do not practice. The rabbinic literature preserves a description of seven types of Pharisees which to a large degree create colorful but negative characterizations.[7] Probably only one of these seven types of Pharisees is positive. The Pharisees scrutinized their own behavior. Self-inventory and constructive criticism were virtues that called for genuine spiritual renewal. The Pharisees sought revival through their self-criticism. In a similar way, the ancient prophets in their special passion for God and in their strong concern for a people in need spoke sharply to their generation. They wanted true repentance.

In the Talmud a similar criticism of hypocrisy is given when King Yanai, who fought the Pharisees, is reported to have advised his wife, Queen Alexandra, to make peace with the influential religious movement. In the story, he tells her, "Do not fear the Pharisees . . . but [fear] the hypocrites who ape them."[8] Thus, according to the Talmud, even an enemy of the Pharisees respected the devout within the movement although he recognized that others were hypocritical. The hypocrites acted like Pharisees but were not true Pharisees. While some scholars may question the historicity of this statement from 76 B.C.E., the year when Queen Alexandra came to power, it demonstrates that people were aware of the esteemed qualities of pious Pharisees as well as the hypocritical practices of others.

The rabbis were normally not reluctant to criticize scholars among their ranks even if they were prominent and respected teachers. Ben Azzai was considered one of the outstanding scholars of Scripture of his day. He was so devoted to the study of Torah that he refused to marry. He was not willing to commit to family responsibilities and preferred to dedicate himself fully to the study and teaching of Torah. In one of his famous expositions on the book of Genesis, he began preaching about the commandment concerning procreation, "Be fruitful and multiply . . ." (Gen 1:28). The rabbinic sources describe how he declared that anyone who does not fulfill the obligation to have children has actually diminished the divine image. It is as if he shed innocent blood. His colleagues were quick to point out that while his sermon was great, his practice was inferior and hypocritical.[9] Ben Azzai needed to practice what he preached and get married. If not, he should at least keep quiet on that point. The teacher must exemplify his message by his own life-style. In a similar fashion, Jesus directs criticism at individuals who preach but do not practice.

Unfortunately, the image of the Pharisee in modern usage is seldom if ever positive. Such a negative characterization of Pharisaism distorts our view of Judaism and the beginnings of Christianity. Little recognition is given to the Pharisees and their contributions to religious thought. For example, we Christian scholars accept the fact that the Pharisees built a foundation for later rabbinic Judaism but downplay their influence upon Christian theology. But the theology of Jesus is Jewish and is built firmly upon the foundations of Pharisaic thought. The Pharisees' strong beliefs, spanning from the doctrine of God to the resurrection of the dead, have influenced Christian belief in a much greater measure than is commonly recognized. Theologically, the early Christians were very close to the Phari-sees. Certainly Jewish thought was greatly diversified during the Second Temple period, and the Pharisees were among the many influential religious movements of the time. Here in order to appreciate fully the parable of Jesus, we must appreciate the positive aspects of Pharisaism. The Pharisee's key role in the drama of the story must be fully appreciated. The Pharisee represents piety and holiness and not self-righteous hypocrisy.

Today the negative opinions concerning the Pharisees have influenced the relationship between Christians and Jews. As Christians we tend to view modern Judaism as the final product of the "wicked Pharisaism" we read about in the New Testa-ment. The poison of prejudice flows in two directions. First it flows in the direction of our perception of the Pharisees in the time of Jesus. Second it flows toward our views of modern Judaism. In actuality, modern expressions of both the Jewish and the Christian faiths possess common roots in the rich spir-itual contributions of the Pharisees during the Second Temple period. Our Christian prejudices against the Pharisees make it more difficult for Christians and Jews to talk with one another and listen to each other in genuine esteem.

To appreciate fully the sharp wit, keen humor, and element of shock in Jesus' parable about the Pharisee and the tax collector, readers must understand the mental associations of the two lead actors. While the very mention of a Pharisee evoked an image of righteousness for the original audience, the reputation for tax collectors was vastly different. The tax collector was despised by the people and considered to be severely deficient in piety and holiness. Not only did he collect taxes for an oppressive puppet regime and the pagan government of Rome, but he also was thought to pocket excessive amounts in customs for his own enrichment. Jewish nationalists went even further by rejecting the tax collectors not only as local representatives of political oppression but also as Jews who gave a measure of recognition to foreign gods. In the view of the Zealots, a tax collector might even be considered an idolater. The publicans gathered taxes for the Roman emperor who claimed to be a god. At best, the publican was viewed as a thief; at worst, a traitor and idolater. The tax collector in the parable is the perfect picture of evil: a thief, traitor, and idolater all self-contained in the same person.

Two individuals go up to the temple to pray. One is holy. The other is wicked. Jesus invites the listener to follow the action of the story's plot. The parable begins with the familiar setting of the temple but astonishes the audience with an unexpected outcome.

THE TEMPLE

The temple was a place of prayer (Luke 1:10).[10] But the most prominent feature of the temple worship in the minds of the people was the sacrifice. Within the temple worship, people were permitted to offer individual sacrifices. The parable, however, probably depicts the daily sacrifices *(tamid)* which were offered twice a day, morning and evening. The people would go up to the temple during these sacrifices and gather for worship. During the Second Temple period, prayers were added to the service. The people would pray during the time of incense. The picture created by the opening of the parable suggests that two individuals went up to the temple to pray at the appointed time of the daily sacrifices. Jesus begins his story by saying, "Two men went up into the temple to pray. . . ."

Atonement for forgiveness was the aim of the sacrifice in the temple. Psalm 48 describes Mount Zion, the place of temple sacrifices, as the joy of the whole earth. A Jewish interpretation of this verse captures something of the true essence of the sacrifices for the temple worship:

"The joy of the whole earth" (Psalm 48:2) means that not one Israel-
ite was in distress as long as the Temple stood, for when a man
entered there laden with sin and offered a sacrifice, he was forgiven.
Could he have a greater joy than the feeling that he departed from
there righteous?[11]

Hence the worship in the temple as described in the parable
naturally makes reference to the atonement for sin, which was
made efficacious in the daily sacrifice. Though both the Pharisee and the tax collector were present during the time the
sacrifice was offered, only one of the two individuals possessed
the proper attitude toward divine grace.

Surely early church leaders would not have invented this story.
It is a parable of Jesus. The view of atonement in the parable
reflects Jewish thought from the time when the temple stood.
The message of the parable focuses sharply on the attitude of
one's heart. The tax collector expressed his sincere desire to
receive God's mercy. Concerning the tax collector, Jesus proclaims, "I tell you, this man went down to his house justified"
(Hebrew *mutzdak* or *zakhai;* Luke 18:14).[12] He had directed his
heart to God during the time of sacrifice and temple worship.
He beat his breast—an action which showed intense sorrow. He
cried out in deep anguish of heart, "God be merciful to me a
sinner!" The Pharisee, on the other hand, was content. He
viewed himself already as being righteous. He thanked God that
he was not like other people. He stood erect during his prayer
and perhaps located himself in a more prominent position nearer
to the altar.

The tax collector, by way of contrast, stood far away. He did
not stand erect but hit his chest in shame and distress. The
people hearing the story would have placed the tax collector far
away from the altar. He was just in sight of the Pharisee. As the
people prayed in the temple's court during the time of incense
after the daily sacrifice, the tax collector did not feel worthy to
come near. While the prayer of the Pharisee, who outwardly
appeared to be holy, revealed his contempt for other people,
the tax collector reached out to God and asked for divine forgiveness. Though the Pharisee fasted twice a week, he was
unlike the true Pharisees, who sincerely sought the spiritual
renewal of the people through fasting. He merely exalted himself in his own mind. Though other Pharisees desired to tithe
out of concern to fulfill biblical principles, he made extra effort

not only by tithing his income but also by giving a tithe of all that he bought just in case the merchant who sold the goods did not fulfill the duty of the tithe. But his outward form of religious piety was not acceptable to God because of the attitude of his heart. Like the prophets before him, Jesus teaches that sacrifices are not enough in the absence of true heartfelt devotion to God. God desires worship from the heart.

KAVANAH AND JEWISH PRAYER

The Hebrew word *kavanah* means the intention or true desire of one's heart. Literally it refers to direction. Often the term means concentration. How can a heart be directed to God in prayer? The supreme importance of *kavanah* in the prayer life of the people is emphasized in Jewish literature. The application of the parable of Jesus must be studied in the light of *kavanah,* namely, the direction of one's heart. In the Jerusalem Talmud, the sages of Israel discussed the duty of each individual to recite the *Shema,* "Hear O Israel, the LORD our God, the LORD is one." The rabbis taught that it is not enough just to repeat the words. The intention of the heart is of paramount significance. They taught, "The recitation of the *Shema* must be accompanied by the intention of the heart *(kavanah).*"[13] The word *kavanah* denotes concentration; it refers to heartfelt sincerity. The heart must be directed to God in prayer. If a person who recites, "Hear O Israel, the LORD our God, the LORD is one" does not concentrate with full intention of the heart, then that person has not fulfilled the obligation to pray.[14]

One must remember that recitation of the *Shema* in rabbinic teachings was connected directly to the kingdom of heaven.[15] To recognize God's kingship in one's individual life means to reject all idolatry. Reciting the *Shema* possessed far-reaching ramifications. The Lord is made King. The kingdom of heaven is realized. One cannot merely go through the motions of saying the words. Each person must concentrate and direct his or her heart to God. In Jewish teachings, prayer should be preceded by directing one's heart to God. In fact, the word "direction" (in Hebrew *kavanah*) is used as a verb of action (*kiven et libo* "direct one's heart").

The Mishnah describes the early Chasidim by their vigorous prayer life.[16] They devoted blocks of time before prayer in

order to direct their hearts to heaven. High priority was given to
directing one's heart to God in concentrated prayer. When one
recited the *Shema,* one received the kingdom of heaven. As a
religious duty, one was required to recite the verse as a prayer
to God. What if the person was thinking about something else
other than God while saying the verse? After all, it is possible
to recite the prayer without really meaning it. Is it enough to
mindlessly repeat the affirmation of the *Shema* without directing one's heart to God? What happens if one is going someplace
and becomes distracted? People are able to recite words without focusing their thoughts on God's reign. True prayer, however, requires concentration. The rabbis said that even when
traveling on a journey,

> it is forbidden to receive upon oneself the kingdom of heaven while
> one is walking in the way. First one must stop and stand in place and
> direct his or her heart to God in awe, fear, trembling, and quaking.
> Then one may recite the unity of the Name, "Hear O Israel, the
> LORD our God, the LORD is one" (Deut 6:4). One must pray every
> single word while directing his or her heart to God with sincerity, and
> then one may recite, "Blessed be His glorious name, His kingdom is
> forever and ever." When one comes to the passage, "You shall love
> the LORD your God with all your heart . . . "—if one desires to walk,
> one may. If one desires to stand, one may. If one desires to sit, one
> may. For thus it is written, ". . . and you shall talk of them when you
> sit in your house, and when you walk by the way, and when you lie
> down, and when you rise" (Deut 6:6).[17]

In order to emphasize the magnitude of the *Shema* and to
acknowledge the acceptance of God's reign, each individual
must stand still and direct his or her heart to God when making
the affirmation, "Hear O Israel, the LORD our God, the LORD
is one." Other portions of the ancient liturgy may be recited
while walking. Receiving the kingdom of heaven by praying the
Shema, however, required the direction of one's heart.

The words of the Jewish rabbis, that a person must "direct his
or her heart to God in awe, fear, trembling, and quaking," make
the meaning of prayer in Hebrew thought clear. The sincere
intention of the heart is needed.

THE GOOD AND THE BAD IN JESUS' STORY

The grand personality of Jesus and his sharp wit are revealed
in the colorful parable of the Pharisee and the Tax Collector. As

we listen to the story, a mirror image is reflected. When we attack Judaism and the religious contributions of Pharisees, we miss the message of Jesus. Strong contrasts between good and bad people appear in the story. The holy man disappoints the audience. But the sin-laden individual surprises us by his sincere repentance and genuine humility before God. The religious Pharisee fails while the impious tax collector goes home righteous before God.

The difference between the Pharisee and the tax collector was the *kavanah* of their hearts. As a Jewish theologian, Jesus calls each individual to a genuine heart-controlled relationship with God. The beauty of the story is seen further in the image of the tax collector. God's grace cannot be earned. Even a wicked tax collector is accepted by God when he cries out for divine mercy. It is the same for both the religious and the unholy. Both are needy but in different ways. God loves the tax collector. He loves the Pharisee. But no matter how sinful or impious the individual may appear in the eyes of the good religious people, God's favor possesses no limitation. He loves the publicans and the sinners. It does not matter what they have done. His grace is given to everyone who directs his or her heart to God in sincere prayer.

NOTES

1. These words introduce a major theme of the parable in a concise and fitting manner even if they betray the hand of Luke or an editorial connecting phrase. Often the despising of others will accompany a self-righteous attitude. They go together.

2. John Crossan, *Raid on the Articulate and Borges* (New York: Harper and Row, 1976) 108.

3. George Buttrick, *The Parables of Jesus* (Garden City: Doubleday, 1928) 90. For an extremely important study of the formation of Judaism and Christianity from the rich Jewish religious thought during the days of the Second Temple period, see Flusser, "A New Sensitivity in Judaism and the Christian Message" in *Judaism and the Origins of Christianity*, 469ff. The danger that rigorous piety will produce the fruit of hypocrisy is always present. Compare the prayers cited in Billerbeck, *Kommentar zum Neuen Testament aus Talmud und Midrasch*, 2.240, where one who prays may too easily fall into the trap of self-congratulation. In the parable of Jesus, the Pharisee's attitude is exceedingly repulsive especially when he prays, "God I thank you that I am not like other men . . . or even like this tax collector."

4. See above, p. 46. For a fine color picture of the discovery, see Michael Avi-Yonah, *Views of the Biblical World* (Jerusalem: International Publishing, 1961) 1.63. On the discovery of the chair and its inscription, see Josef Naveh, *On Stone and Mosaic* (Jerusalem: Carta, 1978) 36 (in Hebrew). Compare the early discussion on the seating in the synagogue and the discovery of the seat of Moses by Herbert Gordon May, "Synagogues in Palestine," *Biblical Archaeologist Reader* (Garden City: Doubleday, 1961) 245–46 (reprinted from *Biblical Archaeologist* 7.1 [Feb. 1944] 1–20). See also, Lee Levine, *Ancient Synagogues Revealed* (Jerusalem: Israel Exploration Society, 1981).

5. Cf. Pesikta De Rav Kahana 1:7 (Mandelbaum, 2.12) and Sokoloff, *Dictionary of Jewish Palestinian Aramaic,* 509.

6. Song of Songs Rabbah 1:3 (See the Soncino English translation, 37). See also the discussion of Y. Gilat, *R. Eliezer ben Hyrcanus, a Scholar Outcast* (Ramat Gan, Israel: Bar Ilan University, 1984) 489.

7. See b. *Sotah* 22 a and b and parallels (cf. J. Bowker, *Jesus and the Pharisees* [Cambridge: Cambridge University, 1973], 139–41).

8. See b. *Sotah* 22b and E. Schürer, *The History of the Jewish People in the Time of Jesus Christ* (rev.; Edinburgh: T. & T. Clark, 1973) 1.219–32.

9. See b. *Yeb.* 63b and parallels.

10. On the temple see S. Safrai, "The Temple," in *The Jewish People in the First Century* (ed. S. Safrai, M. Stern, D. Flusser, and W. C. van Unnik; Amsterdam: Van Gorcum, 1976) 1.865–907. Safrai observes, "During the incense-offering, the people gathered for prayer in the court. Outside the temple people also said prayers, at this time, particularly during the afternoon incense-offering" (p. 888). As Safrai points out, the practice of prayer is mentioned in Luke 1:10 and Jdt 9:1, and is alluded to in Acts 3:1 and the *Protoevangelium Jacobi* 2:4.

11. Exodus Rabbah 36:1 (see the Soncino English translation, 437) and see also the parallel in Midrash Psalms 48:2, W. G. Braude, trans., *The Midrash on Psalms* (New Haven: Yale University, 1958) 1.460–61.

12. David Flusser has suggested that the Greek words *par ekeinon* "rather than the other" are a scribal addition which is reflected in the textual tradition by several variant readings (private communication). If he is right, the allusion of the text would possess a strong sophistication. The hint is more appropriate in live story narration.

13. J. *Ber.* 5a, chap. 2, hal. 5. See there the discussion in the Jerusalem Talmud where different views are explained and defended.

14. Not all the sages of Israel agreed on this matter. See the preceding note.

15. J. *Ber.* 4b, chap. 2, hal. 3.

16. M. *Ber.* 5:1 and parallels.

17. Midrash Tanchuma, *lech lecha* 1 (early edition, 19a), and cf. Tanchuma, Buber's edition, ibid., 29a where Buber views the opening of the section to be taken from the early midrash called *Yelamdenu Rabbenu.*

PART 4

THE JEWISH MESSIAH AND THE POLITICS OF ROME

In the secret of His passion which Jesus reveals to the disciples at Caesarea Philippi the pre-Messianic tribulation is for others set aside, abolished, concentrated upon Himself alone, and that in the form that they are fulfilled in His own passion and death at Jerusalem. That was the new conviction that had dawned upon Him. He must suffer for others . . . that the Kingdom might come.

—Albert Schweitzer

18
The Foundation of the Kingdom

ERHAPS THE TWO MOST IMPORTANT QUESTIONS
Jesus ever asked his disciples are contained in the
story of Peter's great confession (Matt 16:13–14;
Mark 8:27–28; Luke 9:18–19). The tremendous significance of
these two questions has only intensified with the passing of
centuries. Today people still seek to know who Jesus is. The
first question Jesus asked is: "Who do men say that I am?" In
the second question, Jesus asked the disciples directly, "Who do
you say that I am?"

Who is Jesus? Even Christians who believe in Jesus often
completely misunderstand his purpose and mission. In order to
understand the life and teachings of Jesus, we must take a
journey, not only in time but also in culture, custom, and language.

The message of Jesus must be understood in the context of the
first century. Jesus was Jewish. He spoke Hebrew. He lived and
worked in the land of Israel when his people, the Jews, suffered
under the cruel yoke of the mighty Roman Empire. He lived his
entire life as a religious Jew.

To recreate the setting for Jesus' life and teachings, we must
try to hear his voice again. We must listen to the message of
Jesus in the Gospel texts, but not as modern Christians. We
need to listen to Jesus as if we were first-century Jews. We can
enter this new realm of study and understanding of Jesus' message
by studying the Jewish thought and practice of the people
during time of the Second Temple. This work includes the study
of the rabbinic literature. In the Gospel text Jesus asked an
important question which provides insight into his mission and
calling.

Jesus asked his disciples: "Who do men say that I am?" The
disciples seek to answer the question honestly: "John the Baptist;
but others say, Elijah; and others, that one of the old
prophets has *arisen*" (Luke 9:19). Here we have stressed the

action verb associated with the prophets. The prophet has *arisen* in our midst.

Many Jews of the period associated the image of Elijah with the coming of the Messiah. The mention of John the Baptist also indicates that some people considered him to be the deliverer who would come. The often misunderstood phrase "one of the old prophets has arisen" does not indicate that a dead prophet had emerged from his tomb to preach another sermon. The Jews of the period thought "the prophet" would be like Moses (Deut 18:18). At least this has been suggested by David Flusser, and I am convinced that he is correct. The Scripture text, "I will raise up for them a prophet like you from among their brethren; and I will put my words in his mouth, and he shall speak to them all that I command him" (Deut 18:18), was interpreted as referring to the coming messiah.[1] The prophet who would arise would bring redemption and salvation to God's suffering people.

A prophet is not merely one who speaks in prophecy. In the Bible often he is a miracle-worker. What did the term "prophet" mean to people during the time of Jesus? Moses is called a prophet. God worked his mighty miracles by signs and wonders to redeem his people by Moses the prophet. They were redeemed from Egypt. God delivered his people from bondage and slavery by the miracles performed by the prophet. This is the model for deliverance, healing, and salvation.

Consider the story of the widow at Nain (Luke 7:11–17). When Jesus worked the miracle of giving life to her dead son, the people proclaimed, "A great *prophet* has *arisen* among us" (Luke 7:16). They recognized the prophetic ministry of a miracle-worker.

Luke 7:36–50 tells us about two seekers. The religious Simon was offended at the woman intruder who washed the feet of Jesus with her tears. Simon said, "If this man were *the* prophet, he would have known who and what sort of woman this is who is touching him." The definite article in the words "*the* prophet" is written by the hand of the original scribe of the important uncial manuscript of Vaticanus from the fourth century. It also appears in the sixth-century Zacynthius manuscript (040) and the minuscule 205 (Venice fifteenth century). While this manuscript evidence for adding the definite article is meager in comparison to the textual attestation for "a prophet," the article could have been in Luke's source or deleted from the third

Gospel's text by a scribe at an early time for stylistic reasons. Most textual critics will reject the article, but this does not mean that Simeon was not pondering the mission of Jesus. While the definite article is not incorporated into modern translations, when one considers the context of the remarks it seems that the question required the reference to *the* prophet. The Gospel story makes better sense when one recognizes the possible allusion to the messianic association to God's future prophet.

Simon was asking the question: Is Jesus *the* prophet like unto Moses who is to come? The woman received Jesus' message of love and forgiveness. Jesus saw the need of both seekers. The woman's deeply emotional actions broke the custom and culture of the day. Her action was provocative. Jesus argued that her actions were extensions of the accepted custom of greeting an honored guest. She had been forgiven grave wrongdoings. Simon was too religious to recognize the legitimacy of her action. She loved much for she had been forgiven much. Simon was religious. He had been forgiven little and did not have the same understanding of who Jesus is. Both seekers had needs, and Jesus reached out to both of them. He loved the outsider and the insider. Jesus affirmed the human dignity of the intruder. He loved the outcasts. The kingdom principles from the life and teachings of Jesus demonstrate God's love, forgiveness, and acceptance.

First Jesus asked his disciples, "Who do men say that I am?" The second question is of greater importance: He asked, "Who do you say that I am?" If Jesus asked the inner circle of his closest followers this powerful question, how much more important is it for modern Christians: Who do we say that Jesus is? Do we know Jesus?

The Gospel accounts tell us about all that Jesus said and did (Luke 1:1–4; Acts 1:1). Jesus' teaching and miracles authenticated the answer of Peter when he declared that Jesus is "The Messiah of God" (Luke 9:20). Jesus accepts his reply. In fact, Jesus pronounces a blessing upon Peter. It was traditional for a rabbi to pronounce a blessing upon a student who gave the correct answer to an intriguing question. Jesus blesses Peter:

> Blessed are you, Simon Bar-Jonah! For flesh and blood has not revealed this to you, but my Father who is in heaven, And I tell you, you are Peter, and on this rock I will build my church, and the gates of hell shall not prevail against it. I will give you the keys of the

kingdom of heaven, and whatever you bind on earth shall be bound in heaven, and whatever you loose on earth shall be loosed in heaven (Matt 16:18).[2]

Jesus blesses Peter because he acknowledged who Jesus is. Jesus' career, purpose, and mission are intimately connected to the way we interpret this blessing. Jesus is the Messiah of God. He is not a human-made deliverer. He will not be forced into the mold of politicians and preachers. What did Jesus himself say about his mission? We must hear how Jesus defines his divine task. The work of the kingdom is the work of Jesus' disciples.

Peter, speaking for the inner circle of disciples, affirmed who Jesus is. His recognition of who Jesus is—the Messiah of God— forms the foundation for the church, that is, the movement of Jesus. The word "Peter" means "little rock." The word "church" (*ekklēsia* in Greek, *edah* in Hebrew) refers to the community of Jesus' disciples who live life by following the teachings of their master. It is an extension of the ministry of Jesus. The disciples of Jesus act like him. They do what they see their master doing.

ABRAHAM, THE FOUNDATION STONE

Jewish literature reflects a similar interpretation that is helpful in understanding the words of Jesus. In Jewish thought Abraham was the little rock upon which God would create his world. He is the foundation stone. From Abraham, the patriarch who believed God and because of his act of believing was credited with righteousness, God would make a foundation. From the foundation stone of Abraham, the little rock, God would make many rocks, the people of Israel. He would bring deliverance to a world in need through his people.

> Another interpretation: "From the top of the rocks I see him" (Num 23:9). I see them—those who existed before the beginning of the creation of the world. It may be compared to a king who sought to build. He dug deeply into several places seeking to find a foundation. But he found only swamps and water. But he did not lay it, until finally he dug in one place where deep in the ground he found rock (*petra*). He declared: Here I will build. He laid the foundation and built! Thus when the Holy One sought to create the world, he examined the generation of Enosh and the generation of the flood. He

inquired: How can I create the world when all of these wicked people will rise up to provoke me to anger? Then the Holy One saw Abraham who would arise in the future. He declared: I have a rock upon which I can lay the foundation to build the world. Thus Abraham was called rock, for He said, "Look to the rock from which you were hewn" (Isa 51:1). As to Israel he called rocks, for he said: "Remember thy congregation which thou hast purchased of old" (Ps 74:2).[3]

According to Jewish thought Abraham was the foundation stone upon which other stones would be constructed into a living community of faith. Abraham's faith in the one true God of Israel provided the foundation.

Like Abraham, Peter possessed faith; he also recognized the character of Jesus' ministry. Jesus was of God. He was anointed to fulfill the divine purpose. He was the anointed one of God. Peter's faith is the foundation stone of God's witnessing congregation of believers. The gates of hell shall not prevail against the people of God.

The gates of hell are not weapons attacking the people of God! The action is moving in the opposite direction. God's people are plundering the strongholds of the enemy. When the people of God acknowledge the foundation of the kingdom, nothing can stop them. The gates of hell will not be able to withstand their forceful entry.

The keys of the kingdom of heaven are the divine authority. In rabbinic literature the terms "bind" and "loose" can mean "prohibit" and "allow." But one can see the powerful spiritual implications behind this saying in the context of the Gospels. In Jewish literature the word of a righteous individual has tremendous force.[4] What righteous persons declare on earth has the authority of heaven. The rabbis refer to special individuals for whom God answers prayer. The authority of the believer is the channel of healing for a hurting world.

The kingdom of heaven is realized in this present world. It appears in full force. Many theories have been offered as to the meaning of the kingdom of heaven. It is not a political power. It cannot be established by human efforts. Preachers and politicians do not possess the kingdom. They cannot make the kingdom appear. Neither is the kingdom synonymous with heaven. It is *not* reserved *only* for the distant future. It does not begin in the millennium. For Jesus, the kingdom of heaven is:

1. The power of God—that is, God doing what he wants.

2. The people of God—that is, people doing what God wants.

Jesus said that the kingdom was realized in the present when he worked a miracle. The foundation stone of Peter's faith becomes the springboard for the activities of Jesus' followers. All people can experience God's rule when they obey God's absolutes. He releases his divine power in their lives. Healing, love, forgiveness, and acceptance can be channels of God's power in a hurting world. God's saving activity establishes his kingdom now.

JESUS THE MESSIAH

Modern scholars have come to view the Gospel portrayal of Jesus as the Messiah with skepticism. One scholarly "consensus" recently decided that Jesus did not consider himself to be the Messiah. The story of Peter's confession is discounted as a later and romantic memory of the church. It is said to be inadmissible as evidence for Jesus' teachings.[5]

The Jewish roots of Jesus' teachings, however, suggest that messianism was alive and well in the land of Israel during the Second Temple period. The episode of the Great Confession of Peter, for instance, is clearly paralleled in the Jewish source *Yelamdenu,* which speaks about Abraham's being the foundation stone. This fact alone makes it tenuous to claim that such teachings were outside the realm of Jewish thought. And that the Romans pursued a policy of oppressing those who nurtured Jewish messianic hopes speaks volumes against such assertions.

Clearly Jesus claimed to be the anointed one. The real issue, however, is not whether he claimed to be the Messiah. The core problem rests in his willingness to redefine the messianic idea along creative and original lines. No doubt the Jewish people during the Second Temple period possessed rich diversity in their approaches to messianism. The Essenes of the Dead Sea Scrolls talked about two messiahs, one from the priestly and one from the royal line. The Sadducees probably did not even believe in the coming Messiah. But if and when the Messiah would come, he was expected to develop the plan of final redemption based upon the diverse streams of thought.

Jesus preached the kingdom as God's power on earth. He was keenly aware of his messianic task, but his job description for the Messiah has always been quite different from that of anyone in the church or the synagogue. This should not be surprising. In reality, it should be expected. Even John the Baptist entertained his strong doubts about Jesus. Why should it be surprising when modern scholars are bewildered by Jesus' claims?

In all events, when the Gospels are read in their cultural and historical context, all doubt concerning Jesus' self-awareness should be dismissed. In affirming Peter he accepted the title. Jesus, however, defined the messianic task much differently from his disciples. The Romans were intensely concerned with any who claimed to be Messiah. Such a claim was sufficient for the death penalty.

For Jesus the message of the kingdom rests firmly upon Peter's foundational confession, "You are the anointed one of God." The messianic task is inextricably connected to the activities of the disciples who are called to be ministers of healing in a hurting world. Jesus could not separate the task of the Messiah from the servant of the Lord who brings healing.

NOTES

1. The text of Deut 18:18 was quoted in the Dead Sea Scrolls and related to the coming of the prophet of God's salvation (see T. Gaster, *The Dead Sea Scriptures* (New York: Anchor, 1976) 444; 4QTestim). See Flusser, *Judaism and the Origins of Christianity,* 420. The question revolves around whether Jesus should be identified with the eschatological prophet.

2. The Semitic structure of the saying is characteristic of what are the best sources behind the Synoptic Gospels. It is difficult to say why Luke and Mark chose not to add the saying into their Gospels (if it appeared in their sources). But it is far more difficult to imagine that Matthew made it up. The saying cannot be viewed as a Matthean invention. It is perfect Hebrew, and is paralleled in early Jewish thought. Matthew had access to reliable sources concerning the life and teachings of Jesus.

3. *Yelamdenu,* quoted in Yalkut Shimeoni on Num 23:9, vol. 1, remez 766 (A. Hyman's edition, 487). Cf. the important observation of M. Kister, "Plucking on the Sabbath and Christian-Jewish Polemic," 35, n. 1. Kister observes, "Note also Matt 16:18: 'and on this rock I will build my community'; a striking parallel appears in the Thanksgiving Scroll 6:24–27: 'For you will lay a foundation [Hb. *sod*] on a rock.' As Otto Betz pointed out in *Zeitschrift für die neutestamentliche Wissenschaft* 48

(1957) 49ff., the verse quotes a literary source close to the Thanksgiving Scroll. Indeed, *sod* in the Dead Sea Scrolls means both 'community' and 'foundation' (compare Manual of Discipline 11:8 with Thanksgiving Scroll 7:1, 9). Thus word-plays based on this dual meaning appear in the writings of the Dead Sea sect. Accordingly, the phrase just quoted from the Thanksgiving Scroll could be interpreted: 'for you will found a community on a rock.' See also Isaiah 28:16–18, on which the whole passage is based; note especially the words *yesod musad* in v. 16." See the Hebrew text in J. Licht's edition, 116–17, and the English translation and commentary of M. Mansoor, *The Thanksgiving Hymns* (Grand Rapids: Eerdmans, 1961) 144–46.

4. Compare the mention of "key," meaning authority, in Isa 22:22. See also the important parallel in the Talmud, "Once it happened that . . . no rain had fallen. The people asked Choni the Circle Drawer, 'Pray that rain may fall.' He prayed but no rain fell. Then he drew a circle and stood within it. . . . He exclaimed, 'Master of the Universe, your children have turned to me because they believe me to be a member of your house. I swear by your great name that I will not move from here until you have mercy upon your children!' Rain began to fall. . . . Our Rabbis taught: What was the message the Sanhedrin sent to Choni the Circle Drawer? '. . . You have decreed [on earth] below and the Holy One Blessed be He fulfills your word [in heaven] above.' " (b. *Ta'an.* 23a). This story is discussed more fully above in the chapter "Miracles, Proclamation, and Healing Faith."

5. See the deliberations of the Jesus Seminar published in *Foundations and Facets: Forum* and the *Jesus Seminar Series* published by the Polebridge Press in Sonoma, California. The fellows of the Jesus Seminar come from all levels of scholarship and represent a wide spectrum of religious belief.

19

The Transfiguration of Jesus

WHY WAS JESUS TRANSFIGURED? THE PURPOSE and meaning of the transfiguration of Jesus are seldom fully appreciated (Luke 9:28–36; Mark 9:2–10; Matt 17:1–8). In the academic world such a story is routinely discounted as myth. Among Christian believers, on the other hand, the miraculous nature of Christ's transformed appearance often outshines the deeper significance of the episode in his earthly life and experience. Here we will seek a clearer understanding of the transfiguration of Jesus in light of the miracle's Jewish background and in view of a fresh approach to the synoptic problem.[1] Could this story reveal a glimpse of the divine presence which appears in the midst of human suffering?

THE DEATH OF JESUS

The idea of suffering should not be easily dismissed. The Gospel of Luke records that Moses and Elijah spoke to him about his "departure" in Jerusalem. When New Testament scholars approach the synoptic problem from the position supporting the priority of Mark, they tend to ignore this pivotal text from Luke. While all New Testament scholars study Luke, the mention of death often is considered a pious reflection of the evangelist which he added to Mark's version. After all, Luke used Mark as his source for Jesus' life. Although the word "departure" is missing in Mark, Luke may well have based his mention of the word upon authentic witnesses for the life of Jesus apart from Mark. Here Luke's version is crucial: "And behold, two men talked with him, Moses and Elijah, who appeared in glory and spoke of his departure, which he was to accomplish at Jerusalem" (9:30–31). The word "departure" in Greek is *exodos*.[2] Unlike Mark and Matthew, in Luke's account, the reference concerning Jesus' departure is the foundation for understanding the purpose of the transfiguration.[3] On the one hand, this term portrays the imagery of the story of divine deliverance in the exodus of Israel from Egypt. On the other, it signifies death. In fact, in Greek it is a euphemism for death. In English people will say that somebody "passed away" instead of using the stronger verb "died." In the same way, in Greek, the word *exodos* "departure" was another way of referring to "death."

Here Luke's Gospel distinctly alludes to the death of Jesus. Nevertheless, the uncommon phenomena surrounding the transfiguration point toward an awareness of the divine reality connected with his passion. The appearance of Jesus is changed. Moses and Elijah talk with him. The cloud overshadows the mountain and a voice affirms the authenticity of Jesus' messianic task. In the glory of these supernatural occurrences, Jesus receives information concerning his passion in Jerusalem. In the Greek text of Luke, his death is described in a euphemistic way by the term *exodos*. As a result, the redemptive nature of Jesus' sufferings is suggested by the words of Luke's Gospel.

God's presence in the midst of human suffering appears, therefore, in this dramatic event. The concept of redemption is connected to God's intervention in the natural order. Perhaps the Gospel writer had the Passover in mind when he referred to the "departure" of Jesus instead of his death. Every Passover celebrates the triumphal acts of divine deliverance as the miracles of the biblical account of the exodus are dramatically reenacted. The Jewish people celebrate the Passover by a festive meal. The child at the table asks, "Why is this night different from all other nights?" The story of redemption is retold through the imagery of the Passover meal where unleavened bread, four cups of wine, and the shank bone (recalling the Passover lamb's sacrifice) bring to life a distant memory from the historical experience of slaves who became free. A mixed multitude became a people when they were transfigured from darkness into light and redeemed from the cruel bondage of the Egyptian taskmasters.

The change of appearance accentuates the divine presence. By way of sharp contrast, it is on just such an occasion as this that Moses and Elijah speak with Jesus concerning his death in Jerusalem, when the glory of God appears in the most obvious manner. Death and glory are joined together. The pain of death is considered the most excruciating experience of suffering for every human being. Death is the greatest fear of humankind. Jesus will die, but his death possesses enduring significance in the process of redemption. Is his transfiguration during the visitation from Moses and Elijah a preview of his resurrection? Does it foreshadow the splendor of life after death? In ancient Jewish thought the righteous are transformed in the future world. In the present time they suffer in the form of human frailty, but in the next world they will be transfigured by the divine light. Perhaps the transfiguration should be seen as a preview of what is yet to come. Such is the view concerning the righteous in the world to come which is expressed in the rabbinic commentary on the book of Deuteronomy.

> Rabbi Simeon ben Yochai said: In the future the faces of the right-eous will resemble seven joyous things: the sun, the moon, the firma-ment, the stars, lightning, lilies, and the lampstand of the temple. Whence the sun? From the verse, "But they that love Him be as the sun when he goes forth in his might" (Judg 5:31). Whence the moon? "Fair as the moon" (Song Sol 6:10). The firmament? "And they that are wise shall shine as the brightness of the firmament" (Dan 12:3). The stars? "And they that turn the many to righteousness as the stars" (Dan 12:3). Lighting? "they run to and fro like the lightnings" (Nah 2:5). Lilies (*shoshanim*)? "For the leader; upon *shoshanim*" (Ps 45:1). The lampstand of the temple? "And two olive trees by it, one upon the right side of the bowl and the other upon the left side thereof" (Zech 4:3).[4]

The glory of the divine presence will be revealed in the faces of the righteous in the future world. In the transfiguration of Jesus, the light may be compared to the radiant faces of the righteous. It is somewhat like the face of Moses which glowed after he talked with God and came down from Mount Sinai (Exod 34:29–35). The description of brilliance attempts to ex-press the incomprehensible splendor of God himself. In the Hebrew Bible this stunning glory of the Lord is often called the *kavod yhvh*. It denotes his grand omnipotence as the ultimate power. In the rabbinic literature the splendor of the divine presence is described by the Hebrew terms *ziv shekhinah*. Per-haps the very skin of Jesus shone so brightly that his garments glowed from the light. His countenance is changed, his clothes are dazzling white, and the brightness of the awesome reality of God is revealed. Such glory only comes from the radiance of the divine presence.

TWO PROPHETS: MOSES AND ELIJAH

Of course, the appearance of Moses and Elijah possesses crucial significance for the event. Many scholars have theorized that Moses represents the Law and Elijah the Prophets. On the contrary, here it seems more likely that they both appear to fulfill their commissions as prophets of salvation. In Judaism they are prominent characters both in traditional teachings and in popular folklore. In the Passover celebration, for example, Moses is the key actor in the biblical drama of redemption. He is the prophet who leads the people out of bondage. Elijah is also mentioned during the traditional meal of Passover. In Jewish thought Elijah is often associated with the future deliverance of God's people.

Perhaps the coming of Moses and Elijah on the Mount of Transfiguration should be viewed as portraying the in-breaking of God's redemptive activity. They are prophets who bring salvation to God's people. In one homiletical midrash which preserves holiday sermons and traditional Jewish teachings from the ancient synagogue, a message is given in which both Moses and Elijah fulfill a mission in the process of redemption.

> You find that two Prophets rose up for Israel out of the Tribe of Levi; one the first of all the Prophets, and the other the last of all the Prophets: Moses first and Elijah last, and both with a commission from God to redeem Israel; Moses, with his commission, redeemed them from Egypt, as is said "Come now, therefore, and I will send unto Pharaoh" (Exod 3:10). And in the time-to-come, Elijah, with his commission, will redeem them, as is said "Behold, I will send you Elijah the prophet" (Mal 3:23). As with Moses, who in the beginning redeemed them out of Egypt, they did not return to slavery again in Egypt; so with Elijah, after he will have redeemed them out of the fourth exile, out of Edom, they will not return and again be enslaved—theirs will be an eternal deliverance.[5]

The first prophet is considered to be Moses. He is a prophet, not only because of his teachings in which he spoke the word given to him by God, but also because of the signs and wonders he worked in order to redeem the people of Israel from Egypt. No other biblical account is so imbued with dramatic miracles as is the story of the exodus. Elijah, who was translated to heaven by a whirlwind, is also a miracle-worker. The idea that neither Moses nor Elijah experienced the normative form of human death influenced later Jewish reflections on these great leaders in Israel's history. In this midrash, Moses is the first of the prophets who brought deliverance from Egypt. Elijah is the last of the prophets who will be involved in the final redemptive act of God.

In the Gospels these two prophets of redemption speak with Jesus concerning his death in Jerusalem. Their roles in God's plan of final redemption had far-reaching ramifications for the transfiguration of Jesus. They are prophets who are telling him about what will happen to him in Jerusalem. The meaning of the transfiguration, therefore, is focused upon Jesus and his higher mission as it is pronounced in the voice from heaven.

THE VOICE FROM THE CLOUD

The voice gives meaning to the miracle. The three disciples Peter, John, and James who accompany Jesus up the mountain lack true spiritual perception concerning the significance of the event. In fact, they had become heavy with sleep. Startled by what is happening and so overcome with wonder at what they witnessed, they do not know how to respond. They recognize how good it is to be a part of this extraordinary experience. Peter wants to build tabernacles for Moses, Elijah, and Jesus. His reaction brings to mind the festival of Tabernacles in the sacred calendar of the Jewish faith where the people build temporary dwellings to commemorate God's presence and provision during their desert wanderings. Such a dramatic portrayal of divine favor in which Jesus is transfigured in the company of Moses and Elijah should be remembered by an act of faith. Building three booths is Peter's immediate response. But the voice from the cloud teaches that such energies would be misdirected. Without the voice the higher mission of Jesus would be eclipsed by the excitement associated with Moses, Elijah, and the other unusual happenings on that mountain. The message of the voice during the transfiguration, however, reveals the divine presence, which identifies wholly with human suffering in the person of Jesus. His disciples must direct their work toward the fulfillment of his call to bring healing and wholeness to a broken world.

The mountain setting, the change in the appearance of Jesus, and the voice from the cloud were dramatic evidence for his higher mission. The mountain in Luke 9:28 recalled another high mountain from Exodus 24:15–18, "Then Moses went up . . . The glory of the LORD settled on Mount Sinai, and the cloud covered it." The scene for the event in the life of Jesus is paralleled by the dramatic history of redemption in the Hebrew Bible. The cloud on the Mount of Transfiguration is like the cloud in the Bible which portrayed God's glory in his acts of salvation. The cloud went before the people as God's protection in Exodus 13:21. The Lord himself descends in a cloud in Numbers 12:5. Once again, the Lord appeared in the tabernacle in a cloud which depicted His majestic glory and supernatural power (Deut 31:15). The Lord tells Moses, "Lo, I am coming unto you in a thick cloud, that the people may hear when I speak with you, and may also believe you forever" (Exod 19:9). In 2 Chronicles 5:13–14 all the people gather to praise and exalt the Lord when Solomon's temple is dedicated. As they proclaim the goodness and the mercy of the Lord, the cloud fills the temple, "so that the priests could not stand to minister because of the cloud; for the glory of the LORD filled the house of God." In a similar way the cloud in the story of the transfiguration of Jesus portrays the overwhelming presence of God. The voice of God speaks from the cloud as in Exodus 19:9.

God's declaration at the transfiguration, "This is my Son, my Chosen; listen to him!" focused attention on the person of Jesus and his teachings. In fact, it might be considered an example of "stringing pearls," an approach in Jewish preaching which linked different biblical passages together. The Jewish teachers and scholars would allude to a Bible text by quoting one or two words of the passage. The people of the Book who had committed the Scriptures to heart would understand the hint and recognize the larger context.[6] One could refer to a whole verse by a single word. The method is seen in midrash, an approach to Bible study and exposition. In the course of midrash, the rabbis assume that the listener will know an entire passage of Scripture, even though they cite only part of the Bible text in their teaching. The voice from heaven is like that. Three verses of the Bible are alluded to, although they are only quoted in part. The first two hints are given in a single word. "My Son," *beni* in Hebrew, referred to Psalm 2:7, "You are my son, today I have begotten you." The words "My chosen," *bachiri* in Hebrew, recalled Isaiah 42:1: "Behold my servant, whom I uphold, my chosen, in whom my soul delights; I have put my Spirit upon him, he will bring forth justice to the nations." The command, "Listen to him," is paralleled in the words spoken about the prophet who would come after Moses: "The LORD your God will raise up for you a prophet like me [Moses] from among you, from your brethren—listen to him" (Deut 18:15).

One must remember that in the Hebrew language, the word "listen," *shema*, means so much more than passive hearing. It spells out complete obedience. The voice from heaven called upon the disciples to recognize the higher task of Jesus, his sonship, and his chosen call. The emphasis, however, is placed on obedience. The followers of Jesus must study. They need to understand the teachings of Jesus and put them into practice.

THE PURPOSE OF THE TRANSFIGURATION OF JESUS

What is the meaning of the transfiguration? This is not an easy question to answer definitively. A story which has been told about a great talmudic scholar and his disciples may provide some insight. The famous Jewish scholar Saul Lieberman once asked his class of rabbinical students this question: "Who is the most tragic figure in the Bible?" One student volunteered, "Neither Jacob nor Job, but probably Saul." Lieberman responded by saying, "Not bad for a beginner." Lieberman had the full attention of the entire class when he made his point: "The most tragic figure in the Bible is God." After all, in his infinite love and compassion, God shares in the suffering of the people he loves.[7] Each person is created in the divine image. God has sought out his people by meeting their needs. Though he has shared in their sufferings, they have not always responded to his invitation to live in accordance with his higher purposes. Of course, Lieberman was not thinking of Jesus or the transfiguration. He was, however, demonstrating the nature of God and teaching that in the Bible God shares in the suffering of his people. In that regard God is the most tragic figure in the Bible.

For the followers of Jesus, Lieberman's comments may be a source of enlightenment. In Luke the miracle of the transfiguration is a foreshadowing of Jesus' death. The first and last of the prophets, Moses and Elijah, speak about his exodus in Jerusalem. But even in the face of death, the glory of the divine presence appears in a tangible way. The voice from the cloud challenges the disciples of Jesus. They are called to obey the teachings of Jesus. He is designated "my Son" and "my Chosen" by the divine voice.[8] The anointed one of God is commissioned to fulfill his call in Jerusalem. For the disciples Jesus dies the death of a prophet like the suffering servant in Isaiah 53 who gives himself for others. It is the ultimate image of the one suffering for the many. It is like the words of Isaiah 63:8, "In all their [the people's] afflictions, he [God himself] was afflicted." God shares in the anguish of his people. It means that God's presence can be experienced in the midst of the deepest human suffering and the most intense pain.

The actual meaning of the transfiguration will always remain something of a mystery for Jesus' disciples. First and foremost, the event seems to be a prophecy about the passion of Jesus. The splendor of his appearance, moreover, signals God's overcoming presence in an imperfect world. The transfiguration challenges the followers of Jesus to ponder the way he participated in human suffering. They will always wonder in awe at the mighty works of God in fulfilling his higher redemptive strategy. The climax of the story is heard when the call comes forth from the cloud, "Listen to him!" The tragedy of church history is documented in the failure to obey the voice. The disciples of Jesus must devote themselves to hear, understand, and follow the instructions of their master. When we view his cross and consider his sufferings, we are challenged to recognize God's redemptive presence in a world filled with human need and to act in obedience by putting the teachings of Jesus into practice.

NOTES

1. The synoptic problem deals with the literary relationships between the three Gospels of Matthew, Mark, and Luke. Scholars seek to understand the life and teachings of Jesus through comparative study. Today most biblical scholars attribute the greatest authority to Mark as the first and most accurate record of Jesus' life. Sometimes the mechanical application of this approach tends to minimize the value of Matthew and Luke. See the solid discussion of current scholarship, W. G. Kümmel, *Introduction to the New Testament* (Nashville: Abingdon, 1973), 38–79. For a fascinating critique of the prevailing theory of Markan priority, compare Hans-Herbert Stoldt, *History and Criticism of the Marcan Hypothesis* (Macon, Ga.: Mercer, 1980). Here the account of Luke is of major consideration. On the synoptic problem, see

Lindsey, *A Hebrew Translation of Mark* and my *Jesus and His Jewish Parables*, 129–63.

2. In Hebrew, the Greek word *exodos* would be translated by the term *yetzeah* "going out, departure." This is a literal Hebrew translation. It is the root word used in the famous self-designation of God, "I am the LORD your God who *brought you out* of the land of Egypt . . ." (Exod 20:2). Probably the Greek term *exodos* was used to translate the more shocking Hebrew word *mavet* "death." If so, the Greek translator might be giving his understanding of the cross. It is an exodus rather than a death.

3. See I. H. Marshall, *Commentary on Luke* (NIGTC; Grand Rapids: Eerdmans, 1979) 384: "The word is used of the 'departure *par excellence*,' the Exodus from Egypt (Heb 11:22), and euphemistically of death (Wis 3:2, 7:6; cf. 2 Pet 1:15, significantly in the context of an allusion to the transfiguration). But the precise force here is uncertain; it may refer to: 1. simply the death of Jesus (W. Michaelis, "ἔξοδος," *TDNT* 5.107; Schürmann, I.558); 2. the whole event of Jesus' death, resurrection and ascension as his departure to heaven (cf. 9:51; Zahn, 383); 3. the death of Jesus as an act of salvation, repeating the Exodus conducted by Moses (J. Manek, "The New Exodus in the Books of Luke," *Novum Testamentum* 2 [1955] 8–23); 4. the whole life of Jesus as a 'way' which leads from his *eisodos* (Acts 13:24) to its conclusion in Jerusalem. Although the accent is firmly on the death of Jesus, we should probably not exclude the thoughts of the resurrection of Jesus (since for Luke cross and resurrection belong firmly together) and of the saving significance of the event (Ellis, 142). This event was to be fulfilled by Jesus in Jerusalem."

4. See Sifre Deut. 10–11 (R. Hammer, trans., *Sifre on Deuteronomy* [New Haven: Yale University] 35). Of course the prototype for the event is Moses who is transfigured after receiving the Ten Commandments (cf. Exod 34:29–35 and also Paul's description, 2 Cor 3:18). See also Davies and Allison, *Matthew*, 2.696. The Community Rule of the Essenes, moreover, describes the garments of the righteous in a similar manner: "life without end, a crown of glory and a garment of majesty in unending light" (1QS 4.7–8). As Flusser observed, "Here then we have a garment of light worn by the blessed with their crown of glory." See his introduction to the fine work of H. Schreckenburg and K. Schubert, *Jewish Historiography and Iconography in Early and Medieval Christianity* (Assen: Van Gorcum and Minneapolis: Fortress, 1991), xvii.

5. Pesikta Rabbati, Piska 4:2 (Braude, trans., *Pesikta Rabbati*, 1.84–85).

6. See also the discussion of the teaching of Jesus in Bivin and Blizzard, *Understanding the Difficult Words of Jesus*. Compare also S. Sandmel, *Judaism and Christian Beginnings* (New York: Oxford University, 1978) 9–18 and 113–26. See here the chapter "The Baptism of the Messiah," where another heavenly voice is heard.

7. The anecdote about Lieberman appeared in *Masoret* 2 (Winter 1993) 1. In the article, "In the Company of Great Minds," Yochanan Muffs recalls, "I remember when Lieberman asked me in class, 'You think you know Bible, Muffs? Who is the most tragic figure in the Bible?' I promptly answered, 'Neither Jacob nor Job, but King Saul.' 'Not bad for a beginner,' he said. 'But the most tragic figure in the Bible, according to the rabbis, is God, who is torn between His love for Israel and His realistic understanding of their nature.' "

8. See Daniel Harrington, *The Gospel of Matthew* (Collegeville, Minn.: Liturgical, 1991) 256: "In the context of Jesus' final journey up to Jerusalem the transfiguration balances off the passion predictions and the calls to follow Jesus in his sufferings. It provides a preview of the glory of the resurrection."

20
The Son or the Vineyard?

THE PARABLE OF THE WICKED HUSBANDMEN (LUKE 20:9–19; Mark 12:1–12; Matt 21:33–46), which Jesus tells upon the temple mount during the week prior to his crucifixion, is often thought to explain how the Jewish people were rejected by God and replaced with the church as the new Israel. The old Israel has passed into oblivion according to this interpretation. Here I will suggest that the parable is not about the church but about Jesus himself. In reality, the traditional teaching about this parable fundamentally contradicts the message of Jesus.[1]

Has God rejected the Jewish people? Will God break his eternal covenant with the Jewish people in order to establish a new Israel?[2] Many Christian teachings on this parable say "yes" and proclaim that Israel has been disinherited and replaced. But the question must be asked: Is this the message that Jesus wanted to communicate the week before his passion? Although great validity is given to this approach for the parable, the Bible interpreters who hold the position do not explain the key terms of the illustration or the conclusion of the dramatic story Jesus tells to the priests on the temple mount. For example, what does the key term "husbandmen" mean? What is the significance of the son? Why is he called beloved (Luke 20:13)? Why does Jesus refer to a stone? What in the world did Jesus mean when he said, "Every one who falls on that stone will be broken to pieces; but when it falls on any one it will crush him" (Luke 20:18)? None of these questions are answered adequately by New Testament critics who confidently teach that Jesus wanted to disinherit the Jewish people by telling the so-called parable of the Wicked Husbandmen.

Is it possible that we Christians have been sincerely wrong about this parable? In reality, dogmatic church doctrine may actually conceal the meaning of Jesus' message. A careful study of the parable reveals that Christians who have accepted the traditional explanation of the parable may actually have rejected Jesus' teaching about himself! The parable is not about the church, but Jesus.

What did Jesus teach in this parable? A man had a vineyard. He leased it to husbandmen (tenant farmers). The owner of the vineyard sent his servants to collect his portion of the produce from the tenants. The tenants refuse to pay the assigned distribution to the servants of the owner of the vineyard. Then, in a shocking turn of events, the owner decides to send his beloved (only) son to collect. The tenants kill his son. Does the parable emphasize the vineyard or the son?[3] The leading figure of the entire story is the son. The main theme of the parable focuses upon the vineyard owner's son, not upon the real estate. At the heart of the story, furthermore, Jesus proclaims, "The stone which the builders rejected has become the head of the corner" (Ps 118:22–23). In conclusion, he goes on to make the curious declaration "Every one who falls on that stone will be broken to pieces; but when it falls on any one it will crush him" (Luke 20:18). No one will understand the parable unless the key terms of the parable are defined in their original Jewish setting in life. The final stone saying is a key verse for the story, and the Jewish background provides rich insight into the original message of Jesus.

What should the parable of the Wicked Husbandmen be named? The traditional title of this parable is greatly misleading. It tends to vilify the Jewish people as the "wicked husbandmen," even though the term "tenants" (husbandmen) can be related only to the corrupt temple leadership who received their position of authority from Rome (Luke 20:1, Mark 11:27, Matt 21:23). Other New Testament scholars have suggested that it should be called the parable of "the Vineyard." The traditional title emphasizes the actions of the tenants, that is, the wicked husbandmen. The second suggested title focuses upon the real estate. Is the vineyard the main theme or are the wicked husbandmen the primary emphasis? Parables teach one message. I contend that the most important part of this parable is the son. When the parable's title focuses on the vineyard or the husbandmen, the image of the leading character, that is, the son of the owner, is pushed into the background. When one understands the message of the parable in the original context, it becomes clear that the parable is not primarily concerned with either the wicked husbandmen (tenant farmers) or the vineyard (land). It is a parable about the son. The story focuses upon Jesus himself.

The illustration might more properly be titled the parable of "the Only Son." The name we give a parable is important. It shows how we understand its controlling idea. The message of the parable of the Only Son is seldom, if ever, understood. Those who emphasize the actions of the tenants miss the message. Others who believe that Jesus addresses the issue of the vineyard forget that he is speaking about his own purpose and mission. One must not miss the point of Jesus' illustration. When a person faces death, especially execution, he or she will consider the pain of suffering before thinking about what the church will be like many years into the future.

The message of Jesus will be heard clearly when one begins by defining three key terms in the story: 1. husbandmen, 2. beloved son, and 3. stone. These key terms must be viewed in light of the parable's Jewish context and the stone saying at the conclusion of the gospel text.

1. Husbandmen = tenant farmers who live on the land

First, the husbandmen are not merely farmers. They are tenant farmers who occupy the land in the absence of the land owner. They agree to pay him with a portion of the produce. They live on the land and retain a tremendous amount of control as long as they keep their side of the bargain. They must remember who owns the land and pay him according to their agreement, which was probably about forty per cent.

2. Beloved son = only son

Second, the *beloved son* in the parable (Luke 20:13), should be translated as the *only son*.[4] Linguistic studies in both Greek and Hebrew have argued correctly for this meaning of the term "beloved." Hence the word "beloved" in Greek, *agapētos,* as well as its Hebrew equivalent *yachid,* both mean "only." The son of the story is the vineyard owner's only son (Luke 20:13; see also Mark 12:6, "he had still one other, a beloved [only] son").[5] This point is vital for the plot of the story parable because a normal Middle Eastern family of the period would have consisted of several children. The land owner, therefore, would ordinarily have had more than one heir. The single heir, therefore, heightens the suspense of the story. He has one son. The original audience of the parable understands the plan of the tenants. These tenant farmers devise their scheme and determine their course of action. Since their absentee landlord has only one son and heir, they reason that if they kill his son they will possess the vineyard. After all, they live on the land, the land owner is not present, and the only heir will be dead. They will be able to claim the vineyard for themselves.

3. Stone = Jesus the son of David

Third, in Jewish thought the stone (*even*) mentioned in the end of the illustration would make a clear reference to King David. In the context of the parable, the stone would point toward Jesus as the son of David. This is confirmed by the Jewish interpretations of Psalm 118:22–23 in light of King David's life. At least the Jewish commentaries on this psalm related the stone to King David. At the beginning, young David, who was destined to become the greatest of all the kings of Israel, was rejected by the builders. The rabbis said,

> "The stone which the builders rejected has become the head of the corner" (Ps 118:22): "the builders" [mentioned in the verse] refer to Samuel and Jesse. The words "has become the head of the corner" refer to David because he became the head [that is, the greatest] of the kings.[6]

David was rejected by the builders. They saw his small stature and his red hair (ruddy appearance). They would have preferred one of the other sons of Jesse who appeared to be more handsome and strong. But the young shepherd boy's strength was from within, and David was chosen and anointed with oil. The unassuming young man would become king of Israel, and in the minds of many historians, David was the greatest of them all. The basic idea of this Jewish commentary on Psalm 118 has been explained in one of the Dead Sea Scrolls which preserves Hebrew fragments of the apocryphal Psalm 151. David was not the first choice of Samuel and Jesse, and in the Dead Sea Scroll King David asserts,

> Smaller was I than my brothers and the youngest of the sons of my father, so he made me shepherd of his flock. . . . He sent his prophet to anoint me, Samuel to make me great; my brothers went out to

meet him handsome of figure and appearance. Though they were tall of stature and handsome by their hair, the Lord God chose them not. But he sent and took me from behind the flock and anointed me with holy oil, and he made me leader of his people and ruler over the sons of his covenant.[7]

David as a stone was rejected. But he became, nonetheless, the chief cornerstone. The words of the parable draw a line of comparison between the only son, the stone, and King David, whose illustrious career became the model for the future Messiah.

THE SON, THE STONE, AND THE BUILDERS

Finally, it should be noted that the key terms in the parable make a play on words. They look and sound alike in Hebrew. The word play focuses on the terms "son" (in Hebrew, *ben*), "sons" (in Hebrew, *banim*), or "builders" (in Hebrew, *bonim*), "stone" (in Hebrew, *even*) or in the plural "stones" (in Hebrew, *avanim*). In Psalm 118, the stone is rejected by the builders. In the Jewish commentary the son of Jesse, who is despised and rejected, becomes the stone of the corner. He is David the greatest of the kings.

The Jewish literature tells us about how the builders—Samuel the prophet and Jesse the father of David—rejected the future king. They wanted to anoint one of the other sons of Jesse to be king over Israel in the place of Saul. They did not want David to replace Saul. They preferred one of his brothers. But the Lord spoke clearly that though David was not as handsome in appearance, God looked on the inside and saw his heart. God chose David to be king (1 Sam 16:1–13).

The builders, Samuel the prophet and Jesse, David's father, accepted the word of the Lord, and though David was rejected by the builders, he became the head of the corner. Though Psalm 118 did not have a title ascribing it to David, in Jewish tradition it was related to King David. When Jesus made reference to the psalm in the conclusion of the parable, it was natural for the listeners to understand that the only son of the owner of the vineyard was the son of David.

The people expected the Messiah to come from the house of David. This is seen in the Synoptic Gospels. Jesus is from the house of David. The kingly Messiah was to be called the son of David, *ben david*. The stone in the parable refers to the son of David.

Though the stone is rejected by the builders, it becomes the head of the corner. In the parable the only son of the vineyard owner is killed. Although he is defeated by death, he is the son who becomes the head of the corner. How can he be successful after he is killed?

The parable is a prophecy about Jesus and recalls the earlier predictions Jesus made about his passion. In the prophecies Jesus made concerning his death, one always hears a final word of victory. Jesus tells the disciples, "Behold, we are going up to Jerusalem and everything that is written of the Son of man by the prophets will be accomplished. For he will be delivered to the Gentiles and will be mocked and shamefully treated and spit upon; they will scourge him and kill him, and on the third day he will rise" (Luke 18:31–33). He is the son who is rejected and killed. But on the third day he will rise from death.

THE STONE SAYING

The stone saying at the conclusion of the parable is of primary significance. Without an understanding of the stone saying, readers will miss the message of the parable. Jesus concludes the story with a prediction of his future victory. The death of the only son who is rejected by the builders will not hinder the ultimate success of the son of David. Jesus explains:

> Everyone who falls on that stone will be broken to pieces but when it falls on any one it will crush him (Luke 20:18).

What is preferable? Is it better to be broken to pieces or to be crushed? What is Jesus saying to the crowds of people gathered in the temple?

The somewhat puzzling saying is not about being literally broken or crushed. The emphasis of Jesus in this saying, as throughout the parable, is upon the stone. It does not make any difference whether someone falls on the stone or the stone falls upon someone. The strong point is clear: No matter what happens, the stone remains!

The rabbis relate a similar illustration. They speak about the attacks against the Jewish people. The people of Israel are compared to a stone. It is a stone which cannot be broken by the foreign oppressors who have sought to persecute the Jewish people. The rabbis make a humorous comparison between a pot and a stone. They teach,

> If a stone falls on a pot, woe to the pot! If a pot falls on a stone, woe to the pot! In either case woe to the pot! So whoever ventures to attack them [the people of Israel] receives his deserts on their account.[8]

Like the stone in the saying of Jesus, the stone in the rabbinic teaching remains intact while the pot is broken. The people of Israel are victorious in spite of the attacks against them. It does not matter if the pot falls on the stone or the stone falls on the pot. One can easily sense a note of sharp humor in the colorful saying. Perhaps the people standing upon the temple mount who listened to the stone saying smiled when Jesus said, "Everyone who falls on that stone will be broken to pieces but when it falls on any one it will crush him." The parallel rabbinic saying makes reference to the chosen people. Though the people of Israel are attacked by others, they remain victorious. No matter what happens, the Jewish people survive with a strong faith and a clear identity. If the stone in the poetic saying of Jesus refers to himself, it shows his own high self-awareness. Through personal struggle he could envision ultimate triumph.

THE STONE AND THE SON OF DAVID

Jesus is betrayed by one of his own disciples, Judas, who was among the inner circle of twelve. The corrupt Saducean priests who had received authority over the temple complex were willing to cooperate with the Romans. As builders, neither the Romans nor their Saducean temple leaders were ready to recognize Jesus as the son of David. The high priest Caiaphas received his position from the Roman overlords.[9] He realized that someone who claimed to be the son of David or made allusions to a messianic task must be eliminated to save the people from reprisals by Rome (see John 11:48–49). The question of taxes and Jesus' purification of the temple were strong provocation for the Romans and their allies among the Saducean priests. As a foreign governor, Pilate believed that Barabbas was more dangerous to Rome than Jesus. Since he had to release a prisoner during the feast, he preferred to release Jesus, who was less of a danger in his view. In the end Jesus' saying about his fate came true. Pilate sentenced Jesus and the Romans crucified him.

Jesus is concerned about the hostility he will be required to absorb. He has many supporters among the people on the temple mount, though some of the Sadducees cooperated with the Romans. The parable is a way of talking with those who would cooperate with the Romans. Jesus desires to speak prophetically in a nonthreatening way. Jesus is sharing his pain with those who will listen. The parable of the Only Son portrays Jesus' strong confidence in his special mission.

But one must not forget the pain. Jesus loves all people. His suffering had a higher redemptive purpose. In speaking prophetically about his death, he shared his love with others—even those who desired his death to pacify the Romans and to prevent a national catastrophe. Of great interest is the fact that the large number of people on the temple mount strongly supported Jesus. He spoke the parable to the people (Luke 20:9). Not only does the conclusion of the parable say that the priests and their scribes "feared the people" (Luke 20:19), which clearly indicates that Jesus had many friends among the crowds gathered together on that day, but also when they heard about the fate of the son of the vineyard owner they reacted by saying, "God forbid!" (Luke 20:16). Apparently they were shocked by the fate of the son and did not desire to see his death. Perhaps these supporters of Jesus on the temple mount were like the Pharisees who warned Jesus when Herod Antipas wanted to kill him (Luke 13:31).

In all events, the so-called parable of the Wicked Husbandmen would be better titled the parable of the Only Son. Not only does Jesus speak about his special task as the son of David, but also he speaks about his future victory. The stone remains. Moreover, if the stone saying is studied in light of the passion predictions of Jesus, one sees that each time Jesus mentions his death he also prophesies that on the third day he will rise. The traditional interpretation of the parable has focused upon an ecclesiology. Wrongly such interpretations teach that the parable is about the church. The new Israel replaces the old. In reality, the parable is about Christology. Perhaps it is the most messianic text in the Gospels.

Jesus is saying that though the son (*ben*) will be killed, he is the stone (*even*) which cannot be moved or destroyed. The stone will attain the final victory. The stone rejected by the builders becomes the chief cornerstone. Even in death he will triumph. His victory, moreover, is also the ultimate triumph of the people. Jesus will triumph, and his victory will be complete. Death cannot defeat Jesus the son of David! He is the stone that becomes the head of the corner.

NOTES

1. I have discussed the parable in *Jesus and His Jewish Parables*, 282–316. Here I have summarized the results of my earlier study with some practical application.

2. On this vital theological issue, see the important work of Marvin Wilson, *Our Father Abraham* (Grand Rapids: Eerdmans, 1989) and Clemens Thoma, *A Christian Theology of Judaism* (Mahwah, N. J.: Paulist, 1980). See especially the long foreword to Thoma's book by David Flusser.

3. The strong emphasis on the wrong approach is based upon the verse ". . . he [the owner of the vineyard] will come and destroy those tenants and give the vineyard to others" (Luke 20:16), and the text unique to Matthew, ". . . the kingdom of God will be taken away from you and given to a nation producing the fruits of it" (Matt 21:43). I have treated these texts extensively in my book *Jesus and His Jewish Parables*. Here I would emphasize that the vineyard is merely a part of the background stage which is set to focus attention on the overwhelming figure of the only son. One must listen carefully for the one point that a parable is teaching. Cf. also Flusser, *Judaism and the Origins of Christianity*, 552–74. The time of the corrupt Roman-controlled priesthood of the temple mount had come to an end. They were Sadducees. After the destruction of the temple in 70 C.E., the early church as well as centers of Jewish learning like Yavneh, representing the powerful spiritual revitalization of the Pharisees in the aftermath of the tragic war, flourished. But the Sadducees had faded from history.

4. I greatly appreciate the rich insight of R. L. Lindsey and his treatment of the Gospel of Luke in *A Hebrew Translation of the Gospel of Mark*. Lindsey has shown that Luke preserves the Semitic text of the Gospels and the original Hebrew flavor of the teaching of Jesus. I am grateful to R. L. Lindsey and David Flusser for their comments concerning the "only son" in the parable.

5. On the question of the best translation of the term "only" *agapētos* in the parable see *Jesus and His Jewish Parables*, 309, nn. 15–16. C. H. Turner, in his article "ὁ υἱός μου ὁ ἀγαπητός," which appeared in the *Journal of Theological Studies* 27 (1926) 113–29, made the

point quite clearly. Flusser argued for this meaning of the text (private communication).

6. Midrash Hagadol on Deuteronomy 1:17 (Fisch, 32), and see *Jesus and His Jewish Parables*, 313, n. 37.

7. Psalm 151, the apocryphal psalm attributed to King David which was found among the Dead Sea Scrolls (see also the Greek version in the LXX). See J. A. Sanders, *Discoveries in the Judean Desert, the Psalms Scroll of Qumran 11* (New York: Oxford University, 1965) 48–56. See also the Hebrew article by David Flusser and S. Safrai, "Shire David Hechitzoneyim," in *Sefer Zikaron Layehoshua Grintz* (Tel Aviv: Hakibbutz Hameuchad, 1982) 84, 92. See my discussion, *Jesus and His Jewish Parables*, 313.

8. Esther Rabbah 7:10 and see Billerbeck, *Kommentar zum Neuen Testament aus Talmud und Midrasch,* 1.877, and A. Hyman, *Toldot Tannaim Veamoraim* (Jerusalem: Boys Town, 1963) 3.1189–91.

9. On the trial of Jesus, see especially, Flusser, *Judaism and the Origins of Christianity*, 575–609.

21
Pilate or the Jewish People?

DURING THE TRIAL OF JESUS IN THE TEMPLE COM-
plex, the Roman governor Pilate gives the people
a choice. He had to release a prisoner for the
Passover holiday. Will it be Jesus or Barabbas? By any standard
of justice the trial of Jesus is deemed completely unfair. But the
Jewish people have also suffered in an unfair trial. Through
the centuries the church fathers and Christian historians have
pointed the finger accusingly at God's people and pronounced
sentence: "The Jews killed Jesus." In actuality the Gospels tell
a much different story. Pilate and the influence of Rome were
far more pervasive. Many Christians want to know what really
happened during the trial of Jesus. It is an issue of history.
Nonetheless, traditional interpretations of Jewish hatred have
sometimes become more sacred to the church than the New
Testament record itself. Today people are more willing to leave
prejudice behind. They want to learn from the Gospel.

Who is the major force behind the execution of Jesus upon the
cross? The traditional view of Jesus' trial must be challenged.
The onus of guilt has been borne by the Jewish people collec-
tively. While Pilate asked the people whether they wanted Jesus
or Barabbas, in the historical study of the Gospels another
question must be answered: Who is responsible—Pilate or the
Jewish people? The Gospel of Luke makes it clear that Pilate
himself, the Roman prefect, gave the death sentence (Luke
23:24). According to the New Testament the Romans crucified
Jesus and not the Jews. Following the death sentence that Pilate
pronounced on Jesus, however, the church has put the people of
Jesus on trial. Is the Roman governor Pilate—or are the Jews—
responsible for Jesus' death?

Through the centuries, the church has persecuted the Jewish
people as a whole for the crucifixion of Jesus. Some Christians
have claimed, "The Jews killed Jesus and so we may treat them

as we wish."[1] These same Christians have taught that Pilate was a political leader of vision who saw the innocence of Jesus. Pilate was forced to collude with the Jewish leaders' death plot against Jesus. In fact, in one church tradition Pilate was beatified as a saint. After all, he washed his hands at the trial of Jesus. He listened carefully to the dream that his wife is reported to have had in the Gospel of Matthew. Pilate becomes a wise leader who was more or less coerced by the people according to traditional church teachings. He is a bystander who is led astray by the Jewish leaders. He is merely a governmental official who should not be blamed for the decision of his court. Here a closer examination of the evidence of the Gospels as well as historical documents from the New Testament era make this view impossible. Pilate was not an innocent victim. As the representative of imperial Rome, he was probably the major power behind the trial. Historically, the policies of Rome and its puppets were the reasons for the unjust trial and the crucifixion of Jesus. The effort to place blame upon the Jewish people was intended to shift guilt away from the political powers of the day.

THE FEAR OF ROME

The fear of the Romans was not without justification. As a popular messianic movement, Jesus and his followers were growing in numbers. The Romans maintained an ardent policy of putting down all Jewish messianic movements. Rome ruled the land, and even controlled the Jewish priesthood. The door of the holy office of high priest could only be opened and closed by Roman appointment. Rome held the sacred vestments of the high priest under lock and key. Rome's supreme power over the province and its people could only be maintained through strong force. Crucifixion as a means of capital punishment gives gruesome evidence of the Roman policy of fear which was used as a political weapon in every corner of the empire. The messianic concept in Israel was a religious and political ideology that could not be tolerated in a land held under Roman domination. In John's Gospel the people share their unmitigated fear of Rome with Caiaphas the high priest, "If we let him [Jesus] go thus . . . , the Romans will come and destroy both our holy place and our nation" (John 11:48). The mention of the Romans in the Gospel is unusual. No doubt during the first century Roman

officials and armed soldiers were seen frequently throughout
the land of Israel and especially in Jerusalem. The fear of Rome
probably caused the evangelists to downplay their ubiquitous
presence. While Rome did allow the temple worship for a recognized ancient faith, keeping peace in the holy city was a
challenge. The influx of Jewish pilgrims from all parts of the
known world to observe the high holy days in Jerusalem created
potential risks. The military would prevent disturbances. The
Roman garrisons of armed troops were hated by the people.

The pervasive military presence was a reminder that the day
of independence was over. Freedom of religious conviction was
severely limited. Jewish political autonomy was only a vague
memory. The idea of a future deliverer produced great hope in
the hearts of many in the Jewish nation. Perhaps as in the days
of the Maccabees or of King David himself, the freedom of the
people would again become a reality. A second Moses would
appear and bring liberation. In any case, according to the policy
of imperial Rome the messianic belief of the Jews had to be
strictly monitored and strongly oppressed. History proves that
Rome was willing to use powerful legions, military strength, and
brutal force to suppress Jewish messianic hopes. Consequently,
the intense fear of Roman military intervention as a reaction to
belief in Jesus was not without foundation. As we noted from
John's Gospel, Jews feared that Romans would destroy their
"holy place and nation" (John 11:48).

Although all the high priests were appointed by the Roman
leadership, Joseph Caiaphas betrays his own fear of the government's power when he listened carefully to these words of warning. He responds by saying that it is better for one man to die
than that the whole nation perish. The holy place and the nation
should be preserved. In a short span of less than forty years, the
Romans did destroy the temple. Not long after the death, burial, and resurrection of Jesus, the swift might of the Roman
Empire was revealed when legions of soldiers marched across
the land of Israel making war against the Jewish people. Again,
just some sixty years after the destruction of Jerusalem in 70
C.E., the power of imperial Rome put down yet another revolt
in the land of Israel during the fierce guerrilla war from 132 to
135 C.E. This time the revolt was spearheaded by the messianic
hopes surrounding the charismatic leadership of Bar Kochba.
The destruction of Jerusalem in 70 C.E. was Rome's response to
the messianic hopes of the Jewish people and their longing for

religious freedom and political autonomy. The Romans were serious about fighting against Jewish messianism in all its forms.

THE PHARISEES AND JESUS

While the role of Pilate in the trial of Jesus has been largely minimized in the church, the Pharisees are understood to have wanted Jesus' death. Christian tradition emphasizes the role of the Pharisees. Mistakenly it has been taught that Jesus' theological teachings challenged the Pharisees, and, therefore, they wanted him to die. This popular approach has deep roots in Christian hostility toward ancient Jewish thought and ignores the great similarity between the teachings of Jesus and those of the Pharisees.[2] The theology of Jesus was actually almost identical to that of the Pharisees. In contrast to the Sadducees, Pharisees believed in the oral interpretation of the Torah, the resurrection of the dead, the messianic idea, angels, demons, and the devotion to God who is actively involved in the affairs of creation. Almost all the priests were Sadducees. Caiaphas and his power base could not agree with such Pharisaic views. They believed strongly in God and a literal interpretation of the written Torah. The Sadducees, moreover, were much more willing to cooperate with Rome. While Jesus criticized the hypocritical practices of some Pharisees, he never uttered a negative word about the teachings of the Pharisees. He said that they sit on Moses' seat. Like an insider, Jesus said that their teachings were good, but they did not always practice what they preached (Matt 23:1–2). His sharp criticism of the hypocrisy of some Pharisees is far different from an attack against the theology of Pharisaism.

THE SADDUCEES AND JESUS

During his last days Jesus taught openly in the temple. He sat in the backyard of the Sadducean priests and was confronted by opponents who asked him leading questions. One must remember the triumphal entry into Jerusalem and the purification of the temple, events which certainly captured the attention of the Roman authorities as well as the Sadducees. Three issues were raised by the questions of Jesus' opponents. First they ask about his authority. Then they pose a question about paying taxes to

Caesar. Finally, they press him concerning the resurrection of the dead. Probably all three of these questions would only be raised by Sadducees. The third question about the resurrection is asked in a way that ridicules the Pharisees' theological views. The issue of paying taxes possessed far-reaching political ramifications. Anyone who refused to pay taxes would be linked to the Zealots and would quite possibly face execution. The issue of authority would also be of intense interest to the Sadducean priesthood, especially following Jesus' dramatic entrance into the temple through the eastern gate and the purification of the sanctuary.

THE JEWISH PEOPLE AND JESUS

Unfortunately, traditional Christian teachings portray all the Jewish people as rejecting Jesus and his teachings. The witness of the Gospel texts, however, makes it clear that Jesus had many followers during this period. The evangelists stress that the chief priests feared the multitudes of Jesus' followers who gathered around him in the temple complex (Luke 20:19). The Romans and the Sadducees were convinced that Jesus and his messianic movement posed a danger. But the Sadducean priests who cooperated with the Roman authorities were afraid to arrest him on the temple mount because of the multitudes of Jesus' friends and well-wishers who listened to his message. By necessity they had to wait until a more opportune time when the crowds of the Jewish people were celebrating Passover in their private homes. The temple complex would then be filled with the priests and their local supporters who would be strongly sympathetic to Rome.

From a historical standpoint the reason for Jesus' death was political rather than theological. The Pharisees did not kill teachers for saying the things that Jesus said. In fact, many parallels between the teachings of Jesus and Pharisaic theology have come to light in a comparative study of Judaism in late antiquity. For example, many rabbis taught in parables. Jesus was not brought before Pilate because of his teaching. The motive was political. Anyone suspected of promoting the ancient Jewish idea of the Messiah had to be stopped. The Sadducees would have collaborated with the Roman authorities in their efforts to curtail and cut off messianic movements. The

Pharisees and the common people, on the other hand, would not have been willing to help Rome and those who played by the rules of *Realpolitik* of the Second Temple period.

On the contrary, two New Testament passages demonstrate that the Pharisees would have strongly opposed action against Jesus. The Pharisees warned Jesus that Herod Antipas wanted to kill him. Few Christians are aware of the fact that in Luke's Gospel the Pharisees were so concerned about the well-being of Jesus that they told him about the death plot of Herod Antipas. The same Herod put John the Baptist to death. In Galilee the Pharisees warned Jesus, "Get away from here, for Herod wants to kill you" (Luke 13:31). The Pharisees wanted to save Jesus' life. They desired to protect him against the plans of Herod Antipas. In another text from the book of Acts, Gamaliel saves the lives of Peter and John when the Sadducees sought their death for teaching about what happened to Jesus. Although the priests were against the apostles, it is clear that their attitude was not shared by the Pharisees. In the Acts of the Apostles, the ones who went after Peter and John are identified: "But the high priest rose up and all who were with him, that is, the party of the Sadducees . . ." (Acts 5:17). The apostles probably had many friends and supporters among the Jewish population in Jerusalem because the police forces of the priests were careful not to arrest them with force because they feared the people. If the people realized that they were arresting the apostles, the police would have encountered intense resistance with stone throwing. The record of Acts makes the situation clear: "Then the captain with the officers went and brought them [Peter and the apostles], but without violence, for they were afraid of being stoned by the people" (Acts 5:26). While some caution must be exercised in identifying the people *(laos)* with card-carrying Pharisees, surely most of these folk are indeed Pharisees in theology or possess strong leanings toward Pharisaic faith and practice. Jesus himself asked his disciples to follow the teachings of the Pharisees (Matt 23:2), all the while warning against the "leaven" or hypocritical practices of some Pharisees. Josephus assures us that the Pharisees possessed great influence among the common townfolk.[3] It appears that the Pharisees and the common people supported the apostles so much that they would stone the police who arrested Peter and the apostles.

In the council the leader of the Pharisees, Gamaliel, argued vigorously on behalf of Peter and the apostles. He noted previous messianic movements which all had been put down by the force of Rome. On behalf of the Pharisees, and his own strong convictions, Gamaliel pleaded the cause of the apostles:

> For before these days Theudas arose, giving himself out to be somebody, and a number of men, about four hundred, joined him; but he was slain and all who followed him were dispersed and came to nothing. After him Judas the Galilean arose in the days of the census and drew away some of the people after him; he also perished, and all who followed him were scattered. So in the present case I tell you, keep away from these men and let them alone; for if this plan or this undertaking is of men, it will fail; but if it is of God, you will not be able to overthrow them (Acts 5:36–38).

In a sense, the Pharisees, or at least one of their most respected leaders, protected the early church from the Sadducees.

In reality, it is highly doubtful if Jesus ever appeared before the Sanhedrin. Leaders like Gamaliel would never have allowed such unfair proceedings in a trial. The Greek word *sunedrion* is the term used for council. Sometimes it has wrongly been understood to mean the prestigious high court of the Sanhedrin. During the trial of Jesus, it becomes clear that this was *their* council, that is, the committee of Sadducean priests (Luke 22:66). Primarily they wanted to find a charge such as refusing to pay taxes to Caesar which would help the Romans in their judicial process. They wanted evidence of Jesus' messianic claims for the Roman court. In any case, a meeting of the Sanhedrin under such circumstances is unthinkable.

While some historians believe that the Jewish court was unable to offer the death penalty forty years before the destruction of Jerusalem, this tradition has been seriously challenged. It seems quite probable that a Jewish court had the authority to issue the death penalty. But the trial of Jesus is very much an affair of the Roman officials in charge of Jerusalem. While the Pharisees and the majority of the people opposed such actions, the Sadducean priesthood, who received their power and position from their Roman overlords, felt that it was expedient to cooperate with the empire.

PILATE OR THE JEWS?

Traditional Christian teachings have underestimated the cunning and the devious political mind of Pontius Pilate. Did he try to save Jesus? In the first place, if it is true that Pilate indeed wanted to release Jesus, he could have used his own authority to do so without sending him to Herod Antipas. If the Pharisees in Galilee were aware of Herod's desire to kill Jesus, Pilate may have been aware of the petty ruler's suspicion of Jesus. The Pharisees tried to save Jesus from Antipas. Pilate delivered Jesus into his hands. Herod Antipas was actively involved in the affairs of his district. He maintained his rule through careful surveillance, and he monitored possible rivals or political complications in his little fiefdom. Perhaps Pilate thought that the old fox—who was certainly a son of his father Herod the Great—would do away with Jesus the troublemaker.

Transferring Jesus over to Herod was like sending a notorious criminal to the kangaroo court of the hanging judge. But Pilate apparently was interested in improving his relationship with Herod as well as winning some further political favor for imperial Rome, which he represented. The independently minded son of Herod the Great could handle the matter with less difficulty than the governor of Judea. The action demonstrates the political nature of Jesus' arrest and the miscarriage of justice which he endured in his final hours before the crucifixion. Herod returned the favor. After the torture and ridicule of Jesus, Herod sent him back to Pilate. Both politicians benefited from the prisoner transfer no matter how much mental and emotional distress such maneuvers caused the victim. Luke observed, "And Herod and Pilate became friends with each other that very day, for before this they had been at enmity with each other" (Luke 23:12).

Most discussions of Pilate's role in the trial of Jesus forget two facts. The first is that the Roman governor was required to grant amnesty to someone.[4] During the festival he had to release one prisoner. The second forgotten fact is that the picture of Pilate in the contemporary historical records is far from complimentary. Outside of the church tradition, historians have been unkind to Pilate. He is depicted as a cruel, self-serving tyrant.

At this juncture we will consider the second fact by looking at the historical descriptions of Pilate from first-century sources. Philo the Jewish philosopher pronounces seven accusations against Pilate. One of them is striking in light of Jesus' execution. Philo tells us that Pilate was well known for having prisoners executed without trial. The unfair trial of Jesus verified the account of Philo. Philo offers this description of Pilate's rule:

> . . . the briberies, the insults, the robberies, the outrages and wanton injuries, the executions without trial constantly repeated, the ceaseless and supremely grievous cruelty.[5]

The description of "the executions without trial constantly repeated" is a startling reminder of the cruelty associated with the treatment of Jesus. Pilate sends him to Herod Antipas and then proceeds with a mock trial.

In addition, Josephus tells of Pilate's cold-blooded cruelty. Eventually his callous brutality caused Vitellius to depose him. Pilate caused a slaughter of many devout Samaritans[6] who had become involved in a popular messianic movement. It seems that they had decided to follow a would-be messiah to Mount Gerizim in hopes of finding the hidden sacred vessels which would bring about their redemption. Pilate quickly sent a detachment of cavalry and heavy-armed infantry to massacre the Samaritans. Following the violent incident, Vitellius, the powerful and influential governor of Syria, forced Pilate to return to Rome. Such military action would instill the fear of Rome among the local population, but this time the governor of Judea had gone too far.

Pilate's oppression of the Jewish people is also well documented by Josephus. The Jewish historian recounts how Pilate "introduced by night and under cover the effigies of Caesar which are called standards." Perhaps he wanted to win favor from Tiberius for imposing Roman influence upon the sacred city of Jerusalem. Pilate broke all custom when he introduced the symbols of pagan worship and foreign domination into the city of the sacred temple of the Jewish people. But Pilate was greatly surprised by the results. His action was an expression of Rome's idolatrous practices, and the people demanded that he remove the standards. Pilate's provocation aroused immense excitement and profound indignation.

Crowds of demonstrators besieged Pilate in his residence at Caesarea on the coast of the Mediterranean Sea. Josephus describes the major disturbance that Pilate's ill-willed deed had caused: "Hastening after Pilate to Caesarea, the Jews implored him to remove the standards from Jerusalem and to uphold the laws of their ancestors."[7] The Jewish people were dedicated to their faith and were not willing to let Pilate's precedent become the new law of the Roman Empire. But Pilate would not give up easily. He threatened the crowds with death. Apparently the people had gathered in the great amphitheater of Caesarea to hear Pilate's response to their demands. Pilate had Roman soldiers surround the amphitheater and draw their swords ready for the murderous slaughter of the Jews. Pilate reasoned that when the people faced a choice between death or compliance with the wish of Rome, they would surely give up. He was mistaken. Instead of complying out of fear for their lives, the Jewish people laid their necks down to the ground and motioned for the death sentence to be carried out. They preferred death to the desecration of the holy city and its sanctuary. Pilate was not willing to risk the political ramifications of a major slaughter of the Jews, and so he agreed to have the standards removed from the city. The crowd won, over Pilate's wish.

Pilate was devoted to his career and to the position of Rome with its supreme authority. In another incident Pilate had his way against the wishes of the people. Josephus reports how Pilate robbed the treasury of the temple to pay for an aqueduct which he desired to build in grand Roman fashion. The people objected to embezzlement of the donations designated for the sanctuary. This was thievery of sacred temple funds designed to win favor for Pilate himself and for Rome. The people were not so fortunate on this occasion. When a disturbance developed, Pilate sent trained soldiers armed with cudgels under their garments into the crowd. When he gave the signal, the soldiers began to beat the demonstrators mercilessly with deadly force. Many were killed from the brutality and blood-lust of the soldiers as well as in the mad rush of the crowds to escape from the scene. He kept the money.

Pilate was a Roman official who cared first and foremost about his position and the policies of the empire. He showed little compassion during his ten-year rule (26–36 C.E.). Historians viewed his rule with genuine contempt because of his penchant for brutality and ruthless cunning. In the Gospel of Luke Jesus is told about an incident where Pilate killed Galileans. They were offering their sacrifices to God in worship. Pilate mingled the blood of the people with the blood of the sacrificial animals which they were giving to God. The account reveals Pilate's true character (Luke 13:1).

As seen from the record of the Gospels and Acts, Jesus had many friends among the people as well as devoted disciples.[8] It seems that the major opposition to his ministry came from the Sadducean priests who received their privileged status from the Roman officials. Rome and its political policies are largely responsible for this sad state of affairs. At least the high priest and his vestments were controlled by the rule of Rome. No one should underestimate the power of appointment. The high priest had to comply with the wishes of the imperial empire. Rome was intensely dedicated to eradicating any glimmer of messianism among the Jewish people. The Sadducees and the priesthood were dedicated to the status quo. They believed that the Roman yoke was inevitable and that the high culture of Greco-Roman society possessed many virtues. Jesus and his followers presented a serious problem for the priests and the Roman officials with whom they were all too willing to cooperate. On the one hand, many Jews supported Jesus, while on the other the Romans had a strong motive to arrest him and put an end to his movement.

JESUS OR BARABBAS?

The first forgotten fact in the trial of Jesus is revealed in Pilate's action on the temple mount. He gave the group assembled in the temple a choice between Jesus and Barabbas. The Gospel scene probably occurred in the strong fortress of Antonia in the northwest corner of the temple complex. From this massive fortress the Romans could maintain a tight grip over all activities in the temple precincts. The group gathered in that fortress during the time when most people in Jerusalem were at home in the observance of the Passover was probably primarily composed of Sadducees and priests.

Pilate had to release a prisoner. He gave the group gathered in his fortress the choice between Jesus and Barabbas. The Gospels explain, "For of necessity he must release one unto them at the feast" (Luke 23:17).[9] The custom is affirmed in Matt 27:15, Mark 15:6, and John 18:40. It is most surely an original part of Luke though some very important manuscripts delete it. The mistake probably arose because a scribe skipped a line. At Passover, for whatever reason, Pilate had to release one prisoner.[10] The chief priests are identified as leading the group who assembled before Pilate that night. Judas had helped in the arrest of his master, who was rumored to be the Messiah.

Jesus had offered sufficient provocation by his entry into Jerusalem and by the cleansing of the temple. The priests had tried to secure firm evidence that he claimed to be the Messiah and that he urged the people not to pay taxes. The second charge was false. Nevertheless, either accusation was sufficient for a death sentence from Rome.

Did Pilate have a change of heart and seek justice for Jesus? With all that is known about Pilate, it seems highly unlikely. Pilate's personal ambition and his fierce loyalty to the imperial rule of the Roman Empire explain his cunning behavior.

Pilate's decision to release one prisoner was based on expediency. Which prisoner was less dangerous to Rome and Pilate's own position? Barabbas was an insurrectionist. Jesus was the Prince of Peace. Barabbas preached violent revolt. Jesus preached a different message, "Love your enemies." In Pilate's position it was far better to crucify Barabbas and to release Jesus. If he had to release a prisoner, he much preferred to let Jesus go. But the group of Sadducees and priests gathered in the fortress of Antonia urged Pilate to stop Jesus. Unlike the Pharisee Gamaliel who argued wisely in defense of Peter and the apostles, the Sadducees felt that the Jesus movement threatened the nation. As John's Gospel puts it, ". . . everyone will believe in him, and the Romans will come and destroy both our holy place and our nation" (John 11:48).

Pilate gave the death sentence (Luke 23:24). Roman soldiers carried it out.

PILATE'S KING OF THE JEWS

The animosity of Pilate toward the Jewish people can be seen in the message inscribed upon a sign which he ordered to be placed on the cross of a bloody corpse of a man helplessly suspended between heaven and earth. Jesus had endured humiliation. He had suffered inhumane beatings, stinging ridicule, and the excruciating pain of crucifixion. But Pilate wanted a sign. It read "King of the Jews" in three languages. The priests understood what Pilate was saying. It was the final word. They requested that the sign convey a different message. They asked that the wording of the notice be changed. It should say that Jesus claimed to be king of the Jews. But Pilate was obstinate. What he had written would not be changed. The Sadducees were offended at the idea. For them, Jesus should never be called the king of the Jews. But Pilate wanted to make a political statement in the form of a severe warning. The sign was a threat. It mocked Jewish faith and practice. Pilate's words ridiculed the people. In Pilate's mind Rome had crucified the king of the Jews. His action demonstrated the might of the empire and the weakness of Jewish faith in God's future deliverance.

FAITH, HISTORY, AND THEOLOGY

The faith in Jesus proclaims his ultimate victory over the cruel Roman cross through his resurrection. He overcame death in victory. Viewed through the eyes of faith, Jesus gives life because he is the resurrection.[11] In the faith and the theology of his disciples, the historical circumstances surrounding his death, burial, and resurrection dim in comparison with the supreme significance of the sufferings of Jesus. Nonetheless, the misunderstanding of the historical issues pertaining to his trial and crucifixion has caused untold pain to the Jewish people. Millions more Jews would be alive today if it were not for the church. The pages of church history which Christians have forgotten have been memorized by those who have suffered through strong persecution. The pages of the church's history books have been dyed red with the blood of the Jewish faithful. The facts of Jesus' trial are of great value for history.

Christians should never blame modern Jews for the errors of the Sadducean priests. Neither should they place guilt upon Italians, whose ancestors probably played a much more significant role in the death of Jesus. Certainly Pilate's activities and the policies of the Roman Empire have been largely forgotten in the study of the history of Jesus' trial. Should a young generation of Germans be blamed for the sins of Hitler and the Third Reich? The study of history should prevent a new generation from repeating the mistakes of the past. The uncompromising message of Jesus' love should challenge his followers to demonstrate the truth of his message in action. Love is stronger than hatred. Divine love expressed in human action will overcome racial hatred and prejudice. The church must learn from past mistakes and press ahead to fulfill the law of Jesus expressed in godlike love for others.

While often Christians have wrongly persecuted the Jewish people for killing Jesus, they have forgotten that the theology of the early church viewed his suffering as fulfilling the divine plan of redemption. In the faith of Christendom, Jesus had to endure the death of the cross in order to offer himself for sinful humanity. In Christian theology the real reason for Jesus' death is not related to the historical circumstances of the trial. It was both human need for forgiveness and divine grace that mandated the cross. It was not so much the oppression of the Jewish people by the Roman Empire as it was divine love which was uniquely revealed in the person of Jesus. The theology of Christian faith attaches deep significance to the cross. Without death there is no resurrection. Through his agony upon the Roman cross, he shares with and participates in the sufferings of all humanity. When Christians read Isaiah 53, they see Jesus.

But his suffering should also be recognized as a point of unity with his people. For the Romans he was just another trouble-maker among the Jews who needed to be dealt with severely. Perhaps there is no other point in history where Jesus is so much at one with his people than when he suffered upon the cruel cross of Rome.[12] Many have suffered under various political and ideological systems because they were Jews. Jesus is one of them. Though modern Jews and Christians will view the cross from different vantage points, perhaps both faith communities share something in common when they consider the pain of Jesus. He loved his people and suffered as one of his own.

He made the supreme sacrifice. Unfortunately, in history those called by his name have not always lived by his example of self-sacrificing love. Jesus' sufferings on the cross invoke a challenge upon all who consider his agony. He called upon his disciples to deny themselves and walk in his footsteps. The foundation of his ministry was healing love for others. The sacrificial love of Jesus was deeply rooted in the Jewish understanding of divine compassion for people created in the image of God. It is clearly seen in the cross.

NOTES

1. See the sources in H. Schreckenberg, *Die christlichen Adversus-Judaeos-Texte und ihr literarisches und historisches Umfeld (1.-11.Jh.)* (Bern: Peter Lang, 1982).

2. See especially Flusser's introduction to Thoma, *A Christian Theology of Judaism.*

3. See Josephus, *Ant.* 18.15 (18.1.3). Concerning the Pharisees, he observes, "They are, as a matter of fact, extremely influential among the townsfolk; and all prayers and sacred rites of divine worship are performed according to their exposition. This is the great tribute that the inhabitants of the cities, by practicing the highest ideals both in their way of living and their discourse, have paid to the excellence of the Pharisees" (ibid).

4. See also Matt 27:15, Mark 15:6, John 18:39, and some witnesses for Luke 23:7. David Flusser first called my attention to the significance of this fact. Everyone should read his important discussion of the gospel account in *Judaism and the Origins of Christianity* 575–609. On the amnesty, see also Shmuel Safrai, *Die Wallfahrt im Zeitalter des Zweiten Tempels* (Vluyn: Neukirchener, 1981), 206, and compare m. *Pes.* 8:6, b. *Pes.* 91a and j. *Pes.* 36a. The fine historical and exegetical work of R. Brown, *The Death of the Messiah* (New York: Doubleday, 1994), will continue to be the standard academic publication in the study of the trial of Jesus. As Flusser has shown, however, the Gospel of Luke's version has not received the careful attention it merits as a witness, equal to or greater than Mark in authenticity, for the events in the final days of Jesus. See also the photographs of the Caiaphas ossuary.

5. Philo, *Embassy to Gaius* 10.302.

6. See Josephus, *Ant.* 18.87ff.

7. See Josephus, *Jewish War* 2.169–78 and *Ant.* 18.55–64.

8. See my *Jesus and His Jewish Parables,* 282–316.

9. Most modern translations have deleted Luke 23:17 because the verse is missing in important manuscripts including the highly regarded early papyrus witness $\mathfrak{P}^{75}$. The tradition of the amnesty, however, is firmly established in Matthew, Mark, and John. Did a scribe insert Luke 23:17 into the Third Gospel in order to harmonize it with Matthew and Mark? While this is possible, other factors must be considered. The verse does appear in Luke's text in both the uncial manuscripts of Sinaiticus and Bezae. Taken alone, they are not highly valued, but the combination of the two should not be discounted lightly. Verse 17 is attested in $\aleph$ (D sy$^{s.c.}$ *add. p.* 19), W (θ ψ), 063 f$^{1.13}$ (892^{mg}) $\mathfrak{M}$ lat sy$^{p.h.}$ (bo^{pt}). It is indeed possible that a scribe skipped a line and deleted the verse. Multiple copies without Luke 23:17 could have been made over a wide geographical area. Internally, the story needs this verse for the flow of the narrative. I tend to believe that Luke 23:17 was certainly a part of Luke's source and probably was included originally in his Gospel. For a different view of the amnesty tradition, see the solid arguments of Paul Winter, *On the Trial of Jesus* (Berlin: Walter de Gruyter, 1961) 91–99. For evidence against Winter, see note 4 above. Compare Brown, *The Death of the Messiah,* 2.793–95.

10. The wording in Luke 23:17 makes this point clearer than Matt 27:15, Mark 15:6, and John 18:39. Luke's verse adds the words *anankēn de eichen*, "Now he was obliged" or required to release the prisoner. This addition also indicates that a scribe did not copy the verse word for word from Matthew and Mark in order to harmonize the accounts. Luke 23:17 is probably an original part of Luke and is derived from his trustworthy sources. A scribe probably deleted it when his eye passed from *anankēn de* in verse 17 to *anekragon de* in verse 18. Compare *Death of the Messiah*, 1.794. See note 4 above.

11. John 11:25–26.

12. See my article "The Cross, Jesus, and the Jewish People," *Immanuel* 24/25 (1990) 23–34.

PART 5

THE FUTURE MESSIAH

If the Kingdom is the rule of God, then every aspect of the Kingdom must be derived from the character and action of God. The presence of the Kingdom is to be understood from the nature of God's present activity; and the future of the Kingdom is the redemptive manifestation of his kingly rule at the end of the age.

—George Eldon Ladd

22

The Son of Man in the Teachings of Jesus—Is He Human or Divine?

JESUS CALLS HIMSELF THE SON OF MAN. WHY IS THIS expression his favorite way of speaking about himself?[1] This question has perplexed the finest biblical scholars for centuries.[2] The teaching of Jesus concerning the Son of man is difficult to understand because of its deep roots in Jewish thought contemporary with Jesus. On the one hand Jesus says that the Son of man must suffer and die, but on the other he describes him as king who judges the nations of the world. Not surprisingly, scholars have developed quite different approaches to Jesus' sayings about the Son of man.

Does the term refer to the messianic task? The eminent Oxford scholar Geza Vermes answers no.[3] Does it refer to the humanity of Jesus? The church fathers have answered yes.[4] But many scholars contend that the term "Son of man" on the lips of Jesus most certainly does make reference to the messianic task.[5] They challenge both the position of Vermes on the one hand and the church fathers on the other.

David Flusser has argued, "The one like a man [the Son of man] who sits upon the throne of God's glory, the sublime eschatological judge, is the highest conception of the Redeemer ever developed by ancient Judaism."[6] The phrase "Son of man" could be interpreted as a generic term meaning an ordinary human being. It could also be viewed as a messianic title that describes a superhuman figure.[7] Jesus uses the term "Son of man" in the predictions he made concerning his death. Many theories have been proposed for the meaning of the expression "Son of man" in the teachings of Jesus. The tendency of scholars has been to establish one meaning and impose it upon the texts of the Gospels, separating the original teachings of Jesus from the editorial comments of the later church. Perhaps

another approach should be considered. Here we will suggest
that three different meanings may be ascribed to the technical
term "Son of man" in the Gospels. A distinction must be made
concerning the interpretation of the Son of man sayings. Each
must be carefully examined, and the context allowed to determine the interpretation. Three meanings can be discerned in the
best sources of the synoptic tradition: (1) a generic meaning,
that is, a human being; (2) a superhuman figure based upon a
messianic title for the eschatological coming of the judge of all
humanity; (3) a complex combination of the two previous meanings as in the passion predictions of Jesus, that is, he is a human
being in his sufferings and death (first meaning), and also he is
more than an ordinary human being in his resurrection and
triumph (associated with second meaning). The name "Son of
man" was extremely important to Jesus. The Jewish background
of his message gives fresh insight to this crucial designation in
the sayings of Jesus.

THE SON OF MAN IN JEWISH THOUGHT

First and foremost in consideration of the name "Son of man"
in the teachings of Jesus, we must recognize the conscious effort
of Jesus to refer to early Jewish interpretations of the term "Son
of man" as a messianic title from Daniel 7:13. After all, when
Jesus speaks about the end times, he uses apocalyptic imagery
to communicate his message forcefully. Apocalyptic language
was designed to reveal hidden matters which are known in part
and difficult to grasp fully with the human mind. The apocalyptic teachings often sought to reveal the future coming of redemption. The work of the Messiah is not complete in the first
coming of Jesus. But Jesus taught that the time will come in
which the power and the glory of the Lord will be revealed as
the Son of man appears: "And then they will see the Son of man
coming in a cloud with power and great glory" (Luke 21:27).
The mention of the cloud here in Luke 21:27 was a strong
allusion to Daniel 7:13. In both Daniel and Luke the Son of man
is described as coming with the clouds. It is a vision of the
supernatural power of God.

> I saw in the night visions, and behold, with the clouds of heaven there
> came one like a Son of man, and he came to the Ancient of Days and
> was presented before him. And to him was given dominion and glory

and kingdom, that all peoples, nations, and languages should serve him; his dominion is an everlasting dominion, which shall not pass away, and his kingdom one that shall not be destroyed (Dan 7:13–14).

The term "Son of man" in Daniel probably originally referred to the people of Israel as a collective group. But by the time of Jesus the people were looking for a person who would perform the task of the Son of man. It was natural to associate the term in Daniel with the Messiah. Hence when the early Jewish Bible translators rendered the book of Chronicles from Hebrew into Aramaic, they made a free translation in order to bring out the hidden meanings of the text which spoke about the Messiah. They believed that the task would be fulfilled by an individual rather than a collective group. When they came to the proper name Anani in 1 Chronicles 3:24, they realized that in Hebrew this name means "cloud." It reminded them of Daniel 7:13 where the Son of man is described as coming with the clouds of glory. The translator called attention to the messianic idea in ancient Jewish thought. In order to bring out the natural associations between the term "Son of man" in Daniel, the cloud man Anani, and the royal Messiah, 1 Chronicles 3:24 was translated, "Anani [the man coming with the clouds] is the King Messiah who is to be revealed." These Jewish Bible translator(s) saw a messianic significance for the Son of man in Daniel 7:13.

The term "Son of man," however, possessed a number of meanings in Hebrew and Aramaic. With the lofty associations for the name "Son of man" from Daniel 7:13 in clear view, it is possible to examine the significance of the designation in the words of Jesus.

THE SON OF MAN AS A HUMAN BEING

The words *ben adam* in Hebrew are literally translated by the phrase "son of man" in English. In Hebrew, however, the word for man, *adam,* is the same designation used for the name of the first created human being, Adam. Without going into all the theories in this brief study, it should be noted that some leading biblical scholars have proposed that the term "Son of man" in the Gospels is not a messianic title but rather a generic term for a human being, that is, a son or daughter of Adam, which would include every individual in the human race. While it is true that in Hebrew the words *ben adam* simply refer to a person, often the context of Jesus' sayings proves that Jesus goes beyond this common understanding. He alludes to Daniel 7:13 as well as to the messianic implications associated with the designation.

On the other hand, some sayings of Jesus probably intend the common generic meaning. The context of the saying and the background of each Gospel text should be carefully studied. When Jesus gives a solemn warning against saying any word in opposition to the work of the Holy Spirit, he also mentions the Son of man. I believe that in this context Jesus refers to every person rather than to himself specifically or to the future task of the Son of man in the higher redemptive purpose. The Hebrew imagery of the saying is particularly striking in Matthew's version:

> And whoever says a word against the Son of man will be forgiven; but whoever speaks against the Holy Spirit will not be forgiven, either in this age or in the age to come (Matthew 12:32; Mark 3:28–30; Luke 12:10).

One will receive forgiveness for speaking against a human being. One must beware, however, of what is said concerning the Holy Spirit. No one who utters a word against the Holy Spirit will be forgiven either in the present time or in the age to come. The entire passage is imbued with the rich idiom of the Hebrew language and the beauty of strong parallelism. The son of man here is the antithesis of the Holy Spirit. It refers to a human being and not to Jesus. Here the designation "son of man" is used not as a messianic title but in its generic sense.

The phrase "to speak against" is a Hebrew idiom which describes saying something evil against another person or showing strong opposition to someone. The designation of God as Holy Spirit is also significant. In the Second Temple period when someone said, "Holy Spirit," the people thought of God himself. Possessing a strong sense of esteem, awe, and reverence for God, the people never wished to take his holy name in vain or even come close to profaning the divine presence in any way. As a result, they used synonyms for God's name.

One commonly recognized synonym for "God" in the Gospels is "heaven," which appears so frequently in the words of Jesus when he describes God's reign as the kingdom of heaven. Here one sees his use of the designation "Holy Spirit," which described the sanctity of the divine presence and emphasized the activity of God among his people. Any one who speaks against

God and opposes his work will not be forgiven in this world or the world to come. Of course in the Hebrew of rabbinic literature, the technical terms "this world" (*haolam hazeh*) and "the world to come" (*haolam haba*) are used quite frequently. Here the Gospels preserve an early use of the Hebrew idioms from the time of the Second Temple period. The warning was emphatic and focused upon the activity of God's Spirit among people in need. It is one thing to misunderstand another human being and say something wrong about a person. But one must take extreme caution when speaking about God himself!

While Jesus does make use of the generic meaning of the term "son of man," the context of the Gospels should be studied in order to determine if a deeper significance is given to the name.

THE SON OF MAN AS A SUPERNATURAL BEING

In Jewish apocalyptic thought, the Son of man was sometimes conceived in elevated language that gave him semidivine or supernatural qualities. Even in the words of Daniel, the mysterious figure who comes with the clouds of heaven is referred to as one *like* a Son of man. The word "like" is quite startling. He appears to be a Son of man, that is, a human being, but in actuality he is more than a human being. Certainly the designation "Son of man" increases in its significance when it becomes identified with the sublime figure who brings redemption through superhuman power. He is like a man, but he is so very much more than a man.

In other circles of apocalyptic thinking during the period, striking parallels occur. The book of Daniel echoes the wider spectrum of creative Jewish thinkers whose devout faith in God made them envision his higher purpose in a world of evil. The vivid word pictures used by apocalyptic writers captured the imagination of a suppressed people who longed for divine deliverance. Just as the one true God in his goodness had redeemed a mixed multitude of people from Egypt, so in the future he would deliver an oppressed nation. How can one describe such a miracle? In the book of Enoch, an instrument of God's hand in the unfolding drama of redemptive history is identified by the designation "Son of man." The description of the Son of man is quite similar to Daniel. But one should not jump to the conclusion that the book of Enoch is quoting Daniel. Perhaps the apocalyptic thinker who created the vivid images of the Son of man in Enoch is related to this wider circle which included Daniel and probably others as well.

And there I saw One who had a head of days, And his head was white like wool, And with him was another whose countenance had the appearance of a man, And his face was full of graciousness, like one of the angels. And I asked the angel who went with me and showed me all the secret things, concerning yonder Son of man, who he was, and whence he was, (and) why he went with the Chief of Days? And he answered and said unto me: This is the Son of man to whom belongs righteousness, And righteousness dwells with him; And all the treasures of that which is hidden he reveals Because the Lord of spirits has chosen him, And whose cause before the Lord of spirits triumphs by uprightness for ever.[8]

One is overwhelmed by the presence of the Son of man with his auspicious greatness. In this passage from ancient apocalyptic thought, he is standing beside God himself, the Chief of Days, who of course is the same as the Ancient of Days in Daniel. Here in the book of Enoch, the Son of man is portrayed as being with God: "And with him was another whose countenance had the appearance of a man, And his face was full of graciousness, like one of the angels." Is he an angel? Is he a heavenly being of some kind? His face is so very gracious, and he possesses such striking features that he must be compared to the heavenly hosts of angels. He is more than human in the mind of the apocalyptic writers.

When Jesus referred to himself as the Son of man, the people listening to him already knew something about this mysterious figure from Jewish apocalyptic teachings. Jesus employed the most powerful designation for the future deliverer which could have been used by any teacher. When the church fathers thought that the expression "Son of man" referred to the humanity of Jesus, they missed the deeper significance of the designation in ancient Jewish apocalyptic writings. The term was an elevated way of referring to the messianic task. Jesus used this expression when he spoke about the final judgment.

When the Son of man comes in his glory, and all the angels with him, then he will sit on his glorious throne. Before him will be gathered all the nations, and he will separate them one from another as a shepherd separates the sheep from the goats, and he will place the sheep at his right hand, but the goats at the left. Then the King will say to those at his right hand, "Come, O blessed of my Father, inherit the kingdom prepared for you from the foundation of the world; for I was hungry and you gave me food, I was thirsty and you gave me drink, I was a stranger and you welcomed me, I was naked and you clothed me, I was sick and you visited me, I was in prison and you came to me" (Matt 25:31–36).

In these teachings of Jesus, the Son of man appears with the clouds. Of course, the mention of the clouds would remind the people of the words from Daniel and other traditions of apocalyptic writers. Here the Son of man becomes the king. At least in Matt 25:31 he is called the Son of man, but in verse 34 he is referred to as king. Of great interest is the emphasis on present actions in the sayings of Jesus. He does not define the present in terms of the future but rather the future in terms of the present. In other words, he emphasizes the urgent need of feeding the hungry, welcoming the stranger, clothing the one without, caring for the sick, and visiting the prisoner. What one accomplishes now will set the course of the future. His high ethical morality determines his teachings concerning the final judgment.

The reference to the Son of man is clearly related to the final judgment. He is not a human being in the generic sense. On the contrary, he himself is the king who separates the sheep from the goats.

JESUS' DEFENSIVE USE OF THE SON OF MAN

Jesus made prophetic statements concerning his death. These sayings are extremely difficult to understand. In each of the predictions of his sufferings, he employs the term "Son of man." In an effort to comprehend the deeper import of the designation in the context of the passion predictions, Flusser sometimes called these sayings Jesus' defensive use of the Son of man.[9] Jesus was aware of his fate. He would be betrayed by one of his own disciples. The Sadducees who worked so closely with the Romans would cooperate with the political authorities. They handed Jesus over to Pilate. The Romans would crucify him in the way in which they had crucified so many other Jews. Because of the politics of the empire, the Romans wanted to put a stop to this popular messianic movement before it could get out of hand. Jesus indeed suffered and died, but he predicted that the Son of man would rise again in these complex prophetic sayings concerning his death. In Luke 18:31 Jesus mentions his death which fulfills the words of the prophets:

> And taking the twelve, he said to them, "Behold we are going up to Jerusalem, and everything that is written of the Son of man by the prophets will be accomplished. For he will be delivered to the Gentiles, and will be mocked and shamefully treated and spit upon; they will scourge him and kill him, and on the third day he will rise" (Luke 18:31–32).

Perhaps the greatest fear of a human being is the fear of death. In regard to the humanity of Jesus, he would die as the Son of man. But in regard to that other aspect of the task of the Son of man, he would rise again. In death, Jesus said, "everything that is written of the Son of man by the prophets will be accomplished." This probably alludes to Isaiah 53 where the servant of the Lord suffers for the people. The Son of man dies but will be raised from the dead. In a complex fusion of the two meanings of the designation "Son of man," both aspects of humanity and divinity are somehow brought together.

In reality, here one encounters an element of mystery in the words of Jesus. On the one hand, the name "Son of man" possesses deep significance in Jewish apocalyptic thought. On the other, it could be understood to designate a human being. In the teachings of Jesus, the designation "Son of man" possesses a multifaceted significance. It is his favorite designation for himself. He always refers to the Son of man in the third person. But he identifies his own work with the task of the Son of man. Jesus emphasizes the significance of this name and its root meaning in ancient Jewish thought. No one should claim to understand everything about the interpretation of the challenging designation "Son of man" on the lips of Jesus. But perhaps the wisdom of Flusser provides some direction. There is a defensive use of the term "Son of man" which could be viewed from the position of the faith of Jesus as well as the faith in Jesus. He is a human being, but he is so much more. The Son of man will die, but he will be raised on the third day.

Perhaps the confident affirmation of faith is revealed when Jesus said, "The Son of man has no place to lay his head." When this statement is read in the context of Daniel 7:13–14, it is a paradox which betrays subtle wit. The Son of man does not have a place to lay his head in this world, but in the future he will be the king and judge of all nations. While the tendency among many interpreters has been to view the designation "Son of man" as referring to the humanity of Jesus, the name really means that in his self-awareness Jesus claims that he is so very much more. In fact, it is the highest term used in Jewish thought for the Messiah. The Son of man came to seek the lost. He came to heal hurting people. To him all authority has been given. He is the Son of man who will come with the clouds of glory to judge the nations. He possesses all power and authority.

JESUS AS THE SON OF MAN

Jesus identifies with the designation "Son of man." He uses the name "Son of man" to communicate his purpose to the people. While the term "Son of man" is widely understood to refer to the humanity of Jesus, in Jewish apocalyptic thought it became the recognized title for the most exalted view of the coming Redeemer. In Hebrew the term could simply refer to a human being. Jesus, however, used the name with a profound sense of its quintessential significance in messianic conceptions of the future. On the one hand, he told his disciples that the Son of man would die. On the other, he would rise on the third day. The Son of man would return in the future and complete the messianic task during the last judgment. The sheep will be separated from the goats in the same way that a shepherd herds his flocks.

The teachings of Jesus concerning the future coming of the Son of man must be clearly distinguished from many other descriptions of the final judgment in the wider circles of apocalyptic writings. Like others, Jesus alludes to Daniel 7:13 and to other strong traditions concerning the Son of man. The striking feature of his description of the last judgment, however, appears in his intense concern for the needs of suffering humanity in the present. The high ethic of the kingdom is portrayed as the king speaks about feeding the hungry, providing care for the homeless, and seeing the humanity in each hurting person. Jesus, the Son of man who becomes king in this elevated portrayal of the last judgment, declares, "Truly, I say to you, as you did it to the least of these my brethren, you did it unto me" (Matt 25:40). Does one discover a hidden reference to the Son of man? The disciples of Jesus should seek to see the Son of man in every human being.

NOTES

1. Some scholars have contended that Jesus used the third person in order to indicate someone other than himself. "Son of man" refers to someone other than Jesus according to this view. Albert Schweitzer strongly supported this view. The use of the third person suggested something else to Geza Vermes. He has argued that the words "Son of man" in the native speech of Jesus are an Aramaism which is another way of saying "I." These views should be carefully studied. The evidence of the Gospel texts, however, does not support either of these carefully argued positions. Here we will see that often "Son of man" was used by Jesus in the third person to refer to himself and his mission.

2. See the study by W. Horbury, "The Messianic Associations of 'the Son of man.' " Horbury provides a basic bibliography and surveys the major scholarly discussions of the term "Son of man." He is convinced that the term most probably possessed messianic associations during the time of Jesus.

3. See Vermes, *Jesus the Jew*, 188–91.

4. See, e.g., Epistle of Barnabas 12:10, "See again Jesus, not as son of man, but as Son of God, but manifested in a type of the flesh." "Son of man" refers to the humanity of Jesus, according to this understanding, and "Son of God" refers to his divinity.

5. One of the finest treatments of this debate is Horbury, "The Messianic Associations of 'the Son of man.' " David Flusser has discussed the issue in the context of Melchizedek in the Dead Sea Scrolls. See his "Melchizedek and the Son of man," in *Judaism and the Origins of Christianity*, 186–92.

6. Flusser, *Jesus*, 103.

7. S. Mowinckel, *He That Cometh* (New York: Abingdon, 1954) 347: "By this term [Son of Man] Jesus means to express something essential to His mission as God's representative and the mediator of the kingdom of God; He uses it to interpret His Messianic mission."

8. 1 Enoch 46:1–3, and see Black, *The Book of Enoch*, 48, 205ff.

9. Private communication. Here I believe that Flusser possesses a rich insight into the self-awareness of Jesus. I must admit that I feel quite inadequate to express his thought with all his vibrance and characteristic genius. This sensitive issue needs further research.

Epilogue

I do indeed think that we can now know almost nothing concerning the life and personality of Jesus, since the early Christian sources show no interest in either, are moreover fragmentary and often legendary; and other sources about Jesus do not exist. Except for the purely critical research, what has been written in the last hundred and fifty years on the life of Jesus, his personality and the development of his inner life, is fantastic and romantic.

—Rudolf Bultmann

23

Jesus in the Company of Scholars and Theologians

FLUSSER AND THE THEOLOGIANS

David Flusser, an Orthodox Jew who teaches at the Hebrew University, has often related a true experience which shocked him. He was lecturing in Germany before a group of Protestant theologians, some of whom served as pastors. He described his work as a New Testament scholar researching the life and teachings of Jesus in Israel at the Hebrew University. Flusser remarked that through a careful method of linguistic analysis and comparative study, the actual words of Jesus could be heard and understood.

One theologian present completely rejected Flusser's comments. He explained before the learned servants of the church that he had actually studied with Rudolf Bultmann himself. The degree of reverence and awe which are accorded to Rudolf Bultmann in theological settings such as this must be appreciated to fully understand this story. The room was hushed with revered silence.

The theologian continued with a polite way of telling the professor from Israel that he was absolutely mistaken. The words of Jesus are forever lost. No one can hear the voice of Jesus today. In fact, in his extensive studies with Bultmann, they discovered that only one verse in the Gospels comes from Jesus.

Flusser was interested in this active exchange and scholarly interaction. The reference to one verse aroused his curiosity. Flusser asked the question, "Which verse actually goes back to Jesus?"

The theologian replied, "I forgot."

As far as I know, Flusser has never published this anecdote, but I am certain that it has had a profound impact upon him. The shock effect of an ordained minister saying that only one verse in the Gospels goes back to Jesus is really not that surprising when the influence of Bultmann's genius is appreciated. Facts are not important. In a scientific age of learning, the preaching of the church must be seen as the essence of faith—not what Jesus may or may not have said. The words of Jesus are insignificant. The word preached, however, brings faith in a new era. But the real shock for Flusser was in the fact that the minister had forgotten the only verse linked to Jesus of Nazareth.[1]

The incident raises a troubling question: How important is Jesus for Christian theology?

JESUS AND THE THEOLOGIANS

"I do indeed think that we can now know almost nothing concerning the life and personality of Jesus," Bultmann declares, "since the early Christian sources show no interest in either, are moreover fragmentary and often legendary; and other sources about Jesus do not exist."[2] Hence the Christian sources fail to communicate the teachings of Jesus. Bultmann even pioneered the widely accepted theory of "double dissimilarity" which means that if a saying of Jesus is paralleled in either Christian or Jewish sources it must be rejected as inauthentic.[3] After all, the writers of the Gospels were trying to make sermons. The evangelists of the church were immersed in the Hellenistic culture of their syncretistic age. They culled as much information from the wisdom of the church and the synagogue as possible. Then they secondarily attributed universal wisdom and clever sayings to Jesus. But they knew nothing about the historical Jesus.

Was the church interested in preserving accurately the teachings of Jesus? Would parallel teachings from Judaism be readily incorporated into the Gospels and attributed to Jesus? I believe that Bultmann's approach is based upon a weak foundation. First, the disciples of Jesus desired to preserve his teachings. Probably the first generation employed Jewish methods of mastering oral tradition in their efforts to remember precisely the words of Jesus. No doubt Bultmann's approach is partially true in that the church tended to interpret sayings for new problems far removed from the life setting of Jesus. While the first presupposition for double dissimilarity holds some claim to the truth, Bultmann's second assertion must be completely rejected.

It is highly unlikely that the editors of the Gospels or subsequent generations of the church knew enough about Judaism
to ascribe Jewish teachings to Jesus.

Moreover, there was a strong antagonism against Judaism.
The movement was in the opposite direction. The tendency was
to de-Judaize Jesus of the Gospels. This prevalent antagonism
against things Jewish intensified at an early period with the rise
of Marcionism. As the church rejected Marcion and his teachings, it was also influenced by the spirit of the age that created
his extremely powerful movement. To prove the authenticity of
Christianity involved a process of delegitimizing Judaism.

The memory of Jesus was first preserved by Jews and for
Jews. The Hebrew oral culture of the first generation of his
followers provided the means to begin. The teachings of Jesus
were memorized and recited by his inner circle of disciples.
Soon after his death they sensed the need to write a selective
life of Jesus which focused on the major events and the teaching
message. They told the story of his death, resurrection, and
promise to return. His words concerning God's reign lived in
their hearts. Later the story of Jesus' life was translated into
Greek. Outside the Hebrew culture and apart from the original
Jewish setting, many of the life events and the teachings of
Jesus were destined to be misunderstood. Though the life of
Jesus was originally compiled by the Jewish disciples and for the
Jewish disciples, it was preserved by the Gentile church and for
the Gentile church.

Bultmann confidently claims that the Gospel writers showed
no interest in the "life or the personality of Jesus." How would
the compilers of the Gospels respond to this claim? In sharp
disagreement. The genre of modern historical biography had
not been invented and would not be appropriate for presenting
an authentic look at the life and personality of Jesus. If one
applied the same scholarly methods of scrutiny to different
modern biographies of an American president, it would be difficult to discern the historical figure from the presuppositions of
the Democrats and the Republicans. What do we really know
about the life and personality of figures like FDR or JFK? The
historians present quite contrary portraits. The historical portrayal of a conservative president by a liberal political analyst
will differ greatly from a similar treatment by a conservative
journalist. One frustrated authority of the turbulent history of
the Middle East commented on the vastly different approaches

to the same historical event. In the Middle East, he observed, there is no history, only versions.[4]

The Gospels present different versions of Jesus which are based upon the authentic memory of those who followed and loved him. As records of history, they must be studied in their original cultural setting and not as modern biography. In fact, Judaism developed a method of preserving oral and written traditions with precision. Source analysis and comparative study must guide the scholar. The language of primary sources is crucial. Complete mastery of Greek and Hebrew, as well as intimate knowledge of rabbinics, form the basic foundation. Because of the method of preserving sayings and life events, much can be known about Jesus. But the entire story is culturally conditioned.

To be fair, however, church leaders did desire to preserve the precious sources concerning Jesus' life and teachings. Without the primitive church none of the Gospels would have survived. While at times some pious scribes were tempted to change the text before them, it seems that on the whole the church revered the Gospel story of Jesus and worked hard to preserve it. But the text had to be interpreted for a new situation. In preaching and teaching, Christian theologians have revealed a remarkable ability to adapt the meaning of Gospel sayings for their own needs. Why change the actual wording of the text? It is far easier to take what is Gospel to the church and reinterpret the meaning for one's own purpose in a new application. Allegory and typology, so intriguing to the popular mind, made this activity a simple process. No doubt the Christian teachers, while creatively discovering answers to their own questions and support for their personal arguments, believed in the sanctity of their interpretation of Jesus. In that process, however, the original force of Jesus' message loses its impact. The new situation in the church takes precedence over the life setting of Jesus in the Gospels.

One well-known exception to this principle is found in the heretic Marcion who worked hard to rewrite the Gospels through an arduous editing process.[5] Instead of adapting the accepted text for his purpose, he ventured out to recreate the Gospel story. He used the Gospel of Luke as a foundation and rewrote the text according to his understanding of Jesus and what he believed to be authentic. Much of his approach was based upon the special revelation knowledge he received from his interpretation of the one he regarded as the only true apostle, Paul. Revelation knowledge of Jesus must supersede historical fact. Marcion loved Paul, but hated the Bible. He sought to remove the Judaism from Christianity. The Hebrew Scriptures were the first to go. Then the Gospels had to be edited to remove references to the Old Testament. Jesus must be made into a revealer of divine knowledge rather than a Jewish messianic figure of history. The strong church opposition to Marcion's work demonstrates that the sayings of Jesus in the New Testament were already given a measure of canonical authority before Marcion. The facts of Jesus' life were important for the church.

Perhaps Marcion would feel very much at home in the company of Rudolf Bultmann. I do not believe he would feel so much at ease with Joachim Jeremias. Bultmann removes the facts and replaces them with faith. Jeremias, on the other hand, would believe that faith is based upon the facts, but the facts must be carefully discerned through proper linguistic analysis of the text. Some modern trends in scholarship have been pulled toward collecting wisdom-type sayings of Jesus from diverse sources such as the *Gospel of Thomas* while disavowing references to the death, resurrection, and return of Jesus the Messiah. These trends tend to justify Marcion's basic presuppositions. They disavow the apocalyptic element of Jesus' teachings. They distort the messianic claims of Jesus. The Jewish roots of Jesus' teachings are twisted and distorted outside the cultural setting and the historical situation in the pseudo-intellectual jargon of a Gnosticism rediscovered. This too is a reinterpretation of Jesus. Are twentieth-century scholars in a better position to understand the essence of Jesus' message than the writers of Matthew, Mark, and Luke? The best evidence for the historical Jesus is found in the canonical Gospels.

Jewish parallels certainly support the authenticity of much in the teachings of Jesus. The second generation of Christians were far removed from Judaism. But Jesus was Jewish. When his teachings are closely related to other similar Jewish sources, it is a sure indication that they probably share a common heritage. Second Temple period Judaism served as a matrix for both blossoming Christianity and ever-strong Pharisaism.

Often Christian theologians have missed Jesus because we have downplayed his Judaism.

JESUS AND THE CHURCH

The tragedy of church history, in my opinion, is the lack of interest in Jesus. Simply having faith in Jesus has replaced responding to his urgent call to active discipleship, which includes serious study of his teachings and intense involvement with the Hebrew Bible. The Torah is the most neglected volume among the people of the church. Abraham Joshua Heschel focuses attention on the core problem.

> There was early in the history of the Christian church a deliberate cultivation of differences from Judaism, a tendency to understand itself in the light not of its vast indebtedness to but rather of its divergencies from Judaism. With the emergence and expansion of Christianity in the Greco-Roman world, Gentile Christians overwhelmed the movement, and a continuous process of accommodation to the spirit of that world was set in motion. The result was a conscious or unconscious dejudaization of Christianity, affecting the church's way of thinking and its inner life as well as its relationship to the past and present reality of Israel—the father and the mother of the very being of Christianity. The children did not arise and call the mother blessed; instead, they called the mother blind. Some theologians continue to act as if they did not know the meaning of "honor your father and your mother"; others, anxious to prove the superiority of the church, speak as if they suffer from a spiritual Oedipus complex.[6]

On the one hand, many lay people, Christian leaders, and leading scholars have recognized the crisis and sought to remedy it. On the other, the spirit of Marcionism that rejects all things Jewish continues to exert a powerful and sometimes unnoticed, as well as unchecked, influence. The church is infested with a harmful attitude which rebels against the Judaism of Jesus by preaching a new religion, at times far removed from his basic teachings.

The captivating speaker and creative Jewish thinker David Wolpe observes, "For Christianity the word became flesh. For Judaism the word remains elusive, intangible. Not incarnation but interpretation is the Jewish lens for peering at the world."[7] For Christians Jesus is the Word, the divine *logos*. Although the Word has spoken, no one is listening. Historically as Christians, we have elevated believing in the Word sublimely above learning the word spoken by Jesus and obeying his commandments. Perhaps that approach should be reversed. After all, learning his word should challenge, guide, and enhance genuine faith in the Word. The sensitive study of Judaism must be a part of such a process.

Inadvertently and unknowingly Bultmann and his followers tended to reject the Jewish roots of Jesus' teachings. Though Bultmann must forever be revered for his original thinking and marked contribution to scholarly inquiry, his approach must be declared stillborn. It has sought to rob Jesus of his Jewish heritage by denying the historical setting of the Gospels in ancient Judaism. The method developed by Bultmann is wrong because the evidence runs against it. The Semitisms of the Gospels point to a source close to Jesus. The Jewish environment described in the Gospels, moreover, is often authenticated by other contemporary historical sources. Scholarly method remains the best resource for discovering a clearer understanding of Jesus' message in the Gospels.

As a valid method of research, Bultmann's approach is dead because it failed to recognize the historical setting for the life and teachings of Jesus in first-century Israel. The Semitisms of the Gospels and the poetic Hebrew parallelisms, moreover, point to the religious genius of Jesus. Numerous scholars such as David Flusser, Joachim Jeremias, and T. W. Manson have often demonstrated the historicity of the Gospels underneath the multiple layers of church interpretations. The wit and humor as well as the colorful personality of Jesus emerge from a careful study of the rich Gospel sources.

Heschel's critique of Christian theology is devastating—and accurate. Many Jews have died because of Christian views of Judaism. Not only have Christians wrongly persecuted the Jewish people because of our erroneous beliefs about Jews and Judaism, but we have robbed ourselves of a treasured heritage which would have been the source of great spiritual enrichment. By rejecting Judaism the church has missed Jesus. The major problem with Christianity today is a failure to appreciate the life and teachings of Jesus. The sickness of a new Marcionism has infected our theological worldview.

The acute Hellenization of Christianity has led us on a path to Athens rather than Jerusalem. The church's search for Jesus must lead us back to the days of the Jewish temple and the rich centers of Hebrew learning. Heschel challenges Christians to consider the pedigree of the gospel message.

What is the pedigree of the Christian gospel? There are the words
with which the New Testament begins: "The book of the genealogy of
Jesus Christ, the son of David, the son of Abraham" (Matt 1:1; see
also 1 Cor 10:1–3; 1 Pet 1:10ff.). Yet the powerful fascination with the
world of Hellenism has led many minds to look for origins of the
Christian message in the world derived from Hellas. How odd of
God not to have placed the cradle of Jesus in Delphi, or at least in
Athens![8]

Jesus was born in Bethlehem of Judea. The cradle of Jesus
was located in the heart of first-century Israel. Jesus lived in
Galilee and knew well the grandeur of Herodian Jerusalem, but
he never visited Athens or Rome. When Jesus was a baby, his
mother and father took him to the temple. He learned the Bible
and Hebrew tradition in synagogue and centers of Jewish learning. He taught in the temple courts and celebrated Passover
with his disciples. But Jesus never saw the glories of the Par-
thenon of Athens or caught the vista of the Palatine Hill or
walked through the great Colosseum of Rome. Sadly the Jewish
heritage of Jesus has often been forgotten or misunderstood.
For his people the Hebrew Bible was esteemed as sacred. The
Sabbath was observed. As an observant Jew, the *Shema Yisrael*
was often on the lips of Jesus. The world of Hellas was vastly
different.

The church needs to be revitalized by a new "Jesusism" based
upon the old Judaism. Jesus did not seek to destroy the Torah
and the Prophets; rather, he came to place these sacred writings
on firmer footing by a more precise interpretation. This new
focus on Jesus does not mean that Gentile Christians need to
convert to Judaism or pretend to be Jews. This would compromise seriously Jewish and Christian identities. Christians mas-
querading as Jews does not reflect an appropriate response to
the reality of the wild olive branch engrafted into the tree. Let
Jews live as Jews and let Christians follow Jesus' teachings! A
new vision of Jesus does mean that Christians must learn to love
the Jewish people and esteem the root which supports the
branch. A new vision of Jesus requires a decision to study his
teachings and to live the life of a disciple.

THE GOSPEL IN THE GOSPELS

The Gospels tell the story of Jesus. Behind these sources stand
the apostolic tradition which upholds the gospel in the Gospels.[9]

Three areas of research greatly enhance our perception of Jesus. First, one must consider the literary relationship between the Gospels and study their texts comparatively. Second, one must be sensitive to the hidden Hebrew behind the life events and sayings of Jesus. Third, one must recognize the Jewish cultural setting for the story of Jesus' life.

The Gospels of Matthew, Mark, and Luke have been preserved in the language of Koine Greek. Indeed, the Greek language was widely spoken during New Testament times. This development began three centuries earlier because Alexander the Great had been able to spread the use of Greek culture and Greek ways throughout his vast empire. However, the historian discovers a strong resistance to the process of Hellenization within some areas of Alexander's domain. This resistance was nowhere more prominent than within the land of Israel, where pious Jews struggled to worship God according to the Hebrew Scriptures and to maintain faithfulness to their ancient beliefs and customs.

One way that the Jewish people resisted the pagan influence of Greece was by maintaining loyalty to the law of God and by speaking their native language. In the letter of Aristeas, for example, we discover a reference to the language of the people. The language of the Torah, Hebrew, is said to be the language of the people, though some have confused this with Aramaic.[10] While it would not be correct to say that Hebrew was the only language understood and spoken by the Jewish people during the time of Jesus, there is abundant evidence that indeed the people's holy books, prayers, studies in the classroom, parables, and quite naturally, then, their everyday speech, was conducted in the language of the Bible—Hebrew.[11]

THE HEBREW JESUS

Embedded in the early church tradition are numerous references to the words of the Lord and hints of a Gospel text written in the Hebrew language. The early church father Papias said that "Matthew compiled the sayings [logia] of Jesus in the Hebrew language and everyone translated it as he was able."[12] The reference to the sayings is based upon the Greek word logia, which most probably refers to the events in the life and teachings of Jesus as well as to the sayings.

The Hebrew Gospel is contained in our Gospels of Matthew, Mark, and Luke. The Matthew that Papias refers to is not the Gospel bearing his name; rather it seems more likely that Papias refers to a written source known to all three of the evangelists: Matthew, Mark, and Luke. Matthew the tax collector followed Jesus. He became a disciple of his master, which included not only a lifestyle but a memorization of Jesus' sayings and teachings. The process of learning the Jewish oral tradition was integral to education during the time of Jesus. In like manner, Matthew learned from his Lord. He preserved the teaching of Jesus by faithfully passing these traditions on to the other followers of the Lord in writing and in the Hebrew language.

However, our Gospels are in Greek. Because of the need to make the gospel known to a larger readership, it soon became necessary to translate the story of Jesus' life in the language spoken by the early Christians outside the land of Israel. Greek was widely spoken and was an effective medium of communication.

Today, as the sayings of Jesus are read and studied, the true meaning and significance of his message is often lost in translation. English is not Greek and is even more removed from Hebrew. The task of translation is intensely complex. Is it possible that any language can be faithfully translated? Those familiar with two languages, that is, the language of the source document and the language of its translation, are best able to discern its meaning, especially if the translation is a careful and literal one. Certainly it is imperative to use all the tools available for the study of the Scriptures. The linguistic study of the texts of our Gospels promises to enrich our understanding of the words of Jesus. Every word spoken by Jesus is of paramount importance.

The Hebrew Gospel can be recovered. Many of us would like to see archaeologists discover a scroll in the desert, but we realize that with a knowledge of Greek and Hebrew, as well as an understanding of the cultural heritage of the Jewish people, it is possible to recover the Hebrew Gospel today. Matthew, Mark, and Luke contain the Hebrew Gospel. The Greek text is better understood in light of its Hebrew background.

Consider the Hebrew meaning behind the familiar words of Jesus, "Think not that I have come to abolish the law and the prophets; I have come not to abolish but to fulfill them. For truly, I say to you, till heaven and earth pass away, not one iota, not a dot, will pass from the law until all is accomplished" (Matt 5:17–18). The Hebrew meaning of law is Torah. Torah was not a negative word for Jesus. Jesus believed that Torah reveals God's will. He believed that it was good and holy. In the eyes of Jesus, the Hebrew Bible taught God's love for all people and provided a guide for daily life. In light of Jesus' high esteem for Torah, Matthew 5:17 is certainly addressing the issue of properly comprehending the driving force of the text which leads to right conduct in every day living.

The Hebrew background of this verse clarifies its deeper meaning.[13] In rabbinic literature, the Greek words from the Gospel which are translated "abolish" and "fulfill" possess dynamic equivalents. The word "abolish" means "to interpret incorrectly." In Greek the word *kataluō* means "abolish," and its dynamic Hebrew equivalent *batel* also means "cancel, abolish, destroy," but *batel* is often used in contexts that deal with interpreting Scripture. One cancels Torah when it is misunderstood. The word "fulfill," moreover, refers to interpreting a passage accurately. In Greek the word *pleroō* means "fulfill." Its Hebrew equivalent *kiyem* is derived from a root, that means "cause to stand" and possesses the sense, "to uphold, to observe, to fulfill, or to place on a firmer footing." It too is used in contexts that deal with interpreting Scripture.[14]

When one misunderstands the proper meaning of Torah, one may not obey the Lord's will and therefore will cancel the law. Hence a person may abolish Torah by misunderstanding the divine revelation. On the other hand, when one understands the proper meaning, one is able to obey God's will and therefore fulfill Torah. The theological polemics within Christianity during the struggle for self-definition caused the church to sever itself almost completely from Judaism. This created an environment in which Marcion's ideas could flourish. In its efforts to achieve self-definition, it was easy for the church to come under Marcion's anti-Judaism spell.

Later during the Reformation period, many Protestant reformers attacked the papacy. They wrongly used the Torah and Judaism as the whipping boy for what they viewed as the incorrect teaching of the official church. It is not unusual for Judaism to become the scapegoat for attacking all that is perceived as evil in the church's doctrine. The good is seen as emanating from authentic Christianity while the bad is portrayed wrongly as coming from Judaism.

As a result, modern English translations of the three key words of Matthew 5:17, "Torah," "abolish," and "fulfill," acquired meanings quite different from their ancient Jewish ones. What did they mean to Jesus and his early followers? The Hebrew word "Torah" is derived from the root *yarah,* which means to shoot an arrow or to teach. Torah means teaching or instruction that is true and straight as if the words of Torah are shot in a direct path like an arrow, with power and force for living life to the fullest. Torah is the divine aim for all people who love God. Torah means God's will, including but going over and beyond the ink dried upon the scrolls of holy writ. Divine revelation of Torah, however, can be interpreted many different ways. Proper interpretation breathes life and power into the divinely spoken words.

If properly understood and obeyed, the divine revelation provides a guide for successful living. Thus the law is fulfilled. Wrong interpretation, on the other hand, cancels the words communicated through divine revelation. As Abraham Joshua Heschel has shown, while the Greeks studied to comprehend and Western thinkers study to apply their knowledge in a practical sense, the ancient Hebrews studied to revere.[15] God gave Torah. He is to be revered. Each human being stands in awe and wonder before God. Hence the task of learning Torah is a sacred undertaking. Study leads to reverence. Reverence leads to obedience. Jesus came to interpret the Torah accurately so that God, who gave it, will be revered and obeyed through proper action. "Abolish" means to obstruct through wrong interpretation. "Fulfill" refers to an understanding of the text that leads to holy living.

These meanings for the words "Torah," "abolish," and "fulfill" are illustrated in a colorful story about King Solomon in Jewish literature. Solomon is remembered for his legendary wisdom. Nonetheless, even wise Solomon could decide to cancel a letter from the Torah. Because of his own desires, he interpreted the Bible in such a way as to cancel its meaning. As the king, Solomon had problems with one of the commandments of the Torah which dealt with the obligations of Israel's royalty. The king of Israel is instructed in Torah, "Only he shall not multiply horses to himself. . . . Neither shall he multiply wives to himself, that his heart turn not away; neither silver and gold" (Deut 17:16–17). The command forbids the king of Israel to increase for himself horses, wives, or money so that his heart not turn away from God. So King Solomon decided to cancel a jot or tittle from the Hebrew words of the verse.

> When God gave the Torah to Israel, He inserted therein both positive and negative commandments and gave commands for a king, as it says, "Only he shall not multiply horses to himself. . . . Neither shall he multiply wives to himself, that his heart turn not away; neither silver and gold" (Deut 17:16–17). But Solomon arose and studied the reason of God's decree, saying: "Why did God command, 'He shall not multiply wives to himself'? Is it not 'that his heart turn not away'? Well I will multiply and still my heart will not turn away.' " Our rabbis say: At that time, the *yod* (smallest letter of the Hebrew alphabet, *y,* the first letter of *yarbeh,* meaning multiply) of the word *yarbeh* (multiply) went up on high and prostrated itself before God and said: "Master of the Universe! Have you not said that no letter shall ever be abolished from the Torah? Behold, Solomon has now arisen and abolished one. Who knows? Today he has abolished one letter, tomorrow he will abolish another until the whole Torah will be nullified." God responded: "Solomon and a thousand like him will pass away, but the smallest tittle will not be canceled from you."[16]

By deleting the smallest letter of the Hebrew alphabet, King Solomon interpreted the commandment according to his own wisdom. In the end he changed it from a negative command, "do not" multiply to yourself horses, wives, and money, to a positive command, giving himself the divine imperative that he must "multiply to" himself many horses, many wives, and much money. He fulfilled the verse according to his own revised version. All this is possible through the wisdom of biblical interpretation. The miraculous power of exegesis should never be underestimated. The legend concerning clever King Solomon tells about his ability to cancel and to fulfill Torah through his own interpretation. This example from rabbinic literature demonstrates that even removing one jot or tittle from a verse could cause the Torah to be abolished. When Jesus used the words "Torah," "abolish," and "fulfill, the people naturally thought of proper interpretation.

When one studies carefully the context of Jesus' saying "I have not come to abolish the law and the prophets, but I have come to fulfill," it becomes clear that he is dealing with verses from the Pentateuch and their proper interpretation. The words "You have heard it said by the ancients" introduce a quotation (Matt 5:26). For instance, Jesus quotes a text from the Ten

Commandments, "Thou shalt not kill." The literal meaning of
the commandment refers to the actual shedding of blood. But
Jesus' interpretation goes beyond the letter of the commandment and reaches to a higher standard of holiness. If one becomes angry with one's neighbor, one has chosen a dangerous
path. As David Flusser demonstrated in his insightful study of
rabbinic parallels to the Sermon on the Mount, if one violates a
minor commandment, such as the prohibition against anger, it
will lead to the transgression of a major commandment, such as
the prohibition against murder.[17] Moreover, in the teachings of
Jesus, if someone teaches others to transgress even a minor (in
Hebrew *kal*) commandment, that is, the "least of these commandments," that one will be considered minor, that is, "least"
(also in Hebrew *kal*) in the kingdom of heaven. When someone
violates a minor *(kal)* commandment, this initiates a path leading to a grave offense (in Hebrew *chamor*, "weighty or major").
The rabbis contrasted the major or weighty *(chamor)* laws such
as the Ten Commandments with others which might seem to be
minor *(kal)*. In the Sermon on the Mount, Jesus contrasts minor
commandments with the major ones. Lust may be considered a
minor offense, but it leads to adultery. Anger leads to murder.

The rabbis also employ this method of exegesis in their interpretation of the Bible. God gave Torah to the people who,
because of their reverence for him, made the study of his commandments vital for daily life. Mention of light (*kal* minor) and
weighty (*chamor* major) laws in the Torah appears in a Jewish
commentary on the book of Deuteronomy. In their "Fear of
Sin" and desire for a holy life, the rabbis taught the manner in
which anger can lead to murder:

> "If any person hates his neighbor, and lies in wait for him, and attacks
> him (and wounds him mortally so that he dies)" (Deut 19:11). From
> there it was deduced: If a man has transgressed a light (*kal*) com-
> mandment, he will finally transgress a weighty (*chamor*) command-
> ment. If he transgressed (the commandment): "You shall love your
> neighbor as yourself" (Lev 19:18), he will finally transgress (the com-
> mandment): "You shall not take vengeance or bear any grudge" (Lev
> 19:18), and (the commandment): "You shall not hate your brother"
> (Lev 19:17), and (the commandment): "That brother may live beside
> you" (Lev 25:36)—until he will (finally) be led to murder. Therefore
> it is said: "If any person hates his neighbor and lies in wait for him
> and attacks him."[18]

The foundation of the insightful commentary is found in Deuteronomy 19:11. The progression of actions conveyed by the sequence of verbs, "If any person *hates* his neighbor, and *lies in wait* for him, and *attacks* him (and *wounds* him mortally so that he *dies*)," naturally suggested to the rabbis that a major sin is usually the final result of a series of minor wrongs. Therefore, one must take heed not to transgress even a light commandment because the danger is too great. The first sin will lead to another even more grave than the former. The fear of sin leads a person to fulfill a light commandment with the same determination as he or she fulfills a weighty commandment.

The Sermon on the Mount in Matthew contains sayings of Jesus concerning proper biblical interpretation. That Jesus fulfilled the Torah certainly does not mean that the prohibitions against adultery and murder have now been lifted. By no means! The words of Jesus place the meaning of Torah on a higher level of righteousness. One must flee all evil, even the minor sin, because once a person begins to tread the path of a seemingly insignificant transgression, he or she cannot determine the limit of evil. Lust leads to adultery. Anger leads to murder. One must pursue the higher standard of righteousness in all aspects of human experience. Jesus did not cancel the Torah. He put it on a firmer footing by interpreting it correctly.

The Judaism of Jesus, the analysis of the relationships between the Synoptic Gospels, the Semitisms in the Greek text, and the Hebrew language teach much about his life and teachings. In his first coming he came as a healer and a teacher. As the suffering servant he went to the cross.[19] He promised his followers that he would return to complete his mission.

Unfortunately, his teachings are today seldom learned or practiced. The urgency of Jesus' call for active discipleship in the kingdom is disturbingly relevant today for a world with so much human suffering. Jesus and his Jewish theology continue to challenge all who have ears to listen.

JESUS THE JEWISH THEOLOGIAN

For the Western mind theology is the study of God or the contemplation of divine things. It is a science of the divine which often endeavors to find coherence and unity in the vast spectrum of our religious belief systems. The paths to the divinely revealed truths are diverse and complex. Natural theology, practical theology, dogmatic theology, historical theology, systematic theology as well as liberation theology, feminist theology, and process theology—these are but a few approaches. While the authority of Jesus is earnestly sought to authenticate these theological systems, the quest for the authentic theology of Jesus is misplaced, neglected, or forgotten altogether. Rather than being acknowledged as the originator of Christian theology, Jesus becomes the inconsequential prop that supports an enormous edifice.

While Jesus is often invited to keep company with scholars and theologians, he is always an outsider. He is a Jew from the Middle East with ways strange to Western eyes. His religious orientation is different. For Westerners, sometimes it becomes a challenge to foster a genuine esteem for Jesus' faith tradition of Judaism. So at best, calling Jesus a Jewish theologian is merely a stepping stone. Perhaps it will enable us to begin the journey from West to East, from a world of systematic coherence to the domain of puzzling inconsistencies and dynamic process. The realm of Jesus' theology is discovered within his community of faith. The passport for entry into that intriguing world is an understanding of the rabbinic mind.

If Jesus is a Jewish theologian, two preliminary questions must be posed. First, does Jewish theology even exist? For some Christian readers such a question seems out of place. For other Jewish readers, however, the question may seem more fitting. The religion of Judaism teaches a way of life to be lived more than it espouses a creed to be believed. Faith is more concerned with action than belief. A giant in his contribution to Jewish learning, Solomon Schechter entertained the entire issue in his intriguing book, *Some Aspects of Rabbinic Theology*. Schechter observed,

> The old Rabbis seem to have thought that the true health of a religion is to have a theology without being aware of it; and thus they hardly ever made—nor could they make—any attempt towards working their theology into a formal system, or giving us a full exposition of it. With God as a reality, Revelation as a fact, the Torah as a rule of life, and the hope of Redemption as most vivid expectation, they felt no need for formulating their dogmas into a creed, which, as was once remarked by a great theologian, is repeated not because we believe, but that we may believe.[20]

Theology as a discipline of study in and of itself runs contrary to Jewish faith and practice. As Schechter perceptively observes, in Jewish eyes, "the true health of a religion is to have a theology without being aware of it." The theological underpinnings of Jewish thought guide the practice of Judaism. But one should not be aware of the theology. God is beyond finite comprehension. Judaism focuses more on active obedience to God's will as revealed in Torah than on theological reflection.

On the other hand, Schechter makes it plain that the old rabbis did indeed possess a theology. The reality of God, the certainty of revelation, the rule of life as discovered in Torah as well as a keen expectation of a future redemption pervaded their thinking while they lived their lives as religious Jews and community leaders. Theology undergirds everything in Jewish life.

Because of the attitude that writing a theological creed or systematizing theological beliefs are unwarranted activities which might even be viewed as harmful or unholy, the second question which must be posed becomes exceedingly difficult.

What is Jewish theology? Perhaps it would be more fitting to discuss Jewish theologians rather than any systematic Jewish theology. The different thinkers and rabbis could be studied for their theological presuppositions. But most religious teachers and community leaders in the history of Israel who are considered to be Jewish theologians would probably like to deny the charge. Being called a Jewish theologian in such an environment would not be considered a compliment. To be a scholar or a creative thinker is a compliment. To be a theologian is almost an insult. On the other hand, the Pharisees and their successors should not be viewed as detached academicians devoid of a theological worldview. They knew what they believed about God and why they believed it.

What some Western observers would call theology among the rabbis, rabbis would view more as a creative process, that is, the spontaneous eruption of interconnected ideas flowing out of a dialectic discussion of God, his world, and human response to the divine initiative.[21] Spiritual values are learned by a dynamic interaction between different personalities; religious giants battle one another in fierce dialogue, like that of Hillel and Shammai, Eleazer and Joshua, or Akiva and Ishmael. Within a process of free exchange and intense debate, they seek the wisdom of Torah and God's will for humanity. The spiritual values come alive in heated arguments that expose the inner soul of the

Torah master's heart. Individual temperament and depth of personality emerge in the intense exchange of ideas and the dynamic interaction of live debate.

Probably the basic theology of Hillel would not differ that much from Shammai. In the area of practical application, however, vast differences would emerge. The theological foundation is a given. Hillel, however, is more human-centered. Shammai's orientation is God-centered. Jesus would have much in common with both of them. In many ways, he is closer to Choni the Circle Drawer or Chanina ben Dosa than to either Hillel or Shammai. Jesus, by way of contrast to the pious ones in the circle of charismatic Judaism, stresses involvement with Torah learning to a greater degree. At least much more of his sayings and parables deal with the practice of faith in everyday living than what history has remembered from the teachings of these charismatic figures of ancient Judaism. Perhaps like Jesus, they too would stress *agada* more than *halakhah*. Jesus and these charismatic wonder-workers of ancient Judaism focus on piety and stress holiness.

Our picture of these historical characters, however, is far from complete. Our view of theology as a discipline, moreover, is more Western and philosophical. As Christians, we study God and systematize belief. The Eastern mind tends to view God through the emotions of human personality and individual experience. God is viewed through the lens of metaphors and parables of real life which make the abstract concepts more concrete.

The problem of defining an orientation to Jewish theology in the first century is complex. The rich diversity of thought and wide range of interests over the expanse of history have created quite different theological views in Judaism. The Judaism during the time of the Second Temple period differed significantly from Judaism in the time of King David. The religions of Judaism and Christianity of today, moreover, have changed drastically from their first-century origins. These modern faith traditions hardly resemble the mother church or the ancient synagogue. The theology of Judaism has experienced major transitions. But all sit at the feet of Moses and stand in awe before the presence of the God of the Hebrew Bible. The two great commandments—"you shall love the LORD your God with all your heart" and "you shall love your neighbor as yourself"—characterize the primary Jewish theological orientation to a living faith tradition. One must love God and esteem others. Judaism has no creed, but Torah is the fact of divine revelation.

So the theology of many Jewish scholars is not to have a theology. At least one should not be overly aware of one's theology. Perhaps blind obedience to the Torah will better reveal the divine presence in everyday experience than the intellectual exchange of conceptual ideas.[22] God is too vast. Mystery and wonder must pervade human perception of God's goodness. Contradictions and inconsistencies are part and parcel of God and his mysteries. One learns by doing. The Eastern mind loves riddles and is fond of mystery. The Western theologian explains much and understands little. The Eastern mindset of Jewish theology reveres God and wonders at his mysteries. All attempts to systematize God will fall short. Stand in amazement. Wonder in awe.

Jesus is like that. He never wrote a creed. He did not occupy himself with systematic theology. But he is a profound theologian even if he would feel uncomfortable with this Western designation. He is a theologian, but his theology is Jewish to the core, being rooted in Torah-faithful Judaism. He stressed action more than belief. His theology emerges in the metaphor of parable and a holy reverence for life. God is good. One must stand in wonder and awe before him.

God is described in word pictures which show the natural affinity between the physical world of human experience and the supernatural world of divine transcendence. God's kingdom is like the permeating action of leaven in the dough. His reign is like the miracle of a mustard seed that grows and grows. The kingdom is here in full force so people can experience God's power of healing and wholeness in the torture of fragmented human existence. God cares about people, and he still works miracles. He is like a compassionate father who loves two lost sons. The incomprehensible God is revealed in the actions of a loving father or in the magnanimity of a generous landowner. The attitude of the heart, moreover, determines whether the temple sacrifice atones for the wrongdoings of the holy Pharisee or the unholy sinner. If one does not forgive, one will not be forgiven. To know God and enter life, one must keep the commandments.

The Jesus of the Gospels is a provocative theologian deeply involved in the realities of Jewish life. The Jewish theology of Jesus begins with the Hebrew concept of God. It encompasses divine compassion and loving-kindness for all humanity. It demands holiness and fear of sin. God seeks healing and wholeness for all people. The Torah reveals God and the human dignity of each person. Jesus came to uphold the Torah and the Prophets, not destroy them.

NOTES

1. Bultmann himself would, of course, be far better able to represent his own views than this well-meaning disciple. This exchange between Flusser and the German theologian occurred in Marburg, Germany, the city of Bultmann. The list of sayings acceptable to scholars would be much longer today. The scholarly process requires careful scrutiny of the Gospels. The current tendency focuses on collecting striking sayings from the canonical and extracanonical sources that give a strong impression that Jesus may have said something like this; compare for instance the reconstructed inventory by John Dominic Crossan, *The Historical Jesus* (San Francisco: Harper, 1991). Crossan prints what he believes to be the sayings of Jesus on pages xiv–xxvi.

2. Rudolf Bultmann, *Jesus and the Word* (New York: Charles Scribner's Sons, 1958) 8.

3. See Rudolf Bultmann, *History of the Synoptic Tradition* (1963 reprint, Peabody, Mass.: Hendrickson, 1993) 205, and compare the discussion of James Charlesworth, *Jesus within Judaism* (Garden City: Doubleday, 1988) 5–7.

4. See Thomas L. Friedman, *From Beirut to Jerusalem* (New York: Farrar, Straus & Giroux, 1989) 49. Friedman quotes Bill Farrell, Middle East correspondent of the *New York Times*, "There is no truth in Beirut, only versions."

5. See J. Quasten, *Patrology* (Westminster, Md.: Christian Classics, 1986) 1.268–72. One of the finest treatments of Marcion remains Adolf von Harnack, *Marcion* (reprint, Darmstadt: Wissenschaftliche Buchgesellschaft, 1985 [German]). More accessible to many readers is the short article by R. McL. Wilson, "Marcion," in *The Encyclopedia of Philosophy* (New York: Macmillan, 1972) 5.155f. Wilson correctly notes some of the distinctions between Marcion's theology and Gnosticism. On Marcion's interpretation of Matt 5:17, see E. C. Blackman, *Marcion and His Influence* (London: SPCK, 1948) 48. See also P. Amidon, *The Panarion of St. Epiphanius* (New York: Oxford University, 1990) 146. Sadly, for information about Marcion, the scholar must rely on what others wrote about him. Marcion's theology is known primarily from what Christian apologists said against his teachings.

6. Abraham Joshua Heschel, *The Insecurity of Freedom* (New York: Schocken, 1972) 169–70.

7. David Wolpe, *In Speech and in Silence: The Jewish Quest for God* (New York: Henry Holt, 1992) 12.

8. Heschel, *The Insecurity of Freedom*, 170.

9. See R. E. Brown, *New Testament Essays* (Milwaukee: Bruce, 1965) 3–35.

10. See Charles, *The Apocrypha and Pseudepigrapha*, 2.95; Charlesworth, *Old Testament Pseudepigrapha*, 2.12: "The Jews are supposed to use Syrian language [i.e., Aramaic], but this is not so, for it is another form (of language) [i.e., Hebrew of the Torah]." The letter of Aristeas is written in Greek. Interestingly it explains that the spoken language of the Jewish people in the land of Israel was Hebrew.

11. The language situation in the land of Israel during this period was more complicated than is indicated here. One question is often raised concerning the Aramaic translations of the Bible. See my study "Targum," *International Standard Bible Encyclopedia*, rev. ed., 4.727–33. In some areas such as Caesarea, Greek would have been used in commerce, and Aramaic was widely spoken in the East. The language of the Jewish people, however, was Hebrew. See also Bivin and Blizzard, *Understanding the Difficult Words of Jesus*, 19–103, and the important article by J. Grintz, "Hebrew as the Spoken and Written Language in the Last Days of the Second Temple," *Journal of Biblical Literature* 79 (1960) 32–47. See my *Jesus and His Parables*, 40–42.

12. See Eusebius, *Ecclesiastical History*, 3.39.16, LCL. Some scholars have mistakenly claimed that the word for "Hebrew" should be understood as "Aramaic." Without discussing the question at length, it should be noted that the work of Grintz, cited in the previous note, has proved that this is incorrect. "Hebrew" in an ancient text means just that— Hebrew.

13. For me, one of the finest treatments of these issues appears in Heschel, *Torah Men Hashamayim*. See also A. Heschel, *God in Search of Man* (New York: Farrar, Straus & Giroux, 1976) 167ff.

14. See W. Bacher, *Die exegetische Terminologie der jüdischer Traditionsliteratur* (Leipzig: Hinrichs, 1905; Hebrew translation by A. Rabinovitz; *Erche Midrash*, Jerusalem: Carmiel, 1970).

15. See Heschel, *God in Search of Man*, 3–12, 73–79, 43–53.

16. Exodus Rabbah 6:1, A. Shinan's edition, 182; and see j. *Sanh.* 20c, chap. 2, hal. 1, where Simeon bar Yochai (ca. 130 C.E.) is mentioned. For the story to make sense in Hebrew, King Solomon would probably have to remove the Hebrew word *lo* which is translated "not" and "neither" in Deut 17:16 as well as the letter *yod*. Perhaps the rabbis read Solomon's emended text with the negative particle *lo* as the possessive pronoun "to him" which, though spelled differently, sounds the same. In this case the possessive pronoun would be repetitive but certainly clear to the Hebrew listener who loves a clever word play. Sometimes the possessive pronoun was confused with the negative

particle, as in Ps 100:3 which should be translated, "It is he that made us, and we are his *lo*," rather than, "It is he that made us, and not *lo* we ourselves."

17. See David Flusser, "A Rabbinic Parallel to the Sermon on the Mount," in *Judaism and the Origins of Christianity,* 494–507. I am exceedingly grateful for Flusser's rich insight into the teachings of Jesus on this passage. Compare Nolland, *Luke,* 2.820: "It is clear that in Lukan understanding the 'law and the prophets' are in no sense superseded but rather added to in the sense of being made yet more rigorous. . . ."

18. Sifre Deut 186/187 on 19:10 (Finkelstein, 267) and see M. Higger, *Masektot Derech Eretz,* 2.312, where a similar saying is attributed to R. Eleazer. See Flusser, "A Rabbinic Parallel," 501, n. 32. See also the Didache 3:1–3. See the fine English translation of Reuven Hammer, *Sifre: A Tannaitic Commentary on the Book of Deuteronomy* (New Haven: Yale University, 1986).

19. Consider the penetrating analysis of the self-awareness of Jesus by the great Jewish philosopher Martin Buber, *Two Types of Faith,* 104f.: "It was written of yet another, of the servant of JHVH (Isaiah 53), that he was 'taken' and 'cut off from the land of the living. . . .' This too is removal, a removal also to a particular, especially elevated office: he shall become a light to the nations (42:6, 49:6) . . . ; through his mediation the salvation of God shall rule unto the borders of the earth (49:6)." See Matthew Black's sensitive discussion of Buber, "The Messianism of the Parables of Enoch," in Charlesworth, *The Messiah,* 167–68.

20. Schechter, *Aspects of Rabbinic Theology,* 12. On understanding the divine concept in Judaism, see the thoughtful treatment of David Wolpe, *The Healer of Shattered Hearts: A Jewish View of God,* and his newer book, *In Speech and in Silence: The Jewish Quest for God.*

21. See Max Kadushin, *The Rabbinic Mind,* 2: "The absence of a definition, instead of being a defect, is what enables the rabbinic value-concept to function easily and effectively. We shall find that the value-concepts are not only undefined but nondefinable." While Kadushin has justly asserted that forming a rabbinic theology is an utter impossibility, even he has succumbed in part to our Western values by giving the title *A Theology of Seder Eliahu* to one of his fabulous books. In the weakness of human language, I believe we can speak about Jewish theology and the connectedness of Jesus to the faith of his community.

22. Compare the rich combination of spirituality, mysticism, and halakhic genius in the reflections of Joseph B. Soloveitchik, *Halakhic Man* (Philadelphia: Jewish Publication Society, 1983).

Afterword

Some time ago I was reading in Hebrew, the fifth chapter of Matthew with a Jewish rabbi. At nearly every verse the rabbi said, "This is in the Bible," or "This is in the Talmud," and he showed me in the Bible and in the Talmud sentences very like the declarations of the Sermon on the Mount. When we reached the words, "Resist not evil," the rabbi did not say, "This is in the Talmud," but asked me, with a smile, "Do the Christians obey this command? Do they turn the other cheek?" I had nothing to say in reply, especially as at that particular time, Christians, far from turning the other cheek, were smiting the Jews upon both cheeks.

—Leo Tolstoy

We are conscious today that many, many centuries of blindness have cloaked our eyes so that we can no longer see the beauty of Thy chosen people nor recognize in their faces the features of our privileged brethren. We realize that the mark of Cain stands upon our foreheads. Across the centuries our brother Abel has lain in the blood which we drew, or shed tears we caused by forgetting Thy love. Forgive us for the curse we falsely attached to their name as Jews. Forgive us for crucifying Thee a second time in their flesh. For we know not what we did . . . "

—Pope John XXIII

. . . remember it is not you that support the root, but the root that supports you.

—Romans 11:18b

Register of Section Division Quotations

Preface—See Martin Buber, *Two Types of Faith,* trans. Norman Goldhawk and Martin Buber (New York: Harper, 1961) 12–13.

Introduction: Jesus The Jewish Theologian—See Abraham Joshua Heschel, "Protestant Renewal: A Jewish View," in Fritz Rothschild ed., *Jewish Perspectives on Christianity* (New York: Crossroad, 1990) 302.

The Messianic Drama of Jesus' Life Events—See Raymond E. Brown, *New Testaments Essays* (Milwaukee: Bruce, 1965) 24.

The Jewish Roots of Jesus' Kingdom Theology—See F. F. Bruce, *The Hard Sayings of Jesus* (Downers Grove: InterVarsity, 1983) 16.

The Jewish Theology in Jesus' Parables—See David Flusser, "Foreword: Reflections of a Jew on a Christian Theology of Judaism," in Clemens Thoma, *A Christian Theology of Judaism* (New York: Paulist, 1980) 16.

The Jewish Messiah and the Politics of Rome—See Albert Schweitzer, *The Quest for the Historical Jesus* (London: SCM, 1981) 386.

The Future Messiah—See George Eldon Ladd, *A Theology of the New Testament* (Grand Rapids: Eerdmans, 1974) 81

Epilogue—See Rudolf Bultmann, *Jesus and the Word* (New York: Charles Scribner's Sons, 1958) 8.

A NOTE ON TRANSLATIONS

In writing the book, the author has made use of numerous critical editions of ancient sources and their English translations.

Even at its best, the art of translation is an inexact science. Occasionally the author has revised standard translations based upon the Hebrew, Aramaic, and Greek texts. The reader is encouraged to examine other translations of these sources and compare them with the book. Such translations have been noted in the documentation for each chapter. See the bibliography for the translations of rabbinic works mostly published by the Soncino Press, Jewish Publication Society, and Jewish Theological Seminary. The Loeb Classical Library (Harvard University Press) has been employed largely for Josephus and Philo.

Unless otherwise noted, the Revised Standard Version has been used for much of the biblical text, interspersed occasionally with the author's translation. At times, other translations have been used, such as the New International Version, Moffatt's translation, or the King James Version. When consulted, these versions have helped to illustrate a point of translation or may agree with a superior textual reading.

The differences among Bible translations are based not only upon style and current English usage but also upon analysis of ancient manuscripts. The translator must first determine which manuscript reading best represents the original writing of the text. In theory, the author is in agreement with the prevalent methods of textual analysis which have guided most of the current English translations. In practice, however, the author has revised some translations on the basis of weighing the manuscript evidence anew in light of the internal and external evidence. The internal evidence and consideration of the Hebrew (and/or Aramaic) background of the sayings of Jesus may tip the balance in favor of a variant reading which may not be universally accepted by the consensus of textual critics today. For the serious Bible student, much can be learned by comparing the different versions one with the other, all of which are trustworthy, possessing their own strengths and weaknesses.

Today perhaps more than at any other time, students may possess strong confidence in available translations of the Bible. Most Bible translations on the market today are more accurate than ever before because they are based upon better manuscript evidence and seek to communicate the message more effectively. The new translations are easier to read and often are accompanied by solid historical information in study helps. Though no translation is able to portray the rich imagery of the text with absolute precision, accurate translations help the modern reader listen to the voice from the past. Knowledge of Hebrew, Greek, and Aramaic, however, is always crucial in biblical analysis and interpretation. At present, fine resources for biblical research are more widely accessible to the general reader.

RABBINIC LITERATURE

The Mishnah (abbreviated as m.) is cited by chapter and verse. Herbert Danby's translation has been widely used and is considered to be a reliable rendering of the Hebrew text. One may also use P. Blackman's translation and commentary with much benefit.

The Babylonian Talmud (abbreviated as b.) is cited according to the Hebrew/Aramaic text. Each reference gives the tractate name and its page number. The pages are numbered a or b. The letter a refers to the front side of the Hebrew page, and b to the back side. The English translation of the Soncino Press preserves the original Hebrew pagination.

The Jerusalem Talmud (abbreviated as j.) is cited according to the tractate and page number in the Krotoschin edition. Each page of the Hebrew/Aramaic text has two columns. On the front side of the page, columns are numbered a and b. On the back side of the page, columns are numbered c and d. The Jerusalem Talmud is sometimes called the Palestinian Talmud and also may be cited by chapter and halakhah verse.

The Midrash Rabbah collection (Genesis Rabbah, Exodus Rabbah, etc.) is cited by section and paragraph. This is also the case for the homiletical midrashim (midrashim is the plural form of midrash), Pesikta Rabbati, and Pesikta De Rav Kahana. The Mekhilta de Rabbi Ishmael on Exodus is cited by chapter and verse. Usually reference has been made to the translation of the Mekhilta by Jacob Lauterbach in his fine English edition. Sifre Numbers is cited by its section. Sifre Deuteronomy is also cited by its section number in the Hebrew text. Often reference has been given to the excellent translation of Reuven Hammer. Sifra on Leviticus is cited by the chapter and verse in the Torah as well as the page number of the Weiss edition.

Not all rabbinic works have been translated into English. In the bibliography, the reader will discover help in locating other translations and finding critical editions in Hebrew and Aramaic.

THE DEAD SEA SCROLLS

For the Dead Sea Scrolls, the author has often made reference to the translation of Geza Vermes, *The Dead Sea Scrolls in English,* interspersed at times with the author's own translation. Vermes does not give verse citations but chapter headings only. Often the author has added reference to the scrolls according to the accepted form—number of cave found, Qumran, name of scroll or number in the collection of the Rockefeller Museum (PAM, Palestine Archaeological Museum), and the scroll column and the line. For instance, 1QS 3.4–6 refers to Qumran cave 1, the Manual of Discipline or Community Rule (the S stands for *serekh* in Hebrew, meaning the rule or discipline of the community), column 3, lines 4–6.

At the time of this writing, no translation has been made of all the Dead Sea Scrolls. Scholars do not always agree on the rendering of the Hebrew texts. Some disagreements involve lacunas in the scrolls where the text is damaged or fragmentary. Others involve questions of the Hebrew and Aramaic languages. Almost all the scrolls are written in Hebrew though some are composed in Aramaic.

The reader is encouraged to compare different translations and editions of the scrolls cited in the bibliography.

Bibliography and Study Aids

PRIMARY SOURCES, EDITIONS, AND TRANSLATIONS

Avot Derabbi Natan. Ed. S. Schechter. Vienna: Ch. Lippe, 1887.

Black, M. *The Book of Enoch.* Leiden: Brill, 1985.

Braude, W. G. *The Midrash on Psalms.* 2 vols. New Haven: Yale University, 1958.

———. *Pesikta de Rab Kahana.* Philadelphia: Jewish Publication Society, 1975.

———. *Pesikta Rabbati.* 2 vols. New Haven: Yale University, 1968.

———. *Tanna Debe Eliyyahu.* Philadelphia: Jewish Publication Society, 1981.

Charles, R. H., ed. *The Apocrypha and Pseudepigrapha of the Old Testament.* 2 vols. Oxford: Clarendon, 1977.

Charlesworth, J. H., ed. *The Old Testament Pseudepigrapha.* 2 vols. New York: Doubleday, 1983–85.

Clark, E. G. *Targum Pseudo-Jonathan of the Prophets.* Hoboken, N.J., 1984.

Cohen, A., and Israel Brodie, eds. *Minor Tractates of the Talmud.* 2 vols. London: Soncino, 1971.

Danby, Herbert. *The Mishnah.* New York: Oxford University, 1977.

The Dead Sea Scrolls on Microfiche. S. Reed, M. Lundberg, E. Tov, and Stephen J. Pfann. Leiden: Brill, 1993.

Díez Macho, A. *Neophyti I.* 6 vols. Text and translations into Spanish, French, and English. Madrid: Consejo Superior de Investigaciones Científicas, 1968–79.

Epstein, I., ed. *The Babylonian Talmud.* 35 vols. London: Soncino, 1935–1978.

Freedman, H., ed. *Midrash Rabbah.* 9 vols. London: Soncino, 1951.

Friedlander, G. *Pirke de Rabbi Eliezer.* New York: Hermon, 1981.

Gaster, T. *The Dead Sea Scriptures.* New York: Anchor, 1976.

Goldin, J. *The Fathers according to Rabbi Nathan.* New York: Schocken, 1974.

Haberman, A. *Megillot Midbar Yehuda.* Tel Aviv: Machbarot Lesifrut, 1959.

Hammer, Reuven. *Sifre: A Tannaitic Commentary on the Book of Deuteronomy.* New Haven: Yale University, 1986.

Herford, T. *Pirke Aboth the Ethics of the Talmud: Sayings of the Fathers.* New York: Schocken, 1975.

Hertz, J. H. *The Authorised Daily Prayer Book.* Hebrew text, English translation with commentary and notes. New York: Bloch, 1959.

Josephus. Ed. and trans. H. J. Thackeray. 10 vols. Loeb Classical Library. Cambridge: Harvard University, 1978.

Klein, M. L. *The Fragment-Targums of the Pentateuch.* 2 vols. Rome: Pontifical Biblical Press, 1980.

Masekhet Semachot. Ed. M. Higger. Jerusalem: Makor, 1970.

Masekhtot Derekh Eretz. Ed. M. Higger. 2 vols. Jerusalem: Makor, 1970.

Mekhilta Derabbi Ishmael. Ed. H. S. Horovitz and Ch. Rabin. Jerusalem: Wahrmann Books, 1970.

Mekhilta Derabbi Ishmael. Ed. M. Friedmann. Reprint. Jerusalem: Old City Press [Vienna, 1870], 1978.

Mekhilta Derabbi Shimeon Bar Yochai. Ed. Y. N. Epstein and E. Z. Melamed. Jerusalem: Hillel Press, 1980.

Mekilta Derabbi Ishmael. Ed. and trans. Jacob Lauterbach. 3 vols. Philadelphia: Jewish Publication Society, 1976.

Midrash Bereshit Rabbah. Ed. Ch. Albeck and J. Theodor. 3 vols. Jerusalem: Wahrmann Books, 1980.

Midrash Devarim Rabbah. Ed. S. Liebermann, Jerusalem: Wahrmann Books, 1974.

Midrash Ekha Rabbah. Ed. S. Buber. Wilna: Wittwa & Gebrüder Romm, 1899.

Midrash Hagadol. 5 vols. Jerusalem: Mosad Harav Kook, 1975.

Midrash Lekach Tov. Ed. S. Buber. Wilna: Wittwa & Gebrüder Romm, 1880.

Midrash Mishle. Ed. S. Buber. Wilna: Wittwa & Gebrüder Romm, 1891.

Midrash Rabbah. 2 vols. Wilna: Wittwa & Gebrüder Romm, 1887.

Midrash Rabbah. Ed. with commentary, Moshe Mirkin. 11 vols. Tel Aviv: Yavneh, 1977.

Midrash Rut Rabbah. Ed. M. Lerner. Jerusalem: Doctoral dissertation at the Hebrew University, 1971.

Midrash Seder Olam. Ed. D. Ratner. New York: Talmudic Research Institute, 1966.

Midrash Shemuel. Ed. S. Buber. Krakau: Joseph Fischer, 1893.

Midrash Shir Hashirim. Ed. Eliezer Halevi Grunhut. Jerusalem, 1897.

Midrash Shir Hashirim Rabbah. Ed. Shimshon Donski. Tel Aviv: Davir, 1980.

Midrash Tanchuma. Ed. S. Buber. Wilna: Wittwa & Gebrüder Romm, 1885.

Midrash Tanchuma. Reprint. Jerusalem: Lewin-Epstein [Warsaw, 1879], 1975.

Midrash Tannaim. Ed. D. Hoffmann. Reprint. Jerusalem: Books Export [Berlin, 1908], no date.

Midrash Tehilim. Ed. S. Buber. Wilna: Wittwa & Gebrüder Romm, 1891.

Midrash Vayikra Rabbah. Ed. M. Margulies. 5 vols. Jerusalem: Wahrmann Books, 1970.

Mishnah. Ed. Ch. Albeck. 6 vols. Jerusalem: Bialik Institute, 1978.

The New Testament in Greek. The Gospel according to St. Luke. Edited by the American and British Committees of the International Greek New Testament Project. 2 vols. Oxford: Clarendon, 1984–1987.

Novum Testamentum Graece. Ed. S. C. E. Legg. 2 vols. Oxford: Clarendon, 1935–1940.

Pesikta Derav Kahana. Ed. S. Buber. Lyck: L. Silbermann, 1868.

Pesikta Derav Kahana. Ed. B. Mandelbaum. New York: Jewish Theological Seminary, 1962.

Pesikta Rabbati. Ed. M. Friedmann. Vienna: Josef Kaiser, 1880.

Philo. Ed. and trans. F. H. Colson and G. H. Whitaker. 10 vols. plus 2 supplementary vols. Cambridge: Harvard University, 1981.

Pirke Derabbi Eliezer. Ed. David Luria. Warsaw: Bomberg, 1852.

Seder Eliyahu Rabbah. Ed. M. Friedmann. Jerusalem: Wahrmann Books, 1969.

Sifra. Ed. J. H. Weiss. Vienna: J. Salsberg, 1862.

Sifra (incomplete). Ed. M. Friedmann. Reprint. Jerusalem: Old City Press [Breslau, 1915], 1978.

Sifra. Ed. L. Finkelstein. 5 vols. New York: Jewish Theological Seminary of America, 1984.

Sifra: An Analytical Translation. Trans. J. Neusner. 3 vols. Atlanta: Scholars, 1985.

Sifre Al Bemidbar Vesifre Zuta. Ed. H. S. Horovitz. Jerusalem: Wahrmann Books, 1966.

Sifre Debe Rav. Ed. M. Friedmann. Reprint. Jerusalem: Old City Press [Vienna, 1864] 1978.

Sifre Devarim. Ed. L. Finkelstein. New York: Jewish Theological Seminary of America, 1969.

Sifre to Numbers. Trans. J. Neusner. 3 vols. Baltimore: Scholars, 1986.

Sperber, A. *The Bible in Aramaic.* 5 vols. Leiden: Brill, 1959–1968.

Taylor, C. *Sayings of the Fathers.* 2 vols. Cambridge: Cambridge University, 1877.

Talmud Babli. Wilna: Wittwa & Gebrüder Romm, 1835.

Talmud Jerushalmi. Krotoshin: Dov Baer Monash, 1866.

Torah Shelemah. Ed. M. Kasher. 43 vols. New York and Jerusalem: Talmud Institute, 1951–1983.

Tosefta.. Ed. M. Zuckermandel. Jerusalem: Wahrmann Books, 1937.

Tosefta. Ed. with commentary, S. Liebermann. 15 vols. New York: Jewish Theological Seminary of America, 1955–1977.

Vermes, G. *The Dead Sea Scrolls in English.* Baltimore: Penguin, 1988.

Visotzky, Burton. *Midrash Mishle.* New York: Jewish Theological Seminary, 1990.

Wacholder, B., and M. Abegg. *A Preliminary Edition of the Unpublished Dead Sea Scrolls.* Washington, D.C.: Biblical Archaeological Society, 1991–1992.

Yalkut Hamakiri. Ed. S. Buber. Berdyczew: Ch. J. Schefftel, 1899.

Yalkut Hamakiri. Ed. J. Z. Kahana-Shapira. Reprint. Jerusalem: Zvi Hirsch [Berlin, 1893], 1964.

Yalkut Hamakiri. Ed. A. W. Greenup. Jerusalem: Hameitar, 1968.

Yalkut Shimoni. Wilna: Wittwa & Gebrüder Romm, 1898.

GRAMMARS AND LEXICAL AIDS

Arndt, W., and F. W. Gingrich. *A Greek-English Lexicon of the New Testament and Other Early Christian Literature.* 2nd ed. Chicago: University of Chicago, 1979.

Blass, F., and A. Debrunner. Trans. and rev. R. Funk. *A Greek Grammar of the New Testament and Other Early Christian Literature.* Chicago: University of Chicago, 1961.

Brown, F. *The New Brown-Driver-Briggs-Gesenius Hebrew and English Lexicon.* Reprint. Peabody, Mass.: Hendrickson [1906], 1979.

Dalman, G. *Aramäisch-neuhebräisches Handwörterbuch.* Frankfurt am Main: J. Kaufmann, 1922.

_____. *Grammatik die jüdisch-palästinischen Aramäisch.* Leipzig: J. C. Hinrich, 1905.

Jastrow, M. *A Dictionary of the Targumim, the Talmud Babli and Yerushalmi, and the Midrashic Literature.* 2 vols. Reprint. New York: Judaica Press, 1975.

Kittel, G., ed. *Theological Dictionary of the New Testament.* Trans. G. Bromiley. 10 vols. Grand Rapids: Eerdmans, 1983.

Kosovsky, B. *Otzar Leshon Hatannaim Lemekilta Derabbi Ishmael.* New York: Jewish Theological Seminary, 1965.

_____. *Otzar Leshon Hatannaim Lasifra.* New York: Jewish Theological Seminary, 1967.

_____. *Otzar Leshon Hatannaim Lasifre Bemidbar Vedevarim.* New York: Jewish Theological Seminary, 1971.

Kosovsky, Ch. *Otzar Leshon Hamishnah.* Tel Aviv: Massadah, 1967.

_____. *Otzar Leshon Hatalmud.* Jerusalem: Ministry of Education and Culture, Government of Israel, 1971.

_____. *Otzar Leshon Hatosefta.* New York: Jewish Theological Seminary, 1961.

Kosovsky, M. *Otzar Leshon Talmud Yerushalmi* (incomplete). Jerusalem: Israel Academy of Sciences and Humanities, 1979.

Levy, J. *Neuhebräisches und Chaldaisches Wörterbuch über die Talmudim und Midraschim.* 4 vols. Leipzig: Brockhaus, 1876–89.

Liddell, H. G., and R. Scott. *A Greek-English Lexicon.* Oxford: Clarendon, 1976.

Lindsey, Robert L. *A Comparative Greek Concordance of the Synoptic Gospels.* 3 vols. Jerusalem: Baptist House, 1985–1989.

Moulton, J. H. *A Grammar of New Testament Greek.* 4 vols. Edinburgh: T. & T. Clark, 1978.

Moulton, W. F., A. S. Geden, and H. K. Moulton. *A Concordance to the Greek Testament.* Edinburgh: T. & T. Clark, 1986.

Stevenson, W. B. *Grammar of Palestinian Jewish Aramaic.* Oxford: Oxford University, 1974.

GENERAL SOURCES AND STUDY AIDS

Abbott, Edwin. *Clue a Guide through Greek to Hebrew Scripture.* London: Adam and Charles Black, 1900.

Abrahams, Israel. *Studies in Pharisaism and the Gospels.* Reprint. New York: KTAV, 1967.

Aland, Kurt, and Barbara Aland. *The Text of the New Testament.* Grand Rapids: Eerdmans, 1989.

Albright, W. F., and C. S. Mann. *The Gospel according to Matthew.* Anchor Bible 26. New York: Doubleday, 1981.

Amidon, P. *The Panarion of St. Epiphanius.* New York: Oxford University, 1990.

Avi-Yonah, Michael. *Views of the Biblical World.* 5 vols. Jerusalem: International Publishing, 1961.

Ayali, M. *Poalim Veomanim.* Jerusalem: Yad Letalmud, 1987.

Baarda, T. A., G. P. Hilhorst Luttikhuizen, and A. S. van der Woude, eds. *Text and Testimony.* Kampen: J. H. Kok, 1988.

Bacher, W. *Die Agada der palästinischen Amoräer.* Strassburg: Karl Tübner, 1892–1899 (translated into Hebrew by A. Rabinovitz. *Agadot Amore Eretz Israel.* Jerusalem: Davir, 1926).

_____. *Die Agada der Tannaiten.* Strassburg: Karl Tübner, 1890 (translated into Hebrew by A. Rabinovitz. *Agadot Hatannaim.* Jerusalem: Davir, 1919).

_____. *Die exegetische Terminologie der jüdischen Traditionsliteratur.* Leipzig: J. C. Hinrichs, 1905 (translated into Hebrew by A. Rabinovitz. *Erche Midrash.* Jerusalem: Carmiel, 1970).

_____. *Tradition und Tradenten.* Leipzig: Gustav Fock, 1914.

Baeck, Leo. *Judaism and Christianity.* New York: Leo Baeck Institute, 1958.

Bailey, Kenneth E. *Poet and Peasant.* Grand Rapids: Eerdmans, 1976.

_____. *Through Peasant Eyes.* Grand Rapids: Eerdmans, 1980.

Beall, Todd. *Josephus' Description of the Essenes Illustrated by the Dead Sea Scrolls.* Cambridge: Cambridge University, 1988.

Beasley-Murray, G. R. *Jesus and the Kingdom of God.* Grand Rapids: Eerdmans, 1986.

Bengel, J. A. *Gnomon of the New Testament.* Philadelphia: Perkinpine & Higgins, 1860.

Ben-Yehuda, Eliezer. *Complete Dictionary of Ancient and Modern Hebrew.* 17 vols. Tel Aviv: La'am, 1959.

Billerbeck, P. *Kommentar zum Neuen Testament aus Talmud und Midrasch.* 6 vols. Munich: C. H. Beck, 1978.

Birdsall, J. N. "The New Testament Text." In *Cambridge History of the Bible.* Cambridge: Cambridge University, 1.308–377.

Bivin, David, and Roy Blizzard. *Understanding the Difficult Words of Jesus.* Arcadia: Makor Foundation, 1983.

Black, M. *An Aramaic Approach to the Gospels and Acts.* Oxford: Clarendon, 1977.

Blizzard, Roy B., Jr. *Let Judah Go Up First.* Austin: Center for Judaic-Christian Studies, 1984.

Boismard, M., and A. Lamouille. *Synopsis Graeca Quattuor Evangeliorum.* Paris: Peeters, 1986

Brown, R. *The Birth of the Messiah.* New York: Doubleday, 1977; revised, 1993.

_____. *The Death of the Messiah.* 2 vols. New York: Doubleday, 1994.

_____. *New Testament Essays.* Milwaukee: Bruce, 1965.

Buber, Martin. *Two Types of Faith.* New York: Macmillan, 1961.

Büchler, Adolf. *Types of Jewish-Palestinian Piety.* London: Jews' College, 1922.

Bultmann, Rudolf. *History of the Synoptic Tradition.* Reprint; Peabody, Mass.: Hendrickson [1963], 1993.

_____. *Jesus and the Word.* New York: Charles Scribner's Sons, 1958.

Chajes, Z. H. *The Student's Guide through the Talmud.* Translated and annotated by J. Schachter. New York: Feldheim, 1960.

Charlesworth, James H., ed. *Jesus and the Dead Sea Scrolls.* New York: Doubleday, 1993.

_____. *Jesus within Judaism.* Garden City: Doubleday, 1988.

_____, ed. *The Messiah.* Minneapolis: Fortress, 1992.

Cohen, B. *Everyman's Talmud.* New York: Schocken, 1975.

Cohn, Haim. *The Trial and Death of Jesus.* New York: KTAV, 1977.

Crossan, John. *The Historical Jesus.* San Francisco: Harper, 1991.

_____. *Raid on the Articulate: Cosmic Eschatology in Jesus and Borges.* New York: Harper and Row, 1976.

Dalman, G. *Jesus-Jeshua.* London: SPCK, 1929.

_____. *Sacred Sites and Sacred Ways.* London: SPCK, 1935.

_____. *The Words of Jesus.* Edinburgh: T. & T. Clark, 1909.

Daniélou, Jean. *The Infancy Narratives.* New York: Herder and Herder, 1968.

Daube, David. *The New Testament and Rabbinic Judaism.* Reprint. Peabody, Mass.: Hendrickson [1956], 1994.

Davies, W. D. *The Setting of the Sermon on the Mount.* Atlanta: Scholars, 1989.

Davies, W. D., and D. Allison. *The Gospel according to St. Matthew.* International Critical Commentary. Edinburgh: T. & T. Clark, 1988–1991.

Dodd, C. H. *The Parables of the Kingdom.* Glasgow: Collins, 1961.

Doeve, J. W. *Jewish Hermeneutics in the Synoptic Gospels and Acts.* Assen: Van Gorcum, 1954.

Elbogen, I. *Jewish Liturgy.* Philadelphia: Jewish Publication Society, 1993.

Encyclopaedia Judaica. Jerusalem: Keter, 1978.

Fisher, Eugene. *The Jewish Roots of Christian Liturgy.* Mahwah, N.J.: Paulist, 1990.

Fitzmyer, J. A. *The Gospel according to Luke.* Anchor Bible 28. New York: Doubleday, 1981.

_____. *A Wandering Aramean.* Chico: Scholars Press, 1979.

Flusser, David. "Blessed Are the Poor in Spirit." *Israel Exploration Journal* 10 (1960) 1–10.

_____. *Jesus in Selbstzeugnissen und Bilddokumenten.* Hamburg: Rowohlt, 1968. (A poor translation into English was published, New York: Herder and Herder in 1969.)

_____. *Judaism and the Origins of Christianity.* Jerusalem: Magnes Press, 1989.

_____. *Die rabbinischen Gleichnisse und der Gleichniserzähler Jesus.* Bern: Peter Lang, 1981.

_____. "Sanktus und Gloria," in *Abraham unser Vater: Festschrift für Otto Michel zum 60. Geburtstag.* Ed. O. Betz, M. Hengel, and P. Schmidt. Leiden: Brill, 1963.

_____. "Some Notes on the Beatitudes." *Immanuel* 8 (1978) 37–47.

_____. "Die Versuchung Jesu und ihr jüdische Hintergrund." *Judaica* 45 (1989) 110–28.

Gehardsson, Birger. *The Testing of God's Son.* Lund, Sweden: Gleerup, 1966.

Gilat, Y. *R. Eliezer ben Hyrcanus, a Scholar Outcast.* Ramat Gan, Israel: Bar Ilan University, 1984.

Gilmore, A. *Christian Baptism.* London: Lutterworth, 1959.

Gros, M. *Otzar Haagadah.* 3 vols. Jerusalem: Mosad Harav Kook, 1977.

Harrington, D. *The Gospel of Matthew.* Collegeville, Minn.: Liturgical Press, 1991.

Hengel, Martin. *Judaism and Hellenism.* London: SCM, 1974.

_____. *Studies in the Gospel of Mark.* London: SCM, 1985.

_____. *The Zealots.* Edinburgh: T. & T. Clark, 1989.

Heschel, Abraham Joshua. *God in Search of Man.* New York: Farrar, Straus & Giroux, 1955.

_____. *The Insecurity of Freedom.* New York: Schocken, 1972.

_____. *Torah Men Hashamayim.* 3 vols. New York: Soncino, 1972–1990.

Horbury, W. "The Messianic Associations of 'the Son of man.' " *Journal of Theological Studies.* 36 (1985) 35–55.

Huck, Albert. *Synopse der ersten drei Evangelien.* Revised by Heinrich Greeven. Tübingen: J. C. B. Mohr, 1981.

Hyman, A. *Toldot Tannaim Veamoraim.* 3 vols. Jerusalem: Boys Town, 1963.

_____. *Torah Haketubah Vehamasurah.* 3 vols. Tel Aviv: Davir, 1979.

Jeremias, J. *Jerusalem in the Time of Jesus.* London: SCM, 1969.

_____. *The Parables of Jesus.* London: SCM, 1972.

_____. *The Prayers of Jesus.* Philadelphia: Fortress, 1984.

Kadushin, Max. *The Rabbinic Mind.* New York: Bloch, 1972.

Kensky, A. "Moses and Jesus: The Birth of a Savior." *Judaism.* 42 (1993) 43–49

Kenyon, Frederic. *Handbook to the Textual Criticism of the New Testament.* London: Macmillan, 1912.

Kister, M. "Plucking on the Sabbath and Jewish-Christian Polemic." *Immanuel.* 24/25 (1990) 35–51.

Klausner, Joseph. *From Jesus to Paul.* London: George Allen & Unwin, 1946.

_____. *Jesus of Nazareth.* New York: Macmillan, 1945.

_____. *The Messianic Idea in Israel.* New York: Macmillan, 1955.

Lachs, S. T. *A Rabbinic Commentary on the New Testament.* Hoboken: KTAV, 1987.

Ladd, G. E. *The Presence of the Future.* Grand Rapids: Eerdmans, 1980.

_____. *A Theology of the New Testament.* Grand Rapids: Eerdmans, 1974.

Lapide, P. *The Sermon on the Mount.* New York: Orbis, 1986.

Lapide, P., and Ulrich Luz. *Jesus in Two Perspectives.* Minneapolis: Augsburg, 1971.

Levey, S. *The Messiah: an Aramaic Interpretation*. Hoboken, N.J.: KTAV, 1974.

Levine, Lee. *Ancient Synagogues Revealed*. Jerusalem: Israel Exploration Society, 1981.

_____. *The Galilee in Late Antiquity*. New York: Jewish Theological Seminary, 1992.

Lindsey, Robert L. *A Hebrew Translation of the Gospel of Mark*. Jerusalem: Dugith, 1973.

_____. *Jesus Rabbi and Lord*. Oak Creek, Wisc.: Cornerstone, 1990.

_____. *The Jesus Sources*. Tulsa: HaKesher, 1990.

_____. "A Modified Two Document Theory of the Synoptic Dependence and Interdependence." *Novum Testamentum* 6 (1963) 239–64.

Lowe, M. "The Demise of Arguments from Order for Markan Priority." *Novum Testamentum*. 24 (1982) 27–36.

Lundström, G. *The Kingdom of God in the Teachings of Jesus*. Richmond: John Knox, 1963.

Mackin, T. *Divorce and Remarriage*. Mahwah, N.J.: Paulist, 1984.

Mann, C. S. *The Gospel according to Mark*. Anchor Bible. New York: Doubleday, 1986.

Mann, Jacob, "Jesus and the Sadducean Priests: Luke 10:25–37." *Jewish Quarterly Review* 6 (1914) 515–422.

Marshall, I. Howard. *The Gospel of Luke*. NIGTC. Grand Rapids: Eerdmans, 1978.

McArthur, H., and R. Johnston. *They Also Taught in Parables*. Grand Rapids: Zondervan, 1990.

McGinley, L. *Form-Criticism of the Synoptic Healing Narratives*. Woodstock, Md.: Woodstock College, 1944.

McNamara, M. *Targum and Testament*. Grand Rapids: Eerdmans, 1968.

M'Neile, A. H. *The Gospel according to St. Matthew*. London: Macmillan, 1949.

McRay, John. *Archaeology and the New Testament*. Grand Rapids: Baker, 1991.

Metzger, Bruce. *The Text of the New Testament: Transmission, Corruption, and Restoration*. New York: Oxford University, 1992.

_____. *A Textual Commentary on the Greek New Testament*. New York: United Bible Societies, 1975.

Meyer, Ben. *Aims of Jesus*. London: SCM, 1979.

Montefiore, C. G. *Rabbinic Literature and Gospel Teachings.* New York: KTAV, 1970.

_____. *The Synoptic Gospels.* 2 vols. New York: KTAV, 1968.

Montefiore, C. G., and H. Loewe. *A Rabbinic Anthology.* New York: Schocken, 1974.

Moore, G. F. "Christian Writers on Judaism." *Harvard Theological Review.* 14 (1921) 197–254.

_____. *Judaism in the First Centuries of the Christian Era.* New York: Schocken, 1975.

Mowinckel, Sigmund. *He That Cometh.* New York: Abingdon, 1954.

Newman, L., and S. Spitz. *The Talmudic Anthology.* New York: Behrman House, 1945.

Nolland, John. *Luke.* Word Biblical Commentary. 3 vols. Dallas: Word, 1989–1993.

Notley, Steven R. "The Concept of the Holy Spirit in Jewish Literature of the Second Temple Period and 'Pre-Pauline' Christianity." Doctoral dissertation at the Hebrew University, 1991.

Perrin, N. *Jesus and the Language of the Kingdom.* Philadelphia: Fortress, 1976.

Pococke, Edward. *A Commentary on the Prophecy of Micah.* Oxford: Oxford University, 1676.

Riches, John. *Jesus and the Transformation of Judaism.* London: Darton, Longman & Todd, 1980.

Safrai, S. "Teaching of Pietists in Mishnaic Literature." *Journal of Jewish Studies.* 16 (1965) 15–33.

Safrai, S., M. Stern, D. Flusser, and W. C. van Unnik, eds. *The Jewish People in the First Century.* 9 vols. 10th in preparation. Amsterdam: Van Gorcum, 1974–.

Sanders, E. P. *Jesus and Judaism.* London: SCM, 1985.

_____. *Jewish Law from Jesus to the Mishnah.* Philadelphia: Trinity, 1990.

_____. *Paul and Palestinian Judaism.* London: SCM, 1977.

Sanders, J. A. *Discoveries in the Judean Desert, the Psalms Scroll of Qumran Cave 11.* New York: Oxford University, 1965.

Sandmel, Samuel. *Judaism and Christian Beginnings.* New York: Oxford University, 1978.

Schechter, S. *Aspects of Rabbinic Theology.* New York: Schocken, 1961.

Schürer, E. *The History of the Jewish People in the Time of Jesus Christ.* 6 vols. Reprint. Peabody, Mass.: Hendrickson [1891], 1993.

———. *The History of the Jewish People in the Time of Jesus Christ.* Revised and edited by G. Vermes, F. Millar, and M. Black. 3 vols. Edinburgh: T. & T. Clark, 1973–1987.

Shelton, J. *Mighty in Word and Deed.* Peabody, Mass.: Hendrickson, 1991.

Sigal, Phillip. *The Halakah of Jesus of Nazareth.* Lanham, Md.: University Press of America, 1986.

Sokoloff, M. *A Dictionary of Jewish Palestinian Aramaic.* Ramat Gan, Israel: Bar Ilan University, 1990.

Soloveitchik, Joseph B. *Halakhic Man.* Philadelphia: Jewish Publication Society, 1983.

Stendahl, K. *The Scrolls and the New Testament.* New York: Harper, 1957.

Stern, David. *Parables in Midrash.* Cambridge: Harvard University, 1991.

Stoldt, Hans-Herbert. *History and Criticism of the Marcan Hypothesis.* Macon, Ga.: Mercer, 1980.

Strack, H. *Einleitung in Talmud und Midrasch.* Revised by G. Stemberger. Munich: C. H. Beck, 1981.

———. *Introduction to the Talmud and Midrash* Atheneum: New York, 1978. (This English translation was done before Stemberger's revision and now an English translation of G. Stemberger is available, Edinburgh: T. & T. Clark, 1989.)

Strauss, David Friedrich. *The Life of Jesus Critically Examined.* Reprint. Philadelphia: Fortress, 1972.

Swete, H. B. *The Gospel according to St. Mark.* London: Macmillan, 1905.

Taylor, V. *The Gospel According to St. Mark.* London: Macmillan, 1941.

———. *The Text of the New Testament: A Short Introduction.* London: Macmillan, 1961.

Tomson, Peter J. *Paul and the Jewish Law.* Assen: Van Gorcum, 1990.

Torrey, Charles C. *Our Translated Gospels.* London: Hodder & Stoughton, 1933.

Urbach, E. E. *The Sages: Their Concepts and Beliefs.* 2 vols. Jerusalem: Magnes Press, 1975.

Vermes, G. *Jesus and the World of Judaism.* London: SCM, 1983.

———. *Jesus the Jew.* London: Collins, 1974.

———. *The Religion of Jesus the Jew.* Minneapolis: Fortress, 1993.

———. "Sectarian Matrimonial Halakhah in the Damascus Rule." *Journal of Semitic Studies.* 25 (1974) 197ff.

Visotzky, Burton. *Reading the Book: Making the Bible a Timeless Text.* Garden City: Doubleday, 1991.

Willis, W. *The Kingdom of God in 20th-Century Interpretation.* Peabody, Mass.: Hendrickson, 1987.

Wilson, Marvin. *Our Father Abraham.* Grand Rapids: Eerdmans, 1989.

Winter, Paul. *On the Trial of Jesus.* Berlin: Walter de Gruyter, 1961.

Wise, M., N. Golb, J. J. Collins, and D. Pardee. *Methods of Investigation of the Dead Sea Scrolls and the Khirbet Qumran Site.* New York: New York Academy of Sciences, 1994.

Wolpe, David. *Healer of Shattered Hearts: A Jewish View of God.* New York: Henry Holt, 1990.

———. *In Speech and in Silence: The Jewish Quest for God.* New York: Henry Holt, 1992.

Young, Brad H. "The Ascension Motif of 2 Corinthians in Jewish, Christian, and Gnostic Texts." *Grace Theological Journal* 9.1 (1988) 73–103.

———. "The Cross, Jesus, and the Jewish People." *Immanuel.* 24/25 (1990) 23–34.

———. *Jesus and His Jewish Parables.* (Mahwah: Paulist, 1989).

———. *The Jewish Background to the Lord's Prayer.* Austin: Center for Judaic-Christian Studies, 1984.

———. " 'Save the Adulteress!' Ancient Jewish *Responsa* in the Gospels?" *New Testament Studies* 41 (1995) 59–70.

Young, Brad H., and David Flusser, "Messianic Blessings in Jewish and Christian Texts," in Flusser, *Judaism and the Origins of Christianity.* Jerusalem: Magnes Press, 1989, 280–300.

Index of Names and Subjects

Index of Ancient Sources

100:3 276
118:22 218
118:22–23 216
128 97
145:1 119

Proverbs
7–8 109
16:9 72
19:14 114
21:21 72
23:25 40

Ecclesiastes
5:12 135

Isaiah
1:18 xvii
6:3 7
11:2 21
22:22 204
28:16–18 204
29:18–19 59
32:17 89, 90
35:5–6 59
38:1–8 36
42:1 17, 18, 210
42:6 276
49:6 276
51:1 72, 201
53 238, 276
53:8 159
54:13 89, 90
61:1 86
64:4 62
66:2 86

Jeremiah
3:12 154
15:1 134
31:9 154
31:20 154

Ezekiel
1:1 23
17:23 82

Daniel
4:12 82
4:21 82
7:13f. 29, 57, 111,
    240, 245, 246, 250,
    251
12:3 207

Hosea
11:11 20

Micah
2:13 51f., 53, 61, 63,
    66, 73

Nahum
2:5 207

Zephaniah
2:3 85, 93

Zechariah
4:3 207

Malachi
3:1 61, 63
3:1–2 62, 66
3:23 208
4:4–5 62

New Testament

Matthew
3:13–17 24
4:1–11 27
5:1 86
5:3 92
5:3ff. 81, 83
5:3–13 85
5:9 85, 88, 89, 93
5:17–18 264, 265
5:26 267
5:32 116

5:38–42 81
5:43 168
5:48 91
6:23 140
6:33 55, 80
9:1–8 41
9:2 41, 180
9:22 180
11:2–15 70
11:9–10 53
11:12 49ff., 51, 54,
    55, 66, 70, 71, 72
11:13 70
12:5 111
12:22–30 70
12:28 70
12:31–37 112
12:32 246
13:31–33 77, 82
15:28 177
16:6 82
16:12 82
16:13–14 197
16:18 200, 204
17:1–8 205
17:5 25
18:1–5 100
19:3–9 117
19:3–12 116
19:13–15 95
19:14 98
19:30 131
20:1–16 129
20:14–15 136
20:16 131
20:24–28 100
21:15b–16 101
21:23 216
21:33–46 215
23:1–3 100–101
23:2 186, 230
25:31ff. 111
25:31–36 248, 249
25:40 251
27:15 235, 239

Mark
1:9–11 24
1:12–13 27
2:1–12 41
2:5 180
2:27–28 108
3:18–30 112
3:22–27 70
3:28–30 246
4:30–32 77, 82
5:34 180
8:15 82
8:27–28 197
9:2–10 205
9:7 25
9:33–37 100
10:11–12 116–17
10:13–16 95
10:52 177
11:22 42
11:27 216
12:1–12 215
12:6 217
15:6 239, 240

Luke
1:1–4 199
1:41 33
1:61 33
2:10 7
2:14 3, 6, 7
3:13 16
3:14 16
3:21–22 17, 24
4:1–13 27
5:17–26 41
5:33–39 155
5:39 155–58
6:1 103
6:20ff. 83
6:20–23 85
6:21 92
7:1–10 44
7:11–17 198
7:16 198

7:18–28 70
7:36–50 198
7:50 177
8:48 180
9:16 123
9:18–19 197
9:19 197
9:20 57, 199
9:28 210
9:28–36 205
9:30–31 205, 206
9:35 25
9:46–48 100
9:51 213
11:5–8 171
11:7 172
11:20 70, 80
12:1 82
12:10 112, 246
13:18–21 77, 82
13:31 222, 230
15:11–32 143–54
15:12 146
15:18 149
15:22–24 148
15:29–30 150
15:31 148
16:8 173
16:16 54, 66, 70, 71, 72
16:18 113, 114, 115, 116, 117
18:1–8 171
18:9 181
18:9–14 181
18:14 190
18:15–17 95
18:17 100
18:31–32 250
20:1 216
20:9 221
20:9–19 215
20:13 215, 217
20:16 221
20:18 215, 220

20:19 229
21:27 244
22:24–30 100
22:66 231
22:67 57
23:7 239
23:12 232
23:17 235, 239, 240
23:24 236

John
1:29–34 24
4:46–54 44
7:22–23 106
10:9 53
11:48 226, 227, 236
18:39 239, 240
18:40 235

Acts
1:1 199
2:4 33
2:8 33
3:1 194
5:17 230
5:26 230
5:36–38 231
8:33f. 161
9:17 33
13:9 33
13:24 213

Romans
11:18b 277

1 Corinthians
5:7 78
10:26 122

Galatians
5:9 78

Hebrews
11:22 213